THE NOUSEUM SAGAS
THE SPIRITUAL TEACHINGS OF
GABRIEL BAAL EYT

THE NOUSEUM SAGAS

THE SPIRITUAL TEACHINGS OF
GABRIEL BAAL EYT

Lord of the Appointed Time

Codex One: Conservations with a Rose-Croix
Codex Two: History and Meta-Theology of the Djinn
Codex Three: Preparations for War

By

Jean-Michel Polyakov
Baron du Mont Saint Germain
Légat Royale au Temple du Mont Carmel

Teaching Tales Publishing Ltd, Atlanta, GA
https://worldsofjmpolyakov.com

THE NOUSEUM SAGAS

THE SPIRITUAL TEACHINGS OF GABRIEL BAAL EYT
Lord Of Creation

Codex One: Conservations with a Rose-Croix
Codex Two: History and Meta-Theology of the Djinn
Codex Three: Preparations for War

Copyright © by Jean-Michel Polyakov and
Teaching Tales Publishing Ltd, Atlanta, GA
https://worldsofjmpolyakov.com/

All rights reserved. Neither the whole nor any part of this book is available for reproduction or transmission in any manner without permission of the copyright holder(s), except for brief quotations embodied in critical articles or reviews.

First Edition 2024
10 9 8 7 6 5 4 3 2 1

ISBN: 979-8-89109-823-7 (Paperback)
ISBN: 979-8-89109-824-4 (Ebook)
ISBN: 979-8-89109-859-6 (Hardcover)

Contents

Preface vii

Codex I: Conservations with a Rose-Croix 1
Chapter 1:   A Meeting in Damascus 3
Chapter 2:   The Oneirion 11
Chapter 3:   The Proof of the Pudding is in the Eating 23
Chapter 4:   Return to Damascus 37
Chapter 5:   Hell 43
Chapter 6:   The System 56
Chapter 7:   Return to Hell 72
Chapter 8:   Gabriel Unveils Sophie's Destiny 76
Chapter 9:   The Triads 93

Codex II: History and Meta-Theology of the Djinn 107
Chapter 10: The Djinn 109
Chapter 11: By Your Djinny, Djinn Chin 126
Chapter 12: Preparation 135
Chapter 13: A Visit with Ariel 142
Chapter 14: Visitors from Camelot 146
Chapter 15: Resurrection Eve 162
Chapter 16: Ariel Was Born on this Marriage Day 181

Codex III: Preparations For War 195
Chapter 17: The Great War Preparations 197
Chapter 18: More Djinn Metaphysics 203
Chapter 19: Camelot 245
Chapter 20: Evil Rises in the Dark of the Night 269
Chapter 21: The End Wars Begin 290
Chapter 22: Let's Do the Time Warp Again 331

About the Author 339

Preface

hese Teachings originate from my adventures in the Oneirion or Trans-Sentient Dreamworld. Most people believe the physical world is the primary plane of existence; it is not. Sentient vehicles seek to enter the Oneirion and expand the Collective Mind. Our intended home is within the Oneirion, for it is only there the universal reference clock stops.

The concept of an aphysical afterlife exists in all historical and modern religions, even if the forms of the idea are divergent. The history of human religion acknowledges the existence of the Oneirion, though not always called so. We see portions of the Oneirion in the multiple heavens and hells of Hinduism and Mahayana Buddhism; the afterlives of Christianity, Zoroastrianism, and Islam; the happy hunting grounds of the American Indians; and the dismal afterlives of the Babylonians, Greeks, and Sumerians.

Materialists claim only the physical exists, and the dreamworlds are epiphenomena associated with brain activity. The minority view is partially correct, but materialists have no sound evidence for scientific materialism. Physical vehicles contain complex neural systems that produce physical images, but our mental functioning is not only material.

Some neuroscientists argue that the human brain is a bioelectrical instrument obligatory for sentient creatures to experience the physical and aphysical worlds. I discuss much of this in the educational portions of this series of Oneirion narratives.

The ratio of aphysical worlds to the physical is transfinite. The Oneirion is the place of the First Emanation of the Formless Creator-Absolute. Its First Emanation assumes a Most Holy Family, corresponding to all sentient races' nuclear family. As the nuclear family is the foundation of humanity, the ideal Sacred Image is a Holy Family. Remember the Law of Correspondence, As Above So Below, As Below So Above.

As the First Emanation is by nature Formless, it will appear in whatever Form is sacred and worshipped by individuals and societies. The First Emanation manifests as an objectified Noun (the mystic heart) or impersonally as a Verb (the elixir of the philosopher's stone).

In other writings, I teach that the Formless First Emanation infuses our universe as the Divine Qualia or Verbs of Knowing, Observing, Presence, Transcendence, Intending, and Caring-Loving.

I travel to the Oneirion in different ways. Sometimes, I simply observe what is happening in a particular world. Other times, I interact as an independent character with other aphysical characters. When I relate a narrative, I merge with the entity of significant interest. Occasionally, like Ātman, I appear in multiple forms simultaneously.

I am an Initiate and the esoteric founder of The Institute for Conscious Evolution and Human Development. I prefer when people address me using my first name rather than my formal name.[1] I abhor adulation and gently correct a seeker who calls me Lord, Master, or Guru, even though I know the speaker desires to honour me.

Call me, Friend, as this term is sufficient. After all, the Immortals were once creatures struggling for enlightenment on some habitable

---

[1] Ezer-el

planet in this universe or another. All are realists with altruistic hearts and honourable intentions.

I understand the severity of this moment for humanity and the critical need for interventional aid. I hope to publish a series of narratives from my experiences on Earth and within the aphysical worlds. Showing humankind that the only viable solution is discarding egoism and hoarding, replacing it with altruism and a fair sharing of the riches of the Earth.

"Love is the only Law, Love tempered by Wisdom. And by Love, I refer to unconditional caring for others, nothing less."

Our universe is full of life forms existing in the collective consciousness of sentient beings. The Mystics and Magi have known this for hundreds of thousands of years, as do poets, writers, and children (until corrupted by wayward adults). Many falsely believe that their only life is in the physical.

We pray that these stories of Gabriel and his friends in the astral worlds bring you to our doors to become helpers and advocates for the enlightenment of our species. Hence, we accomplish our conjoint spiritual purpose. Blessings and Good Wishes for Enlightenment,

Jean-Michel

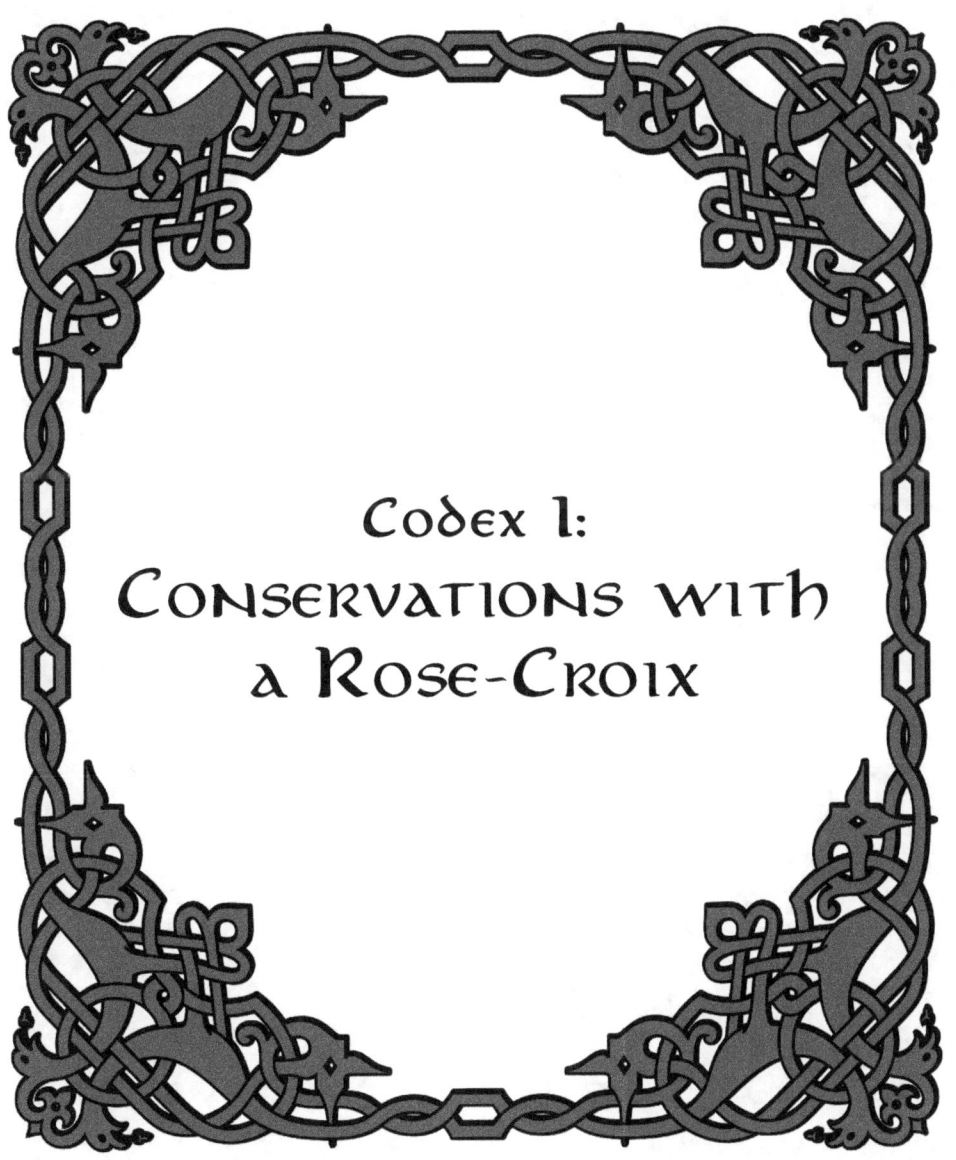

Codex 1:
Conservations with a Rose-Croix

Chapter 1

A Meeting in Damascus

A stunningly beautiful student finds herself sitting on the rooftop of an old house in the foothills overlooking Damascus. The sun sets in the west, and the city radiates a soft orange glow.

On her right sits a man with knee-high brown leather riding boots. He wears faded blue denim pants and a cotton desert shirt from the British army. The shirt sleeves are rolled up and attached to a button by a strip of material sewn onto the outer sleeve of each shirt arm. His blonde hair falls to his shoulders in ringlets, and his eyes are like the vibrant blue of a cloudless California sky. She cannot guess his age, but his presence seems to place him outside of time.

Perhaps JG Bennett was correct when he said orthogonal to clock time is a dimension called Eternity.

The man is neither tall nor short, but his beingness fills the rooftop. He possesses the most charming of smiles. The young lady feels drawn to him most peculiarly, almost magically, as if he could fulfil all her wishes. She realises he has loved many women who have loved him.

A random thought crosses her mind, and instinctively, she looks away from his eyes.

"I will love him one day."

The man sips black coffee fortified with turbinado sugar and fresh lemon rind. A small, tarnished, inscribed copper table from Nebuchadnezzar II (circa 6th Century BCE) is before them. On the tabletop rest, blue-and-white China plates holding dark brown Medjool dates, sugar cubes, Turkish Delight, lemon rind, and a French press filled with the darkest coffee the student had seen. On the right of the tabletop sits an empty blue-and-white porcelain demitasse cup with a matching saucer and a gold spoon for the student.

After what seemed an eternity to the student, the man speaks, "Hello, Sophie. My name is Gabriel Baal Eyt. I summoned you, for I need your help. And yes, my China is Ming Dynasty, especially fired for me by Empress Dowager Xiaoding in 1581. Please sit."

As she sits, Gabriel reaches over, picks up a lemon rind, rubs it around the cup's rim, and drops it into the empty cup. He adds two lumps of turbinado sugar and pours dark coffee into the demitasse cup.

He gracefully picks up the cup and saucer and hands them to Sophie.

"Enjoy the coffee. It is sublime."

Sophie reaches over to pick up the gold spoon and stirs her cup a few times. Laying the spoon onto the saucer, she uses her left hand to lift and hold the saucer while raising the small cup to her lips with her right. Tilting the cup ever so slightly, Sophie feels the elixir contact the taste buds of her tongue. She experiences the wonder of a perfectly roasted and brewed coffee.

After three sips, she replaces the small cup with the saucer and returns the pair to the table.

"Thank you very much. But how did I get here? Where is here, anyway?"

Gabriel smiles, "You are in Damascus, my dear. You are here because I need to tell you about the future of esoteric wisdom for our current epoch. It is an epoch in which humanity turns away from the inward search for its original home to worship two false gods.

"One is Mammon, and the other is Scientific Materialism. The old esoteric schools are failing to redirect humankind. Someone must introduce and grow a new Esotericism. It is this new Esotericism that I am going to share with you and which you will share with the world."

By nature, a talkative person, Sophie finds her mouth vacant of words, her mind and body absent. There is no Sophie, but something is present and aware.

Her mind asks, "Is this real 'I'?"

Gabriel picks up the plate of dark brown dates and offers it to Sophie.

"Take a date and chew it slowly and consciously. You will feel more comfortable. I am sorry, but I needed to show you something."

Sophie follows Gabriel's instructions and chooses a date to eat. She takes small bites, paying attention to texture, sweetness, and flavour. After finishing the date, she returns to her normal state of waking sleep.

"Sophie, I just gave you a taste of real 'I'. Strange, is it not?"

"Most strange. Will you tell me more, Gabriel?"

Gabriel nods his head.

"But this will come later. It is best to begin at the beginning rather than in the middle or, God forbid, the end. Let me explain how I brought you here and why, okay?"

"Yes, please go ahead."

"Sophie, the world is in a dreary, dark place. So dark that my fratres and sorors worry about humanity's questionable future. They begged me to intervene immediately. We do our best to avoid direct intervention, but now and then, we will intervene. I chose you to speak with me this delightful evening. Wait until the full moon rises tonight, and you will see real magick. I have always felt at ease in this place. It is November 1, 1913, my birthday.

"My dear, you fell into a deep sleep this afternoon, allowing me to transport you to Damascus. It is not an effortless task. I brought you here to answer your questions about the universe, the Three Worlds, and God. The answers exist, and I shall give such to you on this visit.

"The world direly needs alternative models of existence. Models generating unique and more functional interrelationships between the material and the spiritual. Maintaining a separation between science and spirituality shall eventually cause an end to life on Earth as we know it. As a working couple, the marriage of science and spirituality can benefit man and the world.

"Sophie, I chose you to bring this message back to our Order and the world so new esoteric knowledge updates the old for the hope of the future. The Rose-Croix have carried the shepherd's crook and worn the shepherd's sandals for uncountable aeons. Cooperating with the demiurgic forces responsible for organising new universes, we search for new planets ready to serve as the Holy Family's evolutionary gardens.

"Whenever we locate a suitable planet, we seed its lands and oceans with the common ancestors of the Archaea needed to birth a lush biosphere over billions of years. A biosphere fit for the gradual evolution of ever more complex life forms. Now and then, a planet's life forms attain a complexity equal to that of human beings. To creatures sufficiently complex to germinate and grow an authentic self, we intentionally provide a seed from which an immortal self can be born if the person desires and works diligently. We call this seed the higher being body, soul seed, or in Greek, *spóros psychis*.

"For immortal souls are necessary to complete Omneity's Plan for this universe. Unfortunately, finalised souls are scarce; we do not have enough to complete the Divine Plan.

"My friends and I were once, as you are now, creatures ready to work consciously so to grow and harvest, one day, an immortal soul. My friends and I exist simultaneously within the Unborn and objective time and space. The attainment of an immortal soul is the *sin qua non* for becoming a Sacred Individual.

"Humanity is facing extinction. Such extinction is a surety unless enough men and women recognise and overcome their genetic propensities for self-love and hoarding. Unless additional men and women seek the proper esoteric training to become capable of assuming the shepherd's crook and sandals to help, men and women will be no more.

"Potentially conscious creatures must band together as a single, conscious humanity to assume the role of the Earth's shepherd. Such is the Law, and it is absolute. This time is quickly approaching, and humanity is not prepared. I am speaking to you, for you will be both a messenger and an innovator. I will do what I can but I prefer not to intervene directly.

"Sophie, you are my little sister, and I must work with you for the benefit of all. Do you accept this chore?"

Gabriel rises from his chair and moves the table away from the two of them.

Sophie stands up, goes to Gabriel, and kisses him on his left cheek. Gabriel places his arms around her back and kisses her forehead, and Sophie lays her head on his left chest.

Moon Maiden is above the horizon, smiling, as she knows what Sophie's heart is saying to Gabriel's heart, and Moon Maiden etches their promises into the scrolls of eternity.

Sophie remains in Gabriel's arms for what seems to her an eternity. She hears the steady beating of his heart and knows she is safe. For as long as she could remember, Sophie hadn't felt safe since early childhood. Her early life had been far from desirable.

Funny, she thought, "It feels like all my past traumas, physical and mental abuse, are slowly being absorbed from my heart and mind. I can feel the invisible scars covering my heart disappearing. Somehow, being in Gabriel's arms is healing my past by closing existing energy drains upon my soul. Truly, he is Rose-Croix."[2]

---

[2] The title Rose-Croix is a French term denoting a fully enlightened Rosicrucian Master incarnate. The term is misapplied in modern Rosicrucian Organizations of the past century or so.

Gabriel withdraws his arms from Sophie's back and helps her sit back in her chair. He offers her a plate of Turkish Delight to restore her mental equilibrium. She takes a single piece and replaces the plate on the table, which he returns to its original position and sits down.

Gabriel said, "Feels better now, eh? Perfected Human Love is the most powerful force in the universe and heals almost anything. I need you to be strong, for the Astral Black Lodge will notice you as a threat soon enough."

Sophie finishes her Turkish Delight. She reaches out, placing her right hand on Gabriel's left.

"Gabriel, thank you from the deepest layer of my heart for restoring me. Somehow, I am reborn. I have never heard of an Astral Black Lodge, and I know the Order is under the direction of the Eternal White Lodge. Please explain."

"Into every suitable universe, the Higher Being Bodies of several Eternal White Lodge members enter to guide its development. Initially, there is only geometry, undifferentiated energy, the Divine Qualia, and the Guides. There is no matter, life, or structure; it is dark and chaotic. Contrary to many philosophical teachings, the primaeval darkness and chaos are lawful and not evil.

"The fiery primeval darkness and chaos expanded and cooled over objective time. Finally, leptons and quarks formed and combined to make neutral atoms. After some 380,000 years post-deflation-reinflation, the photons trapped by early matter could move through space. The universe became transparent for the first time.

"So, the old esoteric adage, 'Darkness pervaded All before Light came, but Light came not forth from the Darkness, for Darkness is the absence of Light,' aligns with modern cosmology. Modern cosmology has shown that the birthing temperature was so high that neither quarks nor leptons could form in the first moments of a birthed universe. The immediate first quanta lacked rest mass and translated at a uniform speed equal to light.

"As the occupied volume of the early universe expanded into unoccupied space, it cooled adiabatically.[3] Such cooling separates the zero charge, zero rest-mass exchange bosons responsible for gravitation and electromagnetism. We believe the separation occurred as the gravitational bosons possessed integral spin two and the photons integral spin one.

"As the universe expands and cools adiabatically, the remaining fundamental forces separated from each other because of spin and charge differentiation. The first nuclear synthesis machines, the stars, formed.

"From a neoesoteric viewpoint, we state, 'For Light, there is no beginning, for Light is the first manifestation of ever-present fundamental information.'

"I do not have time to explain this now.

"Every universe expresses six fundamental Divine Quale: Knowing, Observing, Presence, Transcendence, Intending, and Caring. Such Qualia are inherent qualities or functions seeded into the universe by the Source to manifest pure consciousness. Without these six fundamental Quale, there would be no life and no mind.

"While each of the first five Quale are neutral in valence, the last and supreme Quale, caring or love unconditional, is valence positive, manifesting as pure goodness. Evil is not a fundamental Quale seeded into a new universe. It cannot cross from the prior into the new intact.

"Evil arises from the asocial actions and mental images of sentient creatures inhabiting a new physical universe. If reinforced sufficiently in their conjoint species mind, the individual images merge, forming distinct demonic entities within the Oneirion. Demons are created

---

[3] A thermodynamic system isolated from its surroundings does not exchange heat, mass, or work (all forms of active information) with its environs. It is an adiabatic system.

by-products of normal evolutionary bioprocesses on suitable planets. It is an unfortunate but necessary process for enlightenment.

"The best definition of evil is appropriating the bounties of Nature for self-aggrandisement and devaluing others. Self-aggrandisement manifests as self-serving actions for increased power, wealth, or fame.

"Evil arises whenever the evolutionary drivers for survival, reproduction, and hoarding are knowingly appreciated by intelligent creatures with autobiographical memory and a sense of time. Such intelligence creates the possibility of a sentient creature using its evolutionary traits for selfishness and greed rather than altruism and generosity. Animals such as your species, Sophie.

"So, the First Teaching, Sophie, is that universes are inherently Good and Altruistic. Evil is not coequal to Goodness, as evil is an abomination of Goodness. Evil subverts the universal Good, or Altruism, to serve only egoism."

Sophie is silent for a moment, then says wistfully.

"I have always felt that the Good-Evil twin concept taught originally by Zoroaster and later showing up in Manicheism, Mithraism, and Christianity was incorrect. I understand, and I shall remember this Teaching. It is ancient and new at the same time. I see why you use the term neoesotericism."

"Good. One man's or one woman's evil is not much of an issue because a person's death undoes it. Still, the original evil from mechanical evolution multiplied many times over is a dangerous force that can destroy your species and your planet."

Chapter 2

The Oneirion

"Let me explain," continues Gabriel, "The Swiss psychiatrist Carl Jung[4] did the intellectual world excellent service by postulating the existence of a human, collective unconsciousness, or objective psyche. He originally proposed the collective to explain why certain mental archetypes appear across many cultures. We share his explanation of the contribution of common psychoneurology, shared genetics, and social constructs. Early Jung does not imply a collective psychic mind, though many think so. It was not until the end of his life that Jung suspected his objective psyche was grander than he first imagined.

"We have known for some time that all social animals possess a conjoint species mind existing in the astral or the middle world. The simplest examples appear in the organised, nonlocal behaviour of honeybees, termites, and ants. Part of the cooperative activity arises from chemical and motor messages, and the rest from aphysical sharing.

---

[4] Carl Gustav Jung was a Swiss psychoanalyst (b. 1875 d. 1961)

"For instance, social insects are dissimilar to most creatures. They are unique as they share a common genome and phenotype, enhancing nonlocal cooperation. Their cooperation is partially based upon interactions of electromagnetic fields generated in situ by individual neural nets. The neural nets work to reinforce goal-directed behaviour and extinguish opposing behaviours. Research shows how specific behaviour-inducing pheromones are recruited to induce or inhibit many behaviours.

"I doubt social insects possess a conjoint species mind, which includes conscious content. Clearly, they share one unconsciousness.

"Based upon work conducted long ago, we found human beings possess a very sophisticated conjoint species mind. My friend Baron Jean-Michel explained to those in the Order that all potentially conscious creatures possess a physical body. The brain monitors the sensory data available, processing it to form virtual images of physical objects, which it back projects onto them. The brain stores these images and spatial relations as engrams.[5]

"Our brains also monitor the spatial distribution of chemicals and electric potentials in our tissues (fine-grained) and, more grossly, the position of our organs. The brain is neurologically aware of the boundary between our squamous tissues and the surrounding air, water, and earth. Using such data, the brain creates a virtual image, mirroring our bodies in our surroundings.

"So, while the brain and body are material objects, our egotic awareness exists only in a mirrored virtual world, just as in a dream. And a virtual existence is aphysical.

"Jean-Michel aptly described how humans create and maintain a single awareness in the Dreamworld or Oneirion, both asleep and awake. The source of the collective human consciousness is humanity's

---

[5] Our mundane dreams are constructed using these and related stored images.

capacity to create a separate virtual or dream world to operate within. Physics is not essential now, but it is known to me.

"Sophie, over hundreds of thousands of years, the conjoint human mindbrain created a mental world perched between the material world of bodies and the spiritual world of forms. This world contains nonphysical individuals, sacred images, and possibilities. For convenience, I shall use traditional terminology and call this world the Oneirion, Middle World, or Middle Earth.

"Though I dislike computer analogies, one can picture the Oneirion as the internet whose structure and content arise from the information of billions of personal computers feeding into it. The virtual world comprises subtle energies from quanta necessary for life and mental awareness. We call such fundamental aphysical astral quanta atons, after one of the Egyptian names for the Sun.

"Using the virtual imago of the physical body, these quanta create a virtual duplicate of the physical body's organs, manifesting the kesdjan, astral, soul-personality, or psychic body. This phenomenon is most interesting, for it implies thoughts are more than nebulous epiphenomena without reciprocal effects upon the physical body. Rather, material and mental objects coexist and are mutually necessary for human functioning. As the ancients have said, 'Thoughts and feelings are things.'

"The kesdjan body shares a common awareness with the human body and is what acts in the Oneirion. Are you following, Sophie?"

"I cannot explain what has happened to my mind, but everything you teach seems to sink perfectly into my mind and memory. When you teach, much more than words enter me as knowledge, creating a feeling of clarity and certainty."

"Sophie, I opened your channel to the Noble Organ by removing some limitations.[6] Subsequently, the depth and quality of your soul-personality are more than before. The dimension of Being, your station or *stathmós*, is higher and sufficient for our current needs.

"But there is so much more I must teach you this special evening. I need to explain much more about the structure of the astral or collective dream world.

"Sophie, an ultimate explanation of how the human brain creates dream worlds, is still in the making. For our purposes this evening, the simplest explanation presumes that our virtual or dream realities result from the nervous system's electrical activity, creating an electromagnetic image of the body in space. This electromagnetic body image attracts the more ethereal, non-gravitating, atonic energies. The atonic energies combine with the electromagnetic images of our physical selves, birthing our astral or psychic, which we call the kesdjan body.[7] Your Order calls the atonic energies the vital life force, but not in the same sense as the early vitalists.[8]

"Scientific materialists say that the aphysical worlds cannot exist as measurements of the macroscopic forces; electromagnetism and gravitation cannot detect them. Dark matter is not observable because it does not interact with light, but its presence is inferred by gravitational lensing. Dark energy does not interact with electromagnetic fields but explains the radial acceleration of observable matter. Perhaps there are more strange relations in the physical.

---

[6] The Noble Organ is a higher being vessel which contains all the Wisdom and Love given to this universe in the Beginning.
[7] The term kesdjan came from my essence friend Gurdjieff, which he said is the vessel of the soul. As typical of Gurdjieff he failed to give his students the true meaning which is vessel of the atonic mind.
[8] Vitalism is the theory that the origin and phenomena of life are dependent on a force or principle distinct from purely chemical or physical forces. The Yogins know this life force as one contained within the universal vibratory energy Aum.

"This insistence that aphysical forces cannot exist because they do not interact with the physical as known to science is the philosophical error of misattributing one kind to another.

"Therefore, the existence of aphysical quanta failing to possess mass, spin, or charge, such that we cannot detect them indirectly, is not a proven impossibility. No one denies the reality of their individual dreamworlds full of mental aphysical images. Using Ockham's Razor to simplify is inappropriate, like comparing passion fruit and guava.

"For human beings, the atonic energy not only provides partial independence from the physical body but creates a condition of awareness of some aphysical presence associated with the physical body. This feeling of existence is because the fundamental Quale, Presence, enters what we have called the ergoegotic operator. I know Jean-Michel discussed such matters thoroughly with the Society.

"The atonic energies interconnect our bioelectromagnetic fields and our kesdjan bodies, allowing us to have a collective mind or dream space. The collective mind is aphysical in its construction and function but intimately connects to every physical mindbrain unit. All mindbrains are potentially communicating with each other. Transfer of information is nearly instantaneous, as distances between persons are minute relative to the speed of information transfer occurring at the speed of light.

"This model aptly explains intuition and advanced immediate knowing. It also describes how kesdjan bodies persist following the body's physical death. A kesdjan body is our dream body awareness, so we can live anywhere within the Oneirion when allowed access. As the kesdjan bodies are living entities in the astral worlds, the kesdjan body continues to exist within the collective mind for some time after disconnection from the physical body.

"Kesdjan bodies are mortal but may feel as if they are immortal, for time sense for them is unusual.

"A kesdjan body may appear to live persons under certain circumstances. For example, suppose a person grieves strongly about a deceased loved one. In that case, their sorrow may attract the kesdjan body of the dead relative or friend. The kesdjan body will use its living partner's brain and material self to see, touch, smell, and hear. The mortal may feel it within or project it outward into space as if it were a material object. This explains the rare experience of ethereal beings in real séances and haunted houses.

"Questions, Sophie?"

"Only one question. How does this explain why some people report the existence of demons, angels, and cosmically significant beings?"

Gabriel smiles, knowing that Sophie would ask about demons and angels.

"It will take some time to answer this question, but we can begin. The easiest way to grasp the collective human psyche's existence and functioning is to understand that humankind's common dream world is a more descriptive phrase.

"The collective human sentient psyche came into existence only after our evolutionary forebears came to possess a suitably complex central nervous system. This central nervous system could produce aphysical images, using information stored in memory and spatial and temporal relationships to manifest nocturnal dreaming. Soon, our forebears noticed during sleep, and under the influence of hallucinogens, they coexisted in a dream world.

"One reason people believe that the collective human psyche pre-exists arises from frequent encounters with dead relatives living in various astral worlds.

"A second reason people believe in a pre-existing astral world is because of the appearance of strange creatures during nocturnal dreaming. Not realising that some creatures are only images imagined during diurnal awareness as myths.

"A third reason people believe in a pre-existing astral world is our need to explain physical illness, madness, death, and social inequalities. Based on anthropological studies, humans are hard-wired to objectify the formless as nouns. Why do bad things happen to good people and good things to bad people?

"Therefore, humanity created a grand virtual world filled with imaged demons and angels, mythical creatures, and kesdjan bodies without a physical vehicle out of the atonic energies. The astral is full of every imaginable Heaven and Hell, all available for residency by discarnate kesdjan agents. No wonder there is such confusion about what happens after physical death! Everyone is partially correct, as human desires and fantasies affect how the atonic energies manifest.

"The incredible thing is that these astral entities and objects live within the mindbrains of susceptible persons believing in the actuality of the middle world inhabitants. These mindbrains continue to provide atonic energies to feed such imagined creatures. Given time and mass belief, the astral entities, including vagrant kesdjan bodies, can infect their and other people's minds.

"Once you understand the nature and operational links between the physical and the astral, you will understand how the astral came to possess angelic and demonic layers. In a moment, I will explain who Satan is and the problem humankind has created by bringing such an Image into reality in the world of the Kabbalistic Qlippoth."

Sophie was speechless.

"Please do not think the collective human psyche, the conjoint Dreamworld, or the human astral world is the only astral world. Such middle worlds come into existence through the development of sentient life forms within our universe. Those possessing solid structures and complex central nervous systems (CNS). Over the past several million years, I have accessed astral worlds like yours and found that all hold nearly identical content. To the best of my knowledge, the creators of all experiential astral worlds are humanoid.

"Though not as imagined by the UFO groupies of the New Age Blunder Movement. This error continues to spread in the Oneirion through the efforts of the Infernal Realms' demonic denizens, the Astral Hell Worlds, *der Üntergeist*. Sorry, Sophie, even the ancient ones are not fully unconditional. That is a good reason not to make us perfected angels or gods.⁹

"Sophie, I realise my conversation may seem somewhat tangential and disjointed, but it cannot be any other way. I am feeding you ptahonic and atonic energies so that the two pieces best match your mental processes. Humans, by nature, do best when you provide knowledge that keeps them focused.

"In Islam, it is said that Allah created the magical Djinn in a separate creation. Regardless of how they came to be, humans call these entities demons because of ignorance. Their scripture states that some Djinn despise humans as humans came from clay, and Djinn came from fire. A few Djinn are super-egotistical, as they have given up the opportunity to exchange egoism for altruism. Their beings have crystallised.

This exchange is necessary to create an authentic Higher Being Body (HBB) or Soul.

"A few aberrant Djinn live in the collective human psyche to absorb atonic energies from the kesdjan bodies of the dead and the living. Such feeding is necessary for them to maintain life and egoism. Islam teaches that Iblis, or Satan-el, was not an Angel but a Djinn who lived in the Heavenly Worlds.

"They are selective feeders and will attach to humans who become fixated in their character by crystallising as confirmed egoists. Such humans gave up all desires to develop consciously. These Djinn feed off the creative energy resident within the host's kesjdan body until it is nonfunctional, withered, and mummified. They leave behind a social zombie. The living dead, Christ spoke of in the Gospels."

---

⁹ German for the Under Mind, Soul, or Spirit; contrasted with the Over Mind or Der Übergeist.

Gabriel stopped to observe Sophie's face for signs of understanding, unconscious at first and conscious later. She appeared to be okay and not overloaded.

"Now and then, a Djinn will find a sociopath whose egoism matches their own. In these cases, the Djinn finds feeding off the sociopath does not whither the creature's kesdjan body but increases its absorption of atonic energies, benefiting both creatures. For such persons, their kesdjan bodies can grow to become equal to the Djinn, becoming demons. Such entities are the Qlippoth in Kabbalah and powerful demons in the astral. They can last for aeons of human time, but like the deviant Djinn, they will not survive the end of our time, as all universes start free of evil."

After hearing about anti-souls, Sophie is surprised, asking, "Gabriel, how can this be true?"

Gabriel laughed.

"Sophie, why do all of you believe the forces working in our universe must be benign? No good or bad natural forces exist in the material world or within any creature. A tsunami or volcano has no preference for taking the life of a saint or a serial killer. Natural forces are without valence; it is the same with real magick.

"Physical and psychological forces act under natural law. Suppose a person's intentions arise from excessive egoism. In that case, this person is free to use coercion and physical power to rule as a minor god, presuming he has a sufficiently forceful personality to get others to cooperate. Thus, the strong oppress the meek and the weak, Sophie. It has always been so and will continue until Man becomes a higher species.

"It cannot differ from cosmic forces, my darling. God intended for each person to be free to do what each will do with the soul seed and its agent, the neurological ergoegotic operator.[10] One can make a working soul directed toward the Divine or a long-lasting kesdjan body directed toward oneself. I agree it is an unpleasant rule, but it is necessary and inherently fair in practise.

"So, if one's egoism and feeling of intrinsic self-worth are sufficiently firm, they can activate their ergoegotic operator to contact and draw down powerful cosmic energies. Remember, energies are without innate valence, for valence derives from the person's intentions using such powers.

"If they accumulate sufficient cosmic forces, they attain semi-permanence in the astral worlds. In doing so, they corrupt the kesdjan body, which turns dull black. Those choosing the altruistic possess bright, white kesdjan bodies. So now understand why White and Black Lodges exist in every separate universe.

"When the material universe reappeared, the Source infused into the physical and the aphysical worlds, the Divine Qualia. These Qualia allow four-brain creatures to form a vessel or *kli*[11] by ridding themselves of egoism. God desires every intelligent species to learn to work together to create one unified and perfected *Kli* composed of the individual *kelim*.[12] So fulfilling God's Wish that the universe chooses Altruism and Unconditional Love rather than egoism and self-love.

"This Divine Desire is the source for the concept of Ātman in Hinduism and the Universal Soul in Occidental mysticism.

"So, dearest, now you understand the actual hazard existing within every one of God's creations. Giving freedom to creatures in a universe to choose altruism over egoism invariably results in an ultimate battle

---

[10] An operator in mathematics is generally a mapping or function that acts on elements of a space to produce elements of another space (sometimes required to be the same space).
[11] Hebrew: *kli* is a single vessel, *kelim* are multiple kli.
[12] The *Adam Kadmon* of Kabbalah.

between Good and Evil. Each person must choose which side to fight upon, as the High Initiate Zoroaster taught in the 12th century BCE.

"A successful universe grows toward altruism and God, and it absorbs the individuals composing the Grand Soul into God or moves into the alternative universe as Guides. If the universe becomes mainly Egoistic, the Black Lodge's conscious beings cannot enter the Unborn State and dissolve during the Great Deflation-Inflation.

"Sophie, the growth of the Collective Mind of conscious, sentient beings is the purpose of Creation. As a universe evolves, the mindful portion of all sentient beings' collective minds grows in complexity and understanding, becoming more God-like over long aeons of clock time. Our Order calls the illuminated part of the collective mind *der Übergeist*.[13]

"In a genuine sense, darling, the purpose of every universe is to regenerate and expand the capacity of the previous Mind of God. We can say God created the universe so that the universe can recreate God. I call this God recovering Itself. Cool, eh?"

Sophie sat there, amazed at how much Gabriel knew and understood.

"Gabriel, you are much more than a Rose-Croix. I know you won't tell me exactly who you are, but will I find out one day?"

"At last, some patience. This is good. That question, darling, I will answer later. If I told you now, you would doubt my veracity. But you are correct; I am much more than Rose Croix. I will give you hints, so pay attention."

"I can wait, darling."

"The birth of an altruistic sentient race exists as proven by the evolution of the Djinn race living far away from this solar system. The Djinn race is naturally loving and carries the Holy Scriptures within

---

[13] Der Übergeist is German for the Higher or Over Mind or Spirit.

their kesdjan bodies. Their living religion is like that taught by Yeshua on Earth but without the errors introduced by the latter church. My sister Ariel and I gave this religion to the Djinn hundreds of thousands of years ago. But I will teach you about the Djinn later."

Chapter 3

The Proof of the Pudding is in the Eating

"But, Gabriel, isn't there something we can do on Earth to avoid making veritable demons?"

"There is a solution. It would be a good start if humans eradicated the genes contributing to sociopathy, presuming nothing else happened. Genetic testing of parents before pregnancy would be helpful to prevent the conception of sociopaths. Perhaps, one day, genetic re-engineering will fix these defective genes. It's a marvellous idea, but your species would mess it up. So, leave it alone.

"I think I will take you on a dream journey into the conjoint dream world to show you, in person, so to speak, that all that I have told you is true. Remember, do not believe new things until you can verify and understand. Second Teaching. Are you up for a journey, my dear?"

"I would like to observe all that you have told me first-hand. What must I do?"

"Sit straight in your chair, close your eyes, and allow your presence to move into the quietness within. Imagine our two chairs are inside a side room in the Order's Grand Temple as you rest. Our safe place is filled with soft light and sweet rose incense. As you relax in your chair, allow your kesdjan body to leave its vehicle and stand a few feet away, facing your body. When you see your physical body, I want you to imagine a powerful silver force field composed of atons surrounding it. A force field that can reject all evil attempting to penetrate your physical body while you are away.

"Take about thirty seconds to visualise such a force field, knowing that your physical body can rest and feel safe while your kesdjan body travels with mine. When you finish, allow your kesdjan body to turn to your left, and you will see my kesdjan body standing two yards away. Will your kesdjan body so it is next to mine and take my right hand in your left hand. Perfect, Sophie.

"Now, I want you to imagine that you and I have another force field that will repeal all evil beings so they cannot infect your kesdjan body. I will help you, darling, and stay within the force field so you will feel safe. I do not need such protection as nothing can harm me."

Sophie felt a field composed of pure goodness forming around her. While she could easily see through this atonic sphere, she noticed it glowed with a golden-violet hue.

Laughing, she said, "Gabriel, this is cool. You know how to treat a lady on a first date. What's next?"

Gabriel securely places his arm around her waist, saying, "Here we go, Sophie, off into the wild blue yonder to find some wayward Djinn."

The two kesdjan bodies rose high in the evening sky.

"We're flying, Gabriel. I feel so free."

Soon, Gabriel said, "Look, Sophie, two Djinn are smoking a hookah at a table. Because of our shield, they will not even know we are eavesdropping."

This surprised Sophie because the Djinn did not look like those in the Arabian stories.

"Sophie, astral beings appear to humans in the forms imagined by humans as they inhabit the dream worlds. The Djinn see us as they imagine us to be. Listen carefully. Tell me what you see."

"I see two Djinn sitting at a table with what appears to be a hookah. As they talk, they take puffs from the hookah. I see the charcoal burn hotter when inhaled and see smoke in the tubes, but no smoke comes out when exhaling. Why?"

"Sophie, what do you think they use for tobacco?"

"I don't know, what?"

"The tobacco they smoke is an extract from human kesdjan bodies. It's pure atonic energy, the energy of creativity and individuality. They pluck some out of their marks and then smoke it for nourishment. They see humans as sheep-like creatures, existing mainly for food."

Sophie puts her arms around Gabriel and wrinkles her nose.

"This is disgusting, Gabriel. Can we go somewhere else, please?"

Gabriel takes her hand, and instantly, they enter a murky cave. This cave is inside a monstrous rock mountain within a desolate plain of sand and rocks stretching as far as the eyes can see.

"Sophie, I am taking you into one of the Hell regions, so you will see what usually happens to those creatures who absorb and misuse atonic energies. Many caves like this exist in this world, each containing one individual hasnamuss.

"Gabriel, what is a hasnamuss?"

"Sophie, a hasnamuss is a name created by my student Gurdjieff in the early 20th century. This word means 'someone who outwardly receives much honour and attention as a developed being, but inwardly is nothing but excrement.' He possesses power and position in the eyes of the world, but his end is excretion out of existence (nice pun, eh?). Gurdjieff loved to mix languages to create unfamiliar words.

"There are three kinds of hasnamusses. The difference between types is not egoism corrupting the kesdjan body but how much atonic energy it used and perverted to its use, damaging other beings. We call the worst of such beings eternal hasnamuss. Watch. Soon, you will see what was once a human being."

Before them stood an ugly creature chained to a stone throne by an anklet of steel on its right leg in a chamber lit by several natural gas vents. The beast has dark yellow fur streaked with its excrement. Its face is frozen into a perpetual sneer, its eyes are wicked, empty spheres filled with egoism, and its mouth is full of rotten, yellow teeth. It could not stand up straight, for its spine curved severely forward.

All the creature could say was, "I am God. I am supreme. All bow down to me."

But no one is around to listen or respond. In death, its kesdjan body is as blind as in life.

The cave walls transformed into mirrors at random moments. The creature sees itself as a misshapen, ugly beast, remembering how it had lived its mortal life. For a moment, the creature realises it has become what it is by its actions and feels the pain it inflicted upon those it hurt in its earthly life. In these moments of total clarity, it hears the voices of those it hurt, laughing at the ugly creature it is. Realising it will be so until the end of time, all vermin face extermination.

Gabriel said, "Egoism is not the best path in life, I would say. Do you know there are thousands upon thousands of such creatures in this Hell?"

Knowing the gravity of the situation, Sophie buries her face in Gabriel's chest.

"Gabriel, please take me somewhere pleasant. I can hardly breathe in here."

Gabriel whisks them off to a pleasant meadow in another part of the Oneirion.

Feeling that she is now in a pleasant place, she asks, "Gabriel, did God put that creature in Hell?"

"No, Sophie. God does not reward or punish any kesdjan body after physical death. As you will soon learn, each kesdjan body chooses its afterlife residence based upon its core love. The love which is most precious and most desired. We will visit a dear friend of mine, originally from Sweden, who knows much about the Heavenly and Hellish regions of the astral."

"However, I will answer your question. But you must not forget the Divine Quale: Caring-Compassion, or Unconditioned Love, is the most potent. This Divine Force underlies all cohesion, attraction, and unification forces in the physical and the Oneirion.

"In his distorted mind, this hasnamuss believes he is his world's God and Creator. He has manufactured a place in an imaginary region of the Oneirion, which is most ironic. His wishes to be like God were most imprudent, as he failed to realise that gods can only create in their own image.

"As a hideous, selfish creature, all conscious life in his imagined universe is ugly and knows only to take. All his creatures see him as he really is, destroying his temples. The sole loves in his pretend world are aggrandisement and hoarding. So, he kills one universe to make another, which naturally takes billions of years, and it always turns out to be the same.

"One would think, given his guaranteed failures and his few moments of clarity between creations, that he would come to understand. But, no. He is a blind Samuel and will never see."

"Wow! I can see something great, fair, and good underlying these astral worlds."

"Honey, I want you to meet a dear friend."

Gabriel takes Sophie by her right hand, and the two disappear and reappear elsewhere.

A portly, elderly man hurries toward them. His white, curly hair falls to his shoulders. He dresses in a green velvet coat, knickers, black shoes with silver buckles, and white stockings covering his calves and knees. Sophie guesses he wears clothing popular in early 18th-century Northern Europe. He has the most pleasant face, and kindness surrounds his person.

As the gentleman grew close, he said, slightly out of breath, "Gabriel, my old friend. I see you have brought a student to visit with me. How nice."

Gabriel and the old gentleman share a hug.

"Yes, Emanuel, this is Sophie, and we are on a vital mission this evening for the benefit of the future. I was hoping you could explain to her your visions of Heaven and Hell during your mortal life. Sophie, give this old coot a friendly hug, please. You will adore him."

Sophie hugs Emanuel.

"It is an utmost pleasure to make the acquaintance of such a beautiful and cultured lady. My name is Emanuel Swedenborg. I imagine you have heard my name?"

"Yes, I know a Swedenborgian Church exists, but I have not read your books. I am sorry."

Sophie's face flushes just a little from a tinge of embarrassment.

Emanuel, chuckling, said, "No matter. Today, I will share my visions of Heaven and Hell, which arose from the human astral plane. We stand on the plane onto which the angels of death bring the kesdjan bodies of the recently departed. I spoke of souls in my books, but when I finally passed and arrived here, I learned my visions had been correct but that some of my Lutheran concepts were erroneous.

"When I first got to the entrance plane, Gabriel greeted me and corrected some of my misunderstandings. He explained I would do a great service to the few kesdjan bodies that would reincarnate in the physical. They need refinement in Purgatory. As a mentor, I prepare them for another life by teaching them more about God's Plan. It was sound advice, so I have been here tutoring and mentoring for the past two and one-half centuries. Come with me. I know a nice little coffee and tea shop to talk in. These old legs still get tired."

Emanuel wrinkled his nose. The trio sits at a table in a flower garden resembling one in midsummer England. A plate of freshly baked scones, clabbered cream, and blackberry jam are on the table. Next to it rests a plate of ham, roast beef, watercress, butter, and cucumber tea sandwiches on white bread with no crusts. Emanuel reaches over to lift an old porcelain teapot and pours tea for his guests. Then he offers sugar and cream. After serving everyone dark English tea, Emanuel begins.

"Sophie, when a human being goes through transition, his physical body releases its kesdjan body, and several angels come to meet it. These angels explain they died and came to deliver their kesdjan bodies to an arrival plane between Heaven and Hell. The angels tell them this plane is a school for kesdjan bodies, which God created so that the departed could review how they lived their mortal lives. During the review, the angels point out significant errors made and how such errors happened. They encourage them to begin honest repenting by serving in Heaven to help those they had harmed.

"Sometimes, a new arrival repents and works hard to help those she hurt through greed, selfishness, or just not caring. She feels more substantial and joyful as she repents (Metanoia) and performs Heavenly Community Service. Such joy encourages her to work even harder to cleanse what she thinks is the soul.

"Eventually, one completes their time of service, and the faithful angels transport them to the lowest Heaven. The sincerest repenters have earned the privilege of entering the highest Heaven. They learned to love selfless work so much that they did not want to stop helping God. They discovered that the most significant core love is to love God and those around them more than themselves.

"Purgatory is the best place of all, for it is where kesdjan bodies can decide to become helpers for the Holy Family and become reincarnating individuals. It is infrequent, and this troubles this old heart."

Brightening up and smiling, he said, "Sophie, you have learned the true purpose of Purgatory, eh?"

"Yes, thanks. Even if we misuse our universe's forces, God ensures we have more than one chance to get with the plan if we choose?"

"Yes, Sophie, Our Common Father-Mother is more generous and loving than any creature can imagine, but by choice restricted in what is possible. Freedom to choose is the greatest gift for a Father and Mother to give their children. God is not egotistical, so the Godhead does not want followers. God wants the Greatest Good for All. Unfortunately, freedom of choice in four-brain creatures births evilness with the failure of most universes."

"But, Emanuel, cannot God do whatever God wants?"

"Sophie, it is impossible to say much about God's Actions. Even the angels in the innermost heaven cannot experience God directly. God is beyond quantification and objectification. God is Unfathomable, Inscrutable, Timeless, and so on.

"For instance, for the angels existing within the Celestial, or Innermost, Heaven, loving the Lord does not mean loving an objectification of God as a person. But means loving the Goodness that is the Divine, and to love the Good is to will the Good. Loving one's neighbour does not mean loving a companion concerning her person. It means loving her innate expression of the truth, for loving truth is to will to do the truth.

"Love is the Good, and the Truth is Wisdom. Love is the male valence of gender, and Wisdom is the female. Creation occurs when the male and female reconcile through God's Will. Creation is nothing but a conscious Act or a Good Work. Thus, Gabriel says, 'loving good is to will, and doing good is to love.'

"However, God can only bring something into Creation by partially withdrawing Itself from Itself to create a deficiency to fill. The withdrawal of Itself causes limitations and restrictions on Its Actions and the new universe's possibilities. The great Kabbalist, Rabbi Luria, called this the *tzimtzum*."

"So, what did God withdraw to bring life and mind into a new universe, Sophie? Any idea?"

"I do not know, for I do not understand yet?"

Gabriel intervenes.

"Now, darling, you can answer this question. Stop trying to use your serial reasoning. Just open your intellect to the answer. Based on what you have learned, what is the primary difference between God's essential nature and the physical world? You heard this long ago, so just open your mind."

Sophie stops thinking for a few seconds.

"I know. The universe may be imaginably vast, but it is finite. Everything observable in the universe exists because of discrete geometry, discrete temporality, and discrete, energetic quanta. Continuity is a mathematical idealisation, just as is a null point or an infinite sine wave. Therefore, we all perceive and imagine nouns doing actions as observable objects.

"Therefore, God as the Source must be Mathematical, an Absolute Unity, Absolute Continuity, True Infinity, Unbounded, and Eternal. If the world is discrete, infinitely long sine waves cannot exist. Therefore, the infinite waves needed in quantum mechanical equations are only approximations in our universe. They must exist in God, and God is a mathematical singularity and infinity, present simultaneously. Therefore, the ancients taught, 'In the beginning, God geometrised.'

"The simple answer is that God removed Its Continuity by removing Itself. By disrupting Continuity, there came to be Discreteness and a finite and discrete universe. I know I am correct about what I just said; I did not need to think about it."

Gabriel stretches over and kisses Sophie on her cheek.

"Good job. I knew you knew the answer, my dear. Do you also know I love and adore you?"

Gabriel's comment catches Sophie off-guard, and she blushes and looks at Gabriel with wide eyes.

After a few seconds of silence, she says, "But you just met me. How can you love me? I want to love you and have you love me in return."

"Sweet Sophie, I exist in all your past, future, and present moments. I know where you will be until the end of this universe. I write the destinies of significant sentient creatures, so I know your future. A destiny you will achieve, darling. But we need not worry about this now. Trust me."

Turning to Swedenborg, Gabriel said, "She's a keeper, I think."

Swedenborg nods yes, sips his tea, and reaches for a third scone.

The trio finish the scones and tea sandwiches amidst the stories of Swedenborg. Everyone is silent as to a more serious discussion. Sophie finds him one of the most fascinating people she has ever met.

Soon, afternoon tea time ends.

Swedenborg said, "Sophie, I want to show you something most important and misunderstood by the Doctors of the Church on Earth."

Instantaneously, the trio watches a kesdjan body sinking into the Earth and moving toward the Hell regions.

Sophie hears this person mumbling, "I dislike Heaven. I do not find it at all pleasant or desirable. I need a harlot, and I need some gold. These are available, so I choose Hell over Heaven. Poof, the man disappeared into the lower regions."

Then Sophie saw a young man speaking with his angels. "I understand I made quite a few mistakes and did some injury, and I am genuinely sorry for my ignorance. However, I am glad I can do Heavenly Community Service and do not mind if the Lord desires me to continue. I know I feel the good of love and the need to act respectfully by being useful. Therefore, dear friends, I only request that you find a suitable place of service for me."

The angels smiled and took him by both arms to the middle of Heaven.[14] In a moment, Sophie, Swedenborg, and Gabriel are alone on the plain.

Gabriel asks, "Do you understand the significance of what Emanuel just showed you?"

"Yes, neither God nor His Angels punish or reward anyone. Love is the Supreme Quale in Creation. Everyone chooses their core loves while alive. Purgatory provides a second chance to decide whether one's core loves are proper to Heaven or Hell. The young man saw that his core love was unhealthy and worked to undo what he had done. He chose Heaven. The other man did not want to change his core love of harlots and gold, so he chose Hell. I say this system is the fairest of all."

"Correct, Sophie, you have learned the most important lesson. God Bless you, and enjoy your time with Gabriel. He may never call upon you again, so do not waste his time," said Emanuel, turning to Gabriel, "you might visit this old man more often."

With an enormous wave of goodbye, Sophie and Gabriel are off on more adventures.

Rather than leaving Swedenborg, Sophie found herself and Gabriel back with Swedenborg.

Swedenborg said, "Gabriel, I am shocked you forgot to ask me to explain to Sophie why individual angels, angelic societies, and even the Heavens appear as human beings. And why individuals living in Hell, demons, demon societies, and even the Hells appear as monsters.

---

[14] Swedenborg uses an Octave Model for the afterlife with three Heavens, three Hells, and the intermediate region of Purgatory. Using the heptatonic music scale, the lowest Hell sounds the 'do' note, Purgatory the 'fa' note, the highest Heaven the 'si' note, and the Divine as the unattainable 'Do' note of the Octave.

Sophie has met one of the eternal hasnamusses and saw how he appears as a hideous creature."

Gabriel replied, "I forgot, but then again, I have much to teach Sophie this evening, as I am time-limited. Please explain the concept of the human form to Sophie."

"Sophie, do you remember the first book of the Torah, Bereshit? Christians call it Genesis? For the best understanding, we must go to the earliest available source."

"Yes."

"In Bereshit 1:27 of the Orthodox Jewish Bible, it reads, 'So G-d created humankind in His tzelem (image), in the tzelem Elohim (image of G-d) created He him; zachar (male) and nekevah (female) created He them.'

"The King James Bible reads, 'So God created man in his image, in the image of God, created He him; male and female created He them.' However, I believe the Orthodox version is more accurate.

"In the Orthodox version, God is the unfathomable source. The Elohim, plural and emanated as a human being, is a family of human forms known as the Divine Hexad. The male Elohim is the Emanation of God's Divine Will, Love, Intelligence, and Truth. The female forms are Space and Time.

"Subsequently, whenever a person experiences communion with God, they commune with the Elohim, the First Emanation of God, which provides an experiential form for perception by the inner eyes and ears. I refer to our psychic facilities, which Gabriel calls the ergoegotic operator.

"The proper form of the Elohim is like a human family, grandparents, parents, and children.

"Gabriel teaches how the Source must lie beyond conceptualisation, objectification, definition, and experience. Gabriel teaches that the best a living creature can do is to realise the most transparent realisation or mental picture. This understanding of the Unfathomable Source is discussed in the Teachings of the Kabbalah and the Vedic Schools.

"We know the First Manifested Emanation of Creation by the name Keter and likely arose from the earlier Hebrew concepts of the Elohim. Keter is the head of the Heavenly Man. The Jain religion shares similar concepts as to the structure of Creation. They see the universe in the form of a Man. Enlightened jivas reside in the head as they have exhausted their karmic debt. But I will stick with Kabbalah as I am unfamiliar with Eastern religious philosophy.

"Supporting Keter is the Unknowable Source before Its Self-Manifestation. The Kabbalists picture the First Outpouring of God as three invisible Sefirot lying unmanifest behind Keter, Chokhmah, and Binah. They are known as *Ein, Ein Sof, and Ein Sof Ohr*. These three are reduced to the term *Ein Sof*.

"*Ein Sof* refers to a state characterised by Limitless, Nameless, Unmanifest, Unfathomable, or Without Existence. The Christian Kabbalists call these Divine Will, Divine Good, and Divine Truth.

This concept of a Heavenly being, subordinate to the Source responsible for Creation, exists in many ancient philosophies. The Gnostic Teachings speak of the Dēmiourgos as the Creator of the Universes. Still, they are often thought antagonistic to God. Speaking such is incorrect, for the Highest Beings do not support it. They report that antagonism with the Elohim only arose with conscious creatures.

"The Vedic concept of Brahman-Ātman predates the ancient Hebrew concept of the Elohim. In the Upanishads, Brahman represents the metaphysical, ontological, and soteriological principles inherent in the universe. The Vedas describe Brahman as the universe's Source and Ātman as the highest universal principle, the universe's ultimate reality. Another term used for the Ultimate Self is Ātman.

"Ātman being the primordial reality that creates, maintains, and withdraws within itself the universe, its contents, the cosmic principles, the causes of everything, including all gods. The Divine Being, the God within, the Single Soul, animates the universe and lives within each living being.

"To reinforce this explanation, I will take you to a place where you can see one angel, a society of angels with a similar understanding of good and truth, and Heaven itself."

Swedenborg did as he said. The angel appeared in a human form, and a group of angels appeared in a human form (but the facial features transformed). The Divine allowed Sophie to see that Heaven's fullness was in the image of a human being. At last, Sophie could see all the existing universes, and they, too, assumed the form of a great human being.

When they returned to the tea garden, Sophie said, "This is amazing. Now, I know why the Jain religion teaches the universe is as an immense human being in which the most enlightened reside in the upper head and the lowest in the feet."

Gabriel said, "Isn't it curious, Sophie, how often the plain truth written within Holy Books remains unseen, and few understand the profundity of what is there? Thanks, Emanuel. Goodbye."

And with that, the pair disappeared.

Chapter 4

Return to Damascus

s they travelled to the new destination, Gabriel sang, "Back in the saddle again, out where a friend is a friend. Riding the range once more, Totting my old 44...."

"Gabriel, where did you get that song, Gabriel. It sounds ancient?"

"Ancient. You must be kidding. It is from the days of the Westerns at the movies and on TV. The singer is Gene Autry. Don't they teach history about Americana's substantial contributions to music in school?"

Sophie stuck her tongue out at Gabriel as they arrived back on the roof in Damascus, close to the same time they left.

Gabriel said, "I do not have the luxury on this All-Saints' Day and Night to accumulate validation time in the Astral. We will take more journeys, Sophie. I figured you probably need to tinkle, so the bathroom is downstairs, the first door to the left. I will fix us a bite to eat."

Sophie goes to the bathroom. When she returns, she sees a Greek-style dinner on a Greek table with an ancient amphora sealed with Aleppo Pine resins to prevent oxygen from spoiling the wine.

Ater Sophie sat Gabriel asked, "Sophie, have you ever drunk white or rosé Retsina wine from Greece and Ionia? I recovered the wine in the amphora from a sunken ship in the Mediterranean Sea. The ship sank around 500 BCE, and I did it when you were in the restroom. It is nicely chilled, and the seal is intact."

"I like Greek food and Retsina wine. I think I will enjoy this dinner. Where is the food from?"

"I retrieved the food from a symposium table of Pericles, who is normally frugal. We have barley cakes for bread with olive oil. Appetisers include roasted chestnuts, chickpeas, beans, toasted wheat, and honey cakes. Our fish course is tuna grilled with tomatoes, onions, garlic, and green olives. The meat course is a leg of lamb with a red wine sauce. For dessert, there are figs, raisins, and pomegranates. And twenty-four-hundred-year-old wine."

"How did you get this stuff? What is happening is impossible?"

"Sweetheart, I was on the ship that sunk, and Pericles was a good friend of mine. Why are you so surprised?"

"But Gabriel, how could you have lived in ancient Greece? You can't be over thirty-five?"

Suddenly, she is ravenously hungry and reaches for a plate to try the appetisers. Gabriel opens the amphora and pours two glasses. The wine is rosé and clear. After pouring two portions, Gabriel and Sophie toasted to the God of their hearts and realisation and took the first sip.

"Gabriel, this wine is outstanding. I cannot imagine drinking twenty-four-hundred-year-old wine. Much less enjoying the same food that the great Athenian Pericles was about to eat in 450 BCE. You know how to make a girl fall for you. I mean, you are fun to be with."

Gabriel raises his glass, laughing.

"Sophie, I make this toast for what is within this precious lady. You are a gemstone, and I am immensely enjoying my time with you. But I am not sure I am your polar complement.

"Drink some more wine. Let us eat dinner. I will tell you about my immortal life, but it is a secret.

"Oh, I almost forgot, we need some nice harp music."

Suddenly, two ancient harpists appeared and played the most ethereal music in honour of the many stars.

"I have never met a true mage, Gabriel. You are such, are you not? How else could I be here with such a handsome and considerate man? Why didn't I say something before?"

"Darling, all comes when the need arises. I am a genuine Mage, probably the best in many universes."

Sophie and Gabriel enjoyed the wine, the food, and each other. The moon was high in the sky, and the landscape was blue-tinged, surreal, and enchanting. The shadows of the trees seemed to touch each other for companionship.

Soon, both were drunk, and Sophie was exhausted.

Gabriel takes Sophie downstairs to a bedroom and puts her to bed.

"Sophie, we will continue after you rest. Do not worry. The clock will stop running, and we will lose no time."

Sophie awoke feeling rested and in clarity. She felt as if she had slept for some eight hours. Sophie's first thought upon waking concerned her dream and how real it felt.

It was still dark when she awoke. After washing her face, she returns to the roof. The moon and stars were in the same position as when she went to sleep. Gabriel is standing near the roof's edge and looking into the surroundings.

He hears her footsteps.

"Sophie, nice to see you rested and content in your heart. Come over here, for I want to show you something."

Sophie walks over and stands to Gabriel's left.

"Sophie, what do you see when you gaze from the roof?"

"I see the buildings in front of this house and many lights. Why do you ask?"

"I ask you, for you need to learn about the law of correspondence. Allow me to explain. Suppose you turn around slowly for 360 degrees. In that case, you will see houses of different sizes, varying crooked streets, and narrow alleys separating them. Look and notice that some homes have roof gardens like this one, others are larger, some have many windows, some not so many, some brightly lit, and others less. They all have front doors. Some have courtyards, and some do not. Some have a single floor, and others have two or three.

"However, regardless of detail, Sophie, each possesses the structure to be a house. Large or small, each protects the furniture and people living inside from intruders and inclement weather. Each serves the same purpose, for every home is a place for people to live.

"When we visit a house, each has a kitchen to prepare food for the inhabitants. There is a hearth that burns coal or wood to cook and a place to sit and eat nearby. There are pails for water and bins to store grains and legumes. Each serves the same purpose, even though vast differences may exist in the design.

"Now, Sophie, think about all these houses, joined by many roads and alleys, composing neighbourhoods. These neighbourhoods comprise an ancient city that has existed for thousands of years. This city is similar in composition to many old cities. Each city was built to enhance its dwellers' survival and lifestyle.

"If you think of nations, though they differ in certain belief systems and mores, they serve similar purposes using similar designs. It is correct to conclude that kitchens, houses, cities, and nations correspond to function and basic purposes. In a kitchen in Damascus or England, I see how houses, cities, and nations correspond to each other in kind, though different in degree. Do you understand, darling?"

"I understand, Gabriel. My friend Jean-Michel taught me how cells, organs, creatures, and life upon Earth are similar, though different in degree."

"Our friend Jean-Michel is a genius, Sophie. He flashed through the spiritual levels, for his intuitive understanding is incredible. Our Common Father-Mother chose him a long time ago, his real Name is Ezer-el. I think someday he will join me, Sophie. Did he ever mention this?"

"No, Jean-Michel doesn't brag often. He never boasts; he always tells me that when God asks him to help, he does so and gives credit to God.

"Sophie, when you do well, be proud for one day only. On the second day, your new skill or understanding is now part of the job God wants you to do.'

"You were right, Gabriel. I love Jean-Michel deeply; he is like a brother."

Gabriel smiles, "I am glad, Sophie."

Seeing Gabriel's joy for both was as if the Sun Absolute had awakened to increase the light it sent to Mother Moon. For a moment, Sophie saw Gabriel as an angel or even higher.

Gabriel smiled once more.

"Yes, Sophie, I was a man long ago and in a different universe. I reincarnated many times. During one life, I attained permanence. Though I never found myself in Heaven, I was an Initiate at the end of our time and would survive the end times. Someday, you and Jean-Michel will be like me. An angel who forsakes Heaven for the good of the many. Many hear the call, but few answer.

"Enough about kitchens. I have something much more important to show you. We are going on another astral journey, so sit down and follow the instructions I gave you earlier."

Sophie did as requested, and soon, the pair returned to Swedenborg's Purgatory plane. In front of them stood a handsome, angelic couple. The male angel introduced himself and his wife and gave Sophie some information about the sanctity and joy of spiritual marriage.

After some time had passed in conversation, Gabriel said, "Remember, Sophie, every angel in Heaven has a human form, for this is the form of your species. Watch as your new friends return to the Society of Angels; in which all members are resonant to each other. From this distance, the angel society assumes the form of a rather large angel. Do you see it, Sophie?"

"I do, Gabriel. I see the big angel."

"We are going to move far enough away so you see that Heaven, composed of many angel societies, takes the form of an even grander angel. Do you see it, Sophie?"

"I see, Gabriel, I see. It is like kitchens, houses, cities, and nations. I see why the Elohim in Genesis says, 'We create humankind, in our image will he be.' It is incredible, magnificent. I appreciate the review of what Emanuel taught earlier."

"Good, remember this, Sophie. This observation is most important for understanding the human Oneirion. Come, I will take you closer to the realms of Hell so you see that Hell also assumes a humanoid form. Not beautiful and inviting as with the angels, but hideous."

Chapter 5

Hell

Sophie stands with Gabriel in a desolate and barren landscape. The plain is flat, covered with dirty sand, and dark rock outcroppings. Here and there stand deformed and near-leafless trees. In these trees sat black vultures with blood-red eyes and sharp talons searching for carrion.

Near where the two stood, Sophie saw emperor scorpions scurrying about, tearing and devouring the rotting flesh left upon what looked like a human skeleton stripped of its organs by the vultures.

The sky is dark brown, and no sun is visible, though the lighting is adequate.

"Gabriel, is the skeleton that of a human being," Feeling she wants to vomit.

"I would not say it is the skeleton of a human being, Sophie. It is the skeleton of a demon, once a human being, attempting to escape from Hell and killed by the guarding vultures. A tough way to lose one's kesdjan body."

"Gabriel, I am afraid of this place. Can we leave, please? I believe our perceptions of Hell contain hideous, distorted, humanoid creatures. Remember the hasnamuss we visited. It only makes sense that Hell and its societies would assume the form of monstrous humanoid creatures. I know many paintings and statues of demons have horns, cloven feet, and tails. Such accoutrements reflect the more hedonic and animal side of the passions they prefer. I don't think we need to go see them, right?"

"Sophie, I understand; however, there is an educational benefit in gaining knowledge of the appearance of demons, so you will recognise them. You need to become familiar with the appearances of various demonic classes. You must know how to recognise them when they assume a more acceptable form. Otherwise, you will be vulnerable to their deceitful ways.

"Sophie, I will give you time to prepare for this exercise in hideousness. It is not as bad as it sounds, and the smell is worse than their appearance. Let us go to the tea garden and chat before proceeding."

Soon, both were sitting in the tea garden, waiting for a pot of Earl Grey tea to finish brewing.

Swedenborg sits with them, so he speaks to Sophie.

"I understand Gabriel will take you for a visit to Hell. It is scary initially, but they may not harm you in Hell."

Sophie looks sternly at Gabriel.

"Weren't you going to tell me this? Or did you want to scare the Hell out of me?"

Emanuel finds Sophie's expression funny and laughs, saying.

"I think this is what Martin Luther hoped he could do."

Gabriel replied, "Sorry, I am so used to demons that spending a day with them does not differ from being near a sulphur pool. They can be interesting, though. I hope Your Highness will forgive me?"

"Okay, Gabriel. But do not do this to me again!"

Swedenborg interrupts, "Please, children. Stop bickering and listen up. Now, I remember why I never married."

Both Sophie and Gabriel immediately look at Swedenborg.

Swedenborg begins, "Sophie, all the angels in Heaven and demons in Hell did not exist before advanced sentient beings came into existence. Therefore, both Heaven and Hell are creations of humanity to reflect the quality of the kesdjan images of future inhabitants. Thus, the afterlife portion of the Astral Complex is solely the human conjoint mind's product over many thousands of years. It is free of alien creatures and influences.

"This does not mean only angels, demons, and humans solely populate the human dream and astral world. Other kinds of creatures exist. This area needs more study.

"The creation story in Genesis is only a symbolic explanation of the psychospiritual nature of humanity. It does not explain how the universe came into material existence. Much of the Old and New Testaments are about individuals' psychological development from animal to spiritual. So, the Bible has nonsense, historical, psychoistic, and spiritual levels.

"Subsequently, the proper level for a fundamental understanding of scripture is upon the spiritual. The Hebrew and Christian Testaments refer to man created in the image of Elohim. They relate to the faith of understanding and the will's love. Genesis and Bereshit deal with the spiritual form of man and not specifically with the physical.

"Therefore, the Lord appeared as a man to the prophets, and Daniel wrote, he saw the Son of Man in the clouds of Heaven. Jesus referred to himself as the Son of Man. Such is why angels possess human form. The psychospiritual imago of man is the kesdjan body. The Jains believe the World exists as an original man in their metaphysics. Explaining why the Heavens have human form and why the spiritual universe is human-like.

"Hellish creatures possessed human form before the transition and assumed more grotesque forms in Hell. The hideousness of form is proportional to the heart's stoniness regarding self-love and greed. You will verify what I am telling you soon, my dear.

"Don't worry, Sophie, once you get used to the smell and the difficulty of getting a word of truth from these self-damned souls, it is just unpleasant. They are not that scary in Hell. So, I shall get on with my business. Cheers, Gabriel."

And Swedenborg vanished.

In a moment, Sophie and Gabriel had returned to the desert area they had previously visited. In front of the pair looms a small tunnel leading into a rocky basalt crag. The entrance to the tunnel was the darkest black Sophie had ever seen. The opening was so narrow that Sophie could not see how she or Gabriel could pass through. The darkness seemed to flow out from the entrance, striking her face and causing goosebumps. A shiver of something cold, stale, and sinister was issuing forth from the bowels of the tunnel, smelling of sulphur. A collage of her past life filled her mind, and terror seized her. She grabbed Gabriel's left arm and hid her face.

"Gabriel, please, take me away. I can hardly catch my breath, and my heart is beating so fast I will wet my panties. Please, Gabriel, please."

Gabriel takes her into his arms, saying several words that sound like the angels' language.

"Sophie, the language is Enochian. You will feel the terror draining from your body and into the sand below your feet. I promise you, it shall not return. You will no longer be afraid of what you do not know yet. I promise."

Sophie felt the terror draining out from the soles of her feet and onto the sandy plain. The terror, replaced by some energy from Gabriel entering her physical and kesdjan bodies, calms and strengthens her resolve.[15]

"Gabriel, has part of you merged with my astral body? I feel you inside of me, and I like it very much. I have felt alone all my life, but now I feel connected to someone; I feel I am a part of you, and you are a part of me. It is pure love and goodness. Gabriel, what have you given me? I must know."

Gabriel, still holding her in his arms.

"Sophie, we joined. For the moment, you need not speak to me. You are hearing my thoughts and experiencing my feelings directly. You have assumed the form of an angel, and this is how angels communicate. Enochian is the language of angels' thoughts and deep magick in the human astral. So think, and I will understand. The angelic language will prove useful on our journey into the Hell realms, for demons cannot understand it. Even in the darkest and most evil-infested regions where the Satan archetype dwells."

Sophie thought, "If the feeling I have with you inside of me, Gabriel, is what angels feel in Heaven, I hope I will live there one day. If only people knew this feeling."

Gabriel said, "If they could feel it inherently, they would see they have little freedom of choice. Freedom of choice is the most precious gift in every universe. The inherent right to choose between the good of altruistic love and truth and the good of self-aggrandisement and worldly core loves.

"Freedom of choice allows the astral creation of heavens and hells. While residing in the physical realm, humanity places itself under moral rules beneficial to all members of society. Providing sufficient wealth, social fame, social reputation, family, sexual access, and the fear of corporal punishment and banishment keep many evil hearts in

---

[15] The Higher actualises the Lower to realise the Middle World of possibilities.

check. The core loves of men and women are for a profitable station in life.

"Competition between city-states and nations kept the ruling aristocracy in check. Hence, things work sufficiently well for men and women to work towards living cooperatively. Human history shows that egoism and cruelty often breach society's safeguards, and human madness erupts with its genocide. Eventually, the controls are back in place.

"However, after the first, or physical death, a heinous evil kesdjan body is free of the restrictions placed upon it by physicality and social mores. Freedom from its physical vehicle allows it to persist in the collective human psyche by absorbing and processing the atonic energies associated with and processed by humankind. The atonic energies maintain the form of the kesdjan body as an entity after physical death. The shapes of such kesdjan bodies reflect the quality of its core loves. This explains why angels have pleasant human forms, and demons have hideous ones when seen in the Divine Light."

"But, Gabriel, Jean-Michel once told me that most kesdjan bodies do not reincarnate and eventually disintegrate. How can this be if Heaven and Hell exist?"

"It sounds like I am creating a new story, Sophie. I will explain later. The full report is much more convoluted than Jean-Michel told you. Sometimes, he forgets he knows so much more than most people.

"I explained why we are on this journey and introduced you to Swedenborg. He is a dear old gentleman, but his knowledge is incomplete. I cannot show you the truth in its fullness, for you would not see it at all. I must do this piecemeal.

"Sophie, hold my hand, and we shall easily pass through the entrance. Remember, you and I are not in our physical bodies but in our kesdjan ones. Kesdjan bodies are like water, taking the shape of any container opening."

Gabriel stretches his form into a long pole and pulls Sophie with him.

She does not feel the darkness, nor is she afraid, thinking, "I am totally in love with Gabriel at this moment.?"

Gabriel answered her with a silent laugh, "Sophie, you feel in love with me as I am channelling the protection of Love into you, my dense little friend."

The pair found themselves in an enormous cavern with some rude huts. The men sat apart from each other, sharpening mining shovels and picks. The women appear to grind grain for bread or gruel using a stone pestle and mortar. As Sophie looks around, she sees normal-looking men and women working silently.

Everyone is naked and appears between thirty and forty years old, attractive, and well-endowed. Both have more body hair than is typical for humans, and all the men have firm erections.

Suddenly, a man approaches a woman.

The woman looks up and said, "What do you want? You must work."

The man replied, "I am in lust, harlot. Satisfy my needs; this is my command."

The woman and other women in Hell are harlots; the woman moves from her sitting position to place her behind in front of the man. She is on her knees with her torso extended and held up by her hands on the dirt. Several men and women came and stood by the couple to watch.

The man kneels behind her and rudely takes her as he likes. He moves his hips rapidly, and the woman moans and cries for more thrusts, even though each thrust increases her lust but causes her much pain. The man grunts like a beast and continues until the woman can no longer tolerate the physical pain. She lets out an ear-piercing animal scream. The man did not come.

The man pulls out and stands up, and the woman raises to be on her knees and licks his member clean. Then, the woman's husband appears and pushes the woman to the ground, cursing obscenities. The newcomer and the woman's sexual partner get into a nasty fight for a few minutes. The interloper leaves.

The newcomer takes the woman by the hair, forcing her to have fellatio on him. He slaps her face when he does not come and returns to work with his persistent erection.

"Now, I want you to see how they appear when the divine light shines upon them," thought Gabriel.

In the divine light, Sophie saw that none of the demons was young or attractive. Both men and women were ancient, hairy, and had loose skin. All were dwarfs. Even though the divine light was intense, everyone's skin appeared dull. The eyes were dark and without sparkle.

The ladies' breasts were like the breasts of dogs after birth, hanging down below their waists. There was no fat to the labia, so it hung down between their thighs several inches. All had clitoral hypertrophy.

The old men had loose scrotums hanging down almost to their knees, and their penises were always erect at seven to eight inches. Everyone was unclean and covered in grime.

Once a week, the villagers could see themselves as they really were.

On this day, a pack of Hell hounds entered the village to satisfy the villagers' lust. The men would mount the female hounds with firm erections and brutally violate each hound, even though each female possessed short hairs within their vaginas. The men went into a fornication frenzy and could not stop. Their erections remained even after they had ejaculated. Each man fought for more female Hell hounds, yet dripping with bloody ejaculate with his competitors. Each man takes his animal mate as if he were an animal himself.

The men had bound the female villagers to provide easy access for the hounds. The male hounds are well-endowed and would force themselves into the women. The male hounds possessed short hairs along the sides of their penises, which lacerated the women's vaginas. In the beginning, several male Hell hounds would take turns brutally violating each woman. Still, as the fornication frenzy came onto the woman, the women demanded more sex with the Hell hounds, so the men removed their manacles.

When the fornication frenzy peaked, the Hell hounds disappeared, and the men and women participated in a mass orgy. The men would have oral sex on the bleeding vaginas of the women drinking down the Hell hound ejaculate. Several men would penetrate a woman in three places and pummel her as she begged for more abuse.

The females would violate the mouths and vaginas of each other with their engorged clitorises. The men, not caring about gender anymore, despoiled each other in every way possible.

Finally, exhaustion set in, and everyone fell onto the wet ground in a pile of ejaculate, blood, and excrement.

Sophie asked, "Gabriel, I can see why these people are in Hell, for they are animals. These must be persons from Sodom and Gomorrah?"

Gabriel replied, "Sophie, these men cheated continuously on their wives with whores in mortal life. Life is simple. This entire village is a population of whore-mongers and their whores. The men and their whores are married, and their wives always cheat.

"The men toil in the cinnabar mines to produce red pigment for the harlots' lips. Their free time is spent fighting and catching their wives cheating.

"These activities continue until they exhaust the energies maintaining the kesdjan body. When this energy evaporates completely, their kesdjan bodies fade into nothingness. It is as if they never lived.

"Now remember, Sophie, these people are here because this is where they wanted to be, as their core love was animal sex, and this is all they experience."

"How can people waste the opportunity to rise to the level of beingness of a true human?"

Gabriel said, "The eyes of a demon will always give them away, as they are black and dull compared to human eyes. Now, we are off to a deeper level of Hell."

The pair find themselves in an empty cavern.

Gabriel asked, "Before you experience another part of Hell, I want to return to our last subject. Why do the kesdjan bodies of deceased people go to Heaven or Hell? Both realms serve what purpose?

"But, to explain the latter, we must first explore the spiritual meaning of faith. People cannot find Heaven at the end of physical life, the first death, because they cannot understand faith's true meaning.

"Several opinion surveys, designed to determine the sources supporting the capacity for ordinary people to develop firm convictions, sometimes bordering on delusion, are available. These surveys explored the reasons behind beliefs in the existence of entities and objects whose life is unverifiable. Such belief systems do not differ from those found in myths and origin stories, for instance, a belief in the existence of Satan, UFOs, succubae, angels, demons, Djinn, and so on.

"The examiners found that five to ten per cent of those holding a specific belief based it upon their perceived personal experience. Thirty to thirty-five per cent based their views on the statements of friends and family. Fifty-five to sixty-five per cent based their beliefs on those expressed by a member of an authority group legitimising such opinion.

"Ninety to ninety-five per cent of people accept a belief system with no personal evidence to support such a system. Under authoritative and persuasive pressures, authorities easily spin such persons to buy another belief system, even one contrary to the first.

"The human capacity to believe and act under persuasion and against prevailing mores explains why the human species cannot come to terms with its evolutionary violence. The average person and woman are susceptible to suggestions of racial hatred and genocide by the controlling sociopaths.

"Based upon the archaeological history of human brutality and hate over hundreds of thousands of years and the psychological observations noted above, we conclude the following.

"First, they blindly accept the belief systems expressed by the alpha leaders in their social group. And will act upon them when suitably spun by authority. The secret of spin is to activate greed and egoism in followers. To appeal to what natural evolution and society have taught to be true?

"For instance, those biological actions that one finds enjoyable to the body and the psychoistic personas are right. One should love the things they most desire and work to get them. They seek the good for themselves primarily. To love oneself first is the truth shown to us by all of nature.

"The reason for this blindness is that most persons cannot recognise they possess a potential connection to an individual soul seed. Such a connection is a node to tangible conscience and spiritual truth. Without acknowledging the Noble Organ connecting man to the Divine, men and women restrict themselves to knowing only the natural world's animal truths, such truths arising from biological and social evolution.

"Second, many persons acknowledging religious beliefs lack direct experience of their chosen deity. Nor have they experienced the inherent Qualia of their supposed deity. They only know those psychobiological states aroused by ritualistic activity and prosody of sound. Such reinforcing the dominant social belief of the group.

"Third, a religious system, adopted without access to spiritual knowledge, is not based on critical analysis, but on irrational concepts and magical thinking of one's social group. It is a falsity.

"Whether God, Heaven, Hell, or an Astral world are physically verifiable, it is rational to accept them tentatively based on experiential and sensible inquiry.

"Forming a hypothesis by proper inquiry, based on inner experiences internally consistent with normal psychoneurological processes, is not a belief. Rational inferences predicated upon good faith and personal confidence in the truth of their evidence differ. They see why altruism, with its beneficial action, is necessary.

"The teachings of enlightened beings over recorded history speak to the value of seeking love and truth. Experiencing the inherent Truth within, using Intellect and Wisdom, builds Faith. Sharing the Good that ensues from putting one's faith into action is Charity.

"Faith, Love, Good, Truth, Wisdom, and Charity are present in the words and actions of Yeshua in his testament.[16] He never asks people to believe his words because he spoke them. Yeshua asks people to find the truth in his works within their hearts and gain confidence (faith) to become as he is because of their love of truth and goodness.

"Sophie, based upon what we know about how humans think, feel, and act, ninety per cent of the believers are hell-bound (or annihilated) upon physical death. This is why real estate in Hell is so overpriced compared with Heaven. Economics of supply and demand.

"Simple men and women see how the golden paving stones covering the roads represent tiles composed of inner Faith and Love of Good. Not the mud and dirt of erroneous belief and falsity. I wonder how many people can put aside their evolutionary self-love and greed for possessions for the sake of God and God's Work?"

Sophie replies, "Wow. If you're correct, as the population grows, Hell expands. Why? Because evil grows as the population grows, like compounded interest. Plus, vacancies are few. Most choosing Hell will only be there until their kesdjan bodies exhaust their accumulated energies. Consumption by animal desires must rapidly exhaust such

---

[16] In Volume 2 to this Series, you will learn more of Ariel, Yeshua's Divine Sister for our universe.

energies, and the kesdjan bodies decompose into their component quanta. Allowing choice in one's residence isolates them from the human collective and diminishes effects upon the living."

Gabriel, smiling, is pleased.

"Good job, Sophie. I see you understand. The Divine allows Heaven to protect those who lived righteous lives from those who did not. Although life in Heaven is not forever, being in Heaven is most enjoyable. It makes up somewhat for the hardships and unpleasantness of earthly life. Creation is fair when it can be so. Our Common Father-Mother is not happy that existence must be so brutal to permit the growth of a lasting soul."

"But, Gabriel, are Heaven and Hell the sole possibilities for humans after physical death?"

"No, Sophie, a third path is available for humans to pursue. Persons choosing this path need to possess a strong will and core love to fulfil God's Plan for creation. This core love requires a near-impossible aim to develop a permanent higher-being body. These bodies exist independently of the transient physical and kesdjan bodies. Our School has discussed such men and women with you, calling them beings # 5, # 6, and #7. These are those who consciously become spiritual warriors and Bodhisattvas. Individuals who reincarnate many times to strengthen their higher being bodies.

"But I think I need to save the third path for later. Since my explanation may take some time, returning to Swedenborg's tea garden will be more comfortable," said Gabriel.

Gabriel takes Sophie's right hand and retraces their steps to the tea garden.

Chapter 6

The System

At the tea table, Gabriel said, "Sophie, if you informed ordinary people of my statistics, no one would believe you. So, let me expand my description of the sequestered realms of the astral, known as Heaven and Hell.

"I think I mentioned that Heaven and Hell comprise a small portion of the human conjoint psyche purposely sequestered from contact with that portion of the astral space for living human beings. By this, I mean it neither permits angels nor demons to enter directly into living persons' diurnal and nocturnal realities without the Divine's express permission. There are no exceptions.

"The Divine, in its Endless Mercy, seeks the Salvation of everyone who seeks freedom from unjustifiable self-love and greed. The Divine provides essence angels to watch over mortals. People do not realise such until something very drastic happens, and it seems a miracle they survived.

"The angels are so close to the living kesdjan bodies they can provide additional energies for those who want to open the link between the psychospiritual heart and True Conscience. Opening the connection allows the Divine Qualia to fill them to manifest the good of love and truth.

"The angel watching over us is within us as our nascent higher being body or soul seed. Some soul seeds are ancient, and others young and inexperienced. If people remain as animals and demons, the soul seed vacates the creature without the contamination of sin.

"Thankfully, the system confines all demons absolutely to Hell. As a safeguard, any demon attempting to escape faces an immediate second death, having their kesdjan body torn apart by the guardian vultures you met before. If demons were in the world, humanity would irreversibly convert to evil and subvert the Divine Plan. If such happened, the sole remedy is annihilating humankind, all the human creatures in Hell, and those accessible in the astral. The only ones spared would be those in Heaven and the divine warriors. The third path entities are genuinely immortal. They have made a higher being body or genuine soul and no longer require a kesdjan body.

"The story of Noah and his ark represents a world of demonic evil, requiring God to separate the just and loving from the possessed humans. This required the flood. The tale originated in Sumer and moved to ancient Egypt with Ra and Sekhmet, the blood-thirsty lioness goddess.

One finds It in Kurgan mythology. So much for the literal truth in Genesis.

"Our Common Father-Mother sequesters Heaven to protect its inhabitants, as they no longer possess any human qualities related to mortal life. Such are those Jesus called the meek. They cannot defend themselves as they know nothing more than God's Divine Love and Goodness. They would be devoured by demons whose core loves are power, violence, killing, and greed. So, God wills that no creature harms his beloved children for as long as Heaven exists.

"Heaven does not exist in eternity, Sophie, for human angels do not possess higher being bodies or eternal souls. So, after immense periods, angels fade away as their atonic quanta dissociate from each other and return to the pool of undifferentiated living energies. The kesdjan life span of an angel is proportional to how closely they resonate with Christ and other Avatars. By this, I am referring to how much Divine Light they accumulated in their soul seed, or kli (vessel), over lifetimes of good works and intentions.

"The life span of the kesdjan bodies of demons is proportional to the intensity of the self-love deposited into its kli, as the Infernal Light of Falsity and Evil."

A little surprised, Sophie asked, "Gabriel, it seems rather unjust that the eviler a man or woman was in life, the sturdier the kesdjan body. It sounds like a reward to me than a punishment?"

"Not so, my dear. Those who sinned against God only slightly exhaust their accumulated life energies, and the kesdjan body dissolves quickly. They do not suffer for such a long time. The evil ones desiring to serve or replace Satan upon his Hell Throne exist for aeons. Contending with other demons like themselves, always plotting, constantly at war, endless torture by one's opponents, and so on, without reprieve. A Hell resident can only tolerate it by going mad with hate; in the lowest realms of Hell, perpetual war rages, where no one wins for very long. None trust each other, and everyone is an enemy.

"Imagine the paranoia.

"Eventually, each understands that even the Satans and Mammons in Hell are transient and will be nothing when the universe ends. They also understand that the guardian warriors are immortal and will remain with God and go into the next universe. The anguish of this knowledge is the ultimate punishment they inflicted upon themselves in their insanity.

"But there is more to tell you. Time for some tea, scones, and chatter. Back to our café."

Sophie listens spellbound as Gabriel talks about other sentient lifeforms in our universe seeking enlightenment. Finishing up the tea and scones, Gabriel begins.

"Sophie, please do not be overly anxious about the knowledge and models I am introducing on this journey. Some of this knowledge is new to humanity, some changes older conclusions, and some need discarding. Old and new concepts exist for integration and were never intended for veneration as idols to replace Divine Providence with human prudence. Remember the First, Second, and Third Commandments.

"Humans, by nature, ignore the first three Commandments, as they are born without an open channel to Divine Love and Wisdom, even though their essence is born out of Bliss. This channel concerns the Noble Organ's functional capacity, which you learned about already. Such ignorance manifests from the natural evolutionary tendencies of self-aggrandisement and compelling greed for material possessions. The first three Commandments concern God and Man.

"Most persons partially comply with the Fifth to Tenth Commandments; we can now ignore the Fourth. Visible compliance is possible for these Commandments, as they correspond to commonly prohibited actions in most societies. The majority are happy to violate them if done in privacy or with legal permission.

"Sophie, I think you are coming to understand how far humans and God are apart."

"I understand. But I have a question, Gabriel. You never told me of your home or what you are? Who are you?"

Laughing, Gabriel said, "My dear Sophie, answering questions about where my original home was or how many universes I have worked within is not helpful. I will tell you about the name of the society with which I am associated. We know the members of this Society as the *Conrectoris Verbum Domini*.[17]

"We are not Prophets, Saints, Seers, nor Magicians. Our job is to restore and advance the Word of God given to man so it is helpful again. Our Work is to appear whenever the Word of God has become so corrupted that it no longer serves its intended purpose.

"We are innovators, defenders, and correctors of the Prophets, for Prophets and Saints are kesdjan bodies in Heaven. My kind has forsaken Heaven to serve the Lord by retaining our egos and creating an individualised Higher Being Body, or actual Soul. We sacrificed the Bliss of Heaven to serve as conscious guides to protect humanity from itself. To consciously surrender Heaven is to follow Christ's mission.

"To your awareness, I consciously chose the Third Path, a path you may travel one day. You will find immortality in the Unborn, for you were born more than human and angel. You are too good for Hell and not meek enough for Heaven. Still, for the moment, this is without importance for understanding Hell."

"During earthly life, most people seek after the evolutionary desires for eminence, social position, and exclusive possession. These two desires are not inherent to Divinity or spirituality but arise solely from natural laws in the material universe.

"The dynamic core qualities of eminence, dominance, and hoarding goods arise from the biological necessity for neurological systems motivating animals, promoting each creature's physical survival and reproductive potential.

"We invariably associate the human desire for eminence with social dominance, power, and having a social reputation. The willingness to eminence is not unique to humans if one observes the higher mammals

---

[17] Reformers of the Word of God

and primates, for instance, the dominance orders of wolf packs, baboon troops, and chimpanzee communities.

"Ethological observations and neuroimaging studies of animals show that social importance and behavioural sophistication of eminence increases with cranial capacity, or neurosynaptic volume and density. Humans' psychoneuronal complexity far surpasses any other animal, so much so that humans produce and psychoistically exist in an actual virtual world.

"As best we understand, only humans possess biological personality structures capable of exhibiting morality and character. All mammals and primates display what we call temperament or fundamental emotive biases. Most people spend much of their time operating under temperament. Such dynamic preferences comprise the tendencies to avoid harm, seek novelty, seek social rewards, and persist against difficulty.

"While biological temperaments are primarily hereditary, social learning and personal experience influence character traits. The character exists on three levels of our habitual behaviours. The degrees of personal self-directedness, cooperativeness, and acknowledgement of the necessity for spiritual integration. Character deals with exterior mores, civil and personal, derived from socialisation. We also possess interior mores arising from psychoistic attunement with the Divine Conscience.

"I see the human desire urging people to strive to possess more physical goods necessary for a single person or family at many levels of biological evolution. Such behaviour in humans is understandable, but avarice development is a negative psychoistic exaptation seen only in humans. The proper term to use is the hoarding instinct, an instinctual adaptation to store food for the winter.

"Sophie, biological evolution did an admirable job of survival and reproductive success. The Wallace-Darwin descent with modification theory, coupled with an innate genetic propensity for increasing complexity, explains the existing neuronal hierarchy of creatures.

From mindless, invertebrate neural nets to complex brains capable of generating a vast virtual, aphysical Oneirion of fantasy creatures, human kesdjan bodies, psychic selves, and Heavens and Hell."

Gabriel stopped to see how Sophie was taking everything in.

"A remarkable accomplishment of Mistress Nature, but pointless, I am afraid. A natural creature can't rise above its birth limitations without the infusion of some energy higher than its nature.

"A transfinite set includes many smaller finite sets, but the reverse is impossible. By transfinite, I do not mean infinite but an immeasurably extensive set, so rich that sorting it is impossible given the probable life of any universe.

"For conscious creatures to surpass their inherent biological limitations requires the spiritual worlds to send emissaries to bridge the conceptual and experiential gap between their finite existence and the transfinite of the knowable Divine.

"There is only one actual infinity, the Unfathomable Source, beyond the Limitless, the Eternal, the Timeless, and so on. Our Society opines that the transfinite mathematics of Georg Cantor is mere mathematics. The Greeks were correct. Man can only approach the Infinite but never reach it, for it is always More.

"Every universe occupies an immense multidimensional volume of space potentially available when a prior universe deflates and re-inflates in a few Planck time constants. The energy reinfusing from the old into the new occupies a much more restricted initial volume. Much of the geometric matrix of the universe is empty of manifesting quanta. Subsequently, photons and matter expand at different rates into the potential space.

"Not appreciated is that the multidimensional geometric mesh is infinite in extent and never had a beginning or an end. Universes come and go within portions of this geometric mesh, each transfinite in volume and energy.

"An appreciation of the structure of the Metric is within conscious conceptualisation. The models constructed by our Society are the most extensive and refined, providing a complete understanding of all three ways of Creation. We even know the mechanism for producing the quanta necessary for materiality, life, and consciousness in space's vibratory modes.

"We hypothesise that the physical universe requires a minimum of twelve mathematically imaginary, orthogonal spatial dimensions to produce four spatial dimensions in which solid bodies exist. One of the four dimensions allocated for physical space is not observable and creates an interesting experiential illusion for three-dimensional beings. Losing one dimension explains why the material wave function requires a real and imaginary part.

"In three-space, observers see visible objects are at rest, moving uniformly, or speeding up or down relative to the observer's laboratory reference frame. These observations are illusory because of three-space optical limitations, as we cannot measure at small enough time intervals.

"The Society has discovered that things do not translate in three-space; instead, they appear and disappear temporally as functions of momenergy. They reappear at the same coordinate set or elsewhere. Objects appearing at rest in a laboratory frame are not really at rest but appear and disappear too fast to see without changing coordinates.

"Objects do not move per se; they show up based upon temporal and coordinate information they possess and momenergy. All information moves at the speed of light and rests many times for time intervals too short to observe. Such is possible as quanta in the fourth spatial dimension exist as untied three-dimensional energy knots. This is why they disappear and reappear when nonstationary."

Sophie takes a deep breath. "Gabriel. How do you know stuff that science hasn't even discovered? It is uncanny."

"Based upon the law of correspondence, two other independent sets of mathematically imaginary, orthogonal spatial dimensions coexist for kesdjan and higher being bodies. Kesdjan bodies are only visible in the mental Oneirion from which they arise. Higher being bodies are neither physical nor dreamlike, and we can only observe so in the upper world.

"Still, no one can know with surety whether such energised geometry is equivalent to God. Perhaps it does not matter anymore? Who knows? Questions, Sophie," asked Gabriel as he sips warm tea?

Pondering momentarily, she replied, "You mentioned three modes of Creation. I presume you refer to the appearance of three distinct kinds of quanta in the metric. The material, atonic, and ptahonic. Such vibratory modes of the metric exist as a hierarchy in time. First, the metric must create complex matter suitable for manifesting the aphysical atonic, or living, energies to form, animate, far from equilibrium, autopoietic systems. Second, suitably complex nervous systems allow the emergence of aphysical ptahonic or conscious energies that interact with the Divine. Is this correct?"

"Perfect, my dear. Well done. You are very close to understanding.

"From an energetic point of view, the metric is triune, a trinity. The metric is the Mother, and the one fundamental activating energy is the Father. The triangle's third point reconciles the Mother and Father to actualise the Son-Daughter's creation. Instead of Father, Son, and Holy Spirit or Father, Son-Daughter, and Mother, we find matter, life, and hierarchal consciousness. Each exists independently of the others, but each has one vital energy. Just an analogy, Sophie, do not take it too seriously.

"For God shows six actual faces to the world, the Èixkleidié (Ἐξικλειδά). We call the six the 5 Quale + 1 or 5Q+1. We call these separate forces the Logos or KOPTIC.

"The metric and the three energies are the foundation of the separate worlds of the physical, the astral or kesdjan, and the upper or higher being bodies. While the human body lives physically, the mind lives in the Oneirion. Self-aware creatures lack access to the upper world as they have no higher being bodies. Such bodies are rare and consciously brought into awareness by those who became Immortals to guide humanity and other conscious creatures.

"Earlier, we discussed how the astral plane and its entities are assemblies of atonic energies, duplicating the form and neurological functions of the living physical body. The material world's primary purpose is to construct individual kesdjan bodies that continue to exist after physical death. Recently deceased kesdjan bodies find themselves between the Heavenly and Hellish regions in the intermediate astral world.

"A portion of the intermediate astral is Purgatory, where many kesdjan bodies live for varying times. The purpose of Purgatory is twofold. First, to purify the kesdjan bodies of worldly taints of the good. Second, to remove any heavenly traits of the bad. The conscious efforts of the person can remove such. Those truly desiring salvation correct what they now consider traits unfitting for Elohim's sons and daughters, using methods to purify themselves frequently unpleasantly.

"This is the real meaning of Christian Grace, honey.

"Those persons having lived a godly life quickly move onto Heaven, and those antagonistic to the Divine choose the deepest Hells. The division maintains a balance in the intermediate world and protects those who will choose salvation."

"Our friend Swedenborg perceived the kesdjan body as possessing interior and exterior parts. The interior reflects the Divine, and the outer reflects the physical world. This model is crude but valuable for discussing the ontogeny of the kesdjan body over a lifetime.

"As we learned, as soon as a human zygote divides, it enters eight weeks of embryogenesis in which the major organ and human body form occur. Completion of a functional neonate requires another thirty weeks. When the foetus is ready to face the physical world, it possesses an atonic energy body, duplicating the physical body's functional form, including sensory organs and a central nervous system.

"As the baby follows the phylogeny of its species, its organic body displays more behavioural elements of the standard set of innate and learned human emotional qualities. The central nervous system changes in the organic body are mirrored by those of the atonic body.

As a mirrored pair, both bodies have access to the memories of the other. When the original zygote matures, the system coordinates the organic and atonic bodies in time and space.

"Mirroring explains how the body and mind can affect each other for health or disease. I expect the human mirror neurons are involved somehow.

"During daily functioning, both bodies experience similar desires, feelings, motor actions, and thoughts. The attractions in the organic body imprinting, as desires in the atonic body. Evolution produced several unconscious neurological motivators in all animals possessing a triune brain. The primary motivator is a compelling desire when threatened with enhancing the physical body's survival. As primates, humans have the same passion, when threatened, to fight or flee to improve the physical body's survival. However, both bodies respond when threatened. Still, the survival of the imagined, or cognitive self, is more important for most people.

"Specifically, humans glorify their imagined selves to place them above others. Given the proper genome and epigenetic factors, many believe they are divine, a god or goddess, and more important than others. Such is self-love or self-aggrandisement. Self-love is one of the great sins against the Divine, denying the absolute love and truth underlying Creation.

"There is some truth to this belief as the kesdjan body outlives the organic body for quite some time. Kesdjan bodies are temporal and eventually decompose when measured in Earth time units. Fortunately, neither space nor time exists objectively in the human astral planes; it only exists subjectively, like a nocturnal dream.

"The other primary drive imprinted upon the atonic body by the physical is ownership and possession of things for the use of the self alone. This drive arises from animal adaptation to hoard food in harsh environments. A similar movement to hoard females to enhance a male's genome's survival exists in all animal species. These drives in humans lead to selfishness and greed.

"The kesdjan bodies coexisting with organic bodies and brains, developing toward self-love or greed, will mirror the physical. Such is why the kesdjan bodies, in dreams or after death, have the same desires, or core loves, as the physical-kesdjan pair had in life. Subsequently, organically extreme kesdjan bodies after the first death will migrate toward Hell. Still, such beings must experience Purgatory so they can burn off any divine feelings walled off from their hearts and minds. Swedenborg was correct when he saw a kesdjan body lives either in the 'good and true' or the 'evil and false' after the first death. Heaven will not tolerate evil and falsity, and Hell will not accept good and truth."

As usual, Sophie offered a provocative question.

"Gabriel, I can see that Hellish loves cannot come from the Divine directly but are created by my species by misunderstanding our psychoistic natures. God does not create universes based on self-love. Every universe possesses a fundamental hurdle that conscious life must overcome. God cannot remove a limitation as it would extinguish our freedom to choose our actions.

"God creates or comes into universes, hoping a conscious creature who can access the fundamental Qualia God placed will arise. A species that will discover the inherent flaws in every universe. Discovering they and God can overcome this flaw, allowing that universe to become Divine and in pure altruism. What do you think, Gabriel?"

"Brilliant, utterly brilliant. You understand! I shall marry you, honey. Therefore, you will choose the third path, as I once did."

Hearing the words, 'I shall marry you, honey,' had the most curious effect upon Sophie. Her head swam, her breathing became shallow, and her kesdjan body merged with Gabriel. She felt indescribable happiness, peace, and well-being, which she had never experienced.

She thought, "How can it be that I love and want him so? I have only known him for hours, I guess."

She was about to fall off her chair, and Gabriel stood up to catch her.

"Love is a curious mistress, Miss Sophie."

Sophie's mind clears.

"I love you, Gabriel. I truly do. I don't think I have ever loved anyone else. What is happening to me, Gabriel? Am I going insane?"

Gabriel laughs.

"You are not going insane, honey. You just touched my heart, which is pure love. How are you feeling?"

She stood up, placed her arms around his neck, and kissed him passionately.

"It is wonderful, Gabriel."

When finished, she sat back down in her chair.

"A delightful kiss, Sophie. I enjoyed it, but back to our subject.

"There is more to tell about how kesdjan bodies change as they become fit denizens of Hell. Sophie, most evil persons, at least in the lower classes of society, make no genuine attempts to hide their evilness. I call such plain devils.

"Many upper-class evil persons, often politicians and business executives, are skilled in hiding their inner natures from the world by emulating and fulfilling society's reasonable expectations in front of the community. I call these gilded devils.

"In our society's parlance, we rank the divinity within kesdjan bodies using a three-world hierarchy. Hell splits into three degenerate worlds. They are arranged beginning with the uppermost Hell world, next to the middle, and last, the deepest Hell world. The uppermost Hell region comprises kesdjan bodies with the element Gallium (Ga-70) density, guilty of typical selfishness and greed. The element Copper (Cu-63) symbolises the middle Hell region. A pure copper kesdjan body is equivalent to the god of greed, Mammon. At the bottom is a world composed entirely of elemental Iron (Fe-56). A kesdjan body having the same density as iron would represent pure evil, Satanicalness.

From the deepest Hell, we start with the lowest Heaven, count to the middle, and lastly, the highest. Here, the metallic representatives are noble metals. Silver is a denser element (Ag-107) and symbolises the lowest Heaven, as the angels value truth more than love. The element

Platinum (Pt-195) represents the middle Heaven. In the Platinum world, love is more potent than truth. This Heaven Swedenborg calls Spiritual. Gold (Au-197) represents the uppermost world closest to the Divine and resonates with Divine Love. This world is Swedenborg's Celestial Heaven.

"When a baby is born, its kesdjan body is classifiable similarly to the organic body by the elements, Carbon (C-12), Nitrogen (N-14), Oxygen (O-16), and Hydrogen (H-1). Typically, we sum the molecular weights and use 43 for convenience. If humans did not possess the gift of freedom of choice, the maturing kesdjan body would remain at 43. Freedom of choice is only possible after a species experiences self-love and greed.

"Kesdjan bodies living a life compliant with personal survival and social mortality, but with little feeling for the spiritual experience are common. Having elemental numbers around Gallium but less than silver. Such persons are content to live in Hell's uppermost regions, similar to the environs of mortal life. Often, it is impossible to convince them they died.

"A kesdjan body which converts to Silver during its stay in Purgatory can move into the lowest Heaven. Additional work makes it possible to move into the middle and highest heavens. All a person needs to do is turn away from egoism and towards the Divine. Following the directives of the good of love and truth explains why Heavenly beings are more substantial than Hellish ones. This concept is not new to alchemy or metaphysical schools of the past.

"Sophie, if you remember, in the Chymical Wedding, CRC did not consider himself sufficiently virtuous to pass the ordeal of the scales.[18] But he was the heaviest guest at the wedding, as his heart and

---

[18] Johannes Valentinus Andreae, Chymical Wedding of Christian Rosencreutz (Original in German), 1616. Many English translations.

intellect followed the Divine closely when weighed. I imagine you will ask me why kesdjan bodies needed to determine whether they practise truth and love or falsity and evil?

"If we assigned a weight of 1.00 to an iron kesdjan body of a specific volume, a copper kesdjan is 1.15 times heavier, a silver kesdjan body is 1.93 times more massive, and a gold kesdjan body is 3.52 times denser. As angels do not exist in physical space or clock time, they cannot directly distinguish people's elemental nature. Therefore, they must gauge the kesdjan body's quality by estimating how much they crush the grassy plains of the entrance zone.[19]

"Kesdjan bodies appearing in the intermediate world possessing rusted iron or weathered copper finishes are no better within. Other kesdjan bodies appear with gleaming platinum or bright silver finishes, but they are iron or copper within. These are the gilded devils I referenced earlier. But at least the ungilded creatures did not pretend to be saintly.

"The gilded devils cause some confusion for the angels. Their conditioning is to act as just and decent people, even though they are deceitful, self-conceited, and greedy. The gilded devils work incongruously with their fundamental nature until the exterior patina decomposes. Such patinas evaporate after a few days or weeks in the intermediate zone. So, the kesdjan body must think, feel, speak, and act congruously with its inner nature. In the sequestered zones of Heaven and Hell, each kesdjan body is comfortable in a psychic place befitting its core loves. And so, finds comfort in being with its kind.

"Those kesdjan bodies coming to the intermediate zone seeped in the love of self or love of possessions eventually choose to live in a Hell region proper to their core loves. I showed you one such place the other day. However, many kesdjan bodies contain mixtures of

---

[19] See CS Lewis, The Great Divorce.

silver and copper, with silver predominating. After indoctrination in the intermediate zone, they ask for a cleansing of iron and copper to approach pure silver.

"This is the purpose of Purgatory, Sophie. It is a salvation tool for burning away the iron, copper, and gallium within them. This is necessary to resonate and harmonise with an angelic society. Experiencing Purgatory is psychically painful, but those living there gladly accept the correction they need, for they understand they have another chance to be with the Divine.

"Purgatory separates Heaven and Hell, as persons voluntarily accept time in Purgatory for cleansing of evil and falsity. Kesdjan bodies arriving, prepared for Heaven or Hell, automatically go to their appropriate location by desire and not by current choice. Still, the best plan is to open one's heart to the Divine via the Noble Organ, or Holy Spirit, while living in the physical. The physical is where man has maximum freedom and opportunity to be as close to the Infinite as possible.

"I will delay discussing the third, or the royal, path until we finish our astral exploration of Hell. I will tell you, Sophie, those who follow the third path will attain a state of true siblingship with Yeshua the Christ and Ariel the Holy Comforter."

Sophie and Gabriel entered deep hypnosis and separated their kesdjan bodies for another trip to Hell.

Chapter 7

Return to Hell

Soon, both stand in a tunnel opening onto the deepest level of Hell. Looking into the cavern, Sophie sees it is immense. The tunnel walls and roof seem to diverge away to form a hollow. Dirty ice litters the cavern floor, and a chilling breeze flows from deep ahead. The draft made an eerie sound as it navigates around the field of gigantic calcium-rich stalagmites and stalactites. Here and there, Sophie recognises frozen waterfalls and rivers. Sophie cannot locate any light source illuminating the cavern but still discerns the scenery's details. She thinks it strange that the surrounding space lacked any hellish life.

"Gabriel, why is this place so dreary, icy, and dark? How can I see if there is no source of radiant light?"

"Sophie, this cavern lies so distant from the Divine that the full spectrum of the Light emanating from the Divine Sun inhabiting the centre of Heaven does not enter fully into this cavern. As I taught you, the Divine Light entering our universe is like an undivided mega-caduceus formed by the heads, bodies, and tails of the Six Eternal and Diamond Nāga. The Nāga, or Divine Serpents, infuse the fundamental Quale of the Divine required for biological, conscious, and spiritual evolution from the single cell to the fully enlightened Man and Woman.[20]

"The spectrum of the Light illuminating Hell is without Divine Caring (Love), so there is no warmth. The Light is without Divine Knowing (Wisdom), so only insanity is possible. The Light is without Divine Transcendence, as Hell will not release its inhabitants until the end of time, and the release is their destruction.

"All the inhabitants don't experience the full Light. Only that sufficient to observe, intend, and realise they are present in this Hell. Their kesdjan bodies remain activated only by the worst kinds of self-aggrandisement. Each is intoxicated with self-love and self-serving, existing without trust between each other, lacking compassion for all creatures, and conniving and warring in the most wicked ways. The greatest desire is to be like Satan. Nice place, eh?"

Wrinkling her nose, Sophie said, "Ha-ha. I have a joke for you, Gabriel. Tell me an easy mnemonic for remembering whether stalagmites accrete from the floor or the ceiling?"

"Boy, Sophie, that is an easy riddle, and one needs only to remember a ballerina. The tights go down, and the mites go up."

As Sophie appeared a bit disappointed, Gabriel reminded her.

"Sophie, what do you expect from an Immortal and a smart one?"

Gabriel takes Sophie by the hand, and they find themselves by a vast ice lake. Standing upon the lake's surface, Sophie sees frozen kesdjan bodies in various poses. Naked men and women are everywhere. In the centre of the ice-covered kesdjan bodies is a gigantic, immensely hideous creature covered in icy scales. Sophie finds herself transfixed.

Gabriel interrupts Sophie's mesmerised state of mind.

"Sophie, I want you to shift your focus from the frozen sociopaths to the gigantic frozen being. I am not asking you about size differences;

---

[20] Kundalini Serpent

it is something more subtle I would like you to notice. When you find it, you can answer my riddle, then tell me the answer, please."

Sophie observes the scene for a few minutes, answering, "There is a subtle difference between the frozen sinners and Satan. Each frozen kesdjan body wants to conquer Hell but can do nothing as their bodies cannot move. Within the thoraxes of the once-living kesdjan bodies, I see nothing but a shrivelled, dark, and odious remnant in the place where once beat a human heart. Endless streams of hate issue forth, filling their lungs and exiting from their open mouths. The force of such hatred creates the chilling winds rushing about.

"The gigantic frozen creature with horns, claws, and bat wings is not a creature. It is an Imago generated by the insane minds of the hideous sinners in this cavern. The hatred and rage issuing from their mouths for hundreds of thousands of years, condensing and solidifying to form an Archetype, or Imago, of pure self-love and hate for what is not-self. But, the creatures of this Hell foolishly believe that their Archetype, or Imago, is coequal to the Lord. As all kesdjan bodies must worship that they love most, each region of Hell must have its false and imagined Archetype."

"What you have seen, Sophie, is the truth of Hell. God made Hell to protect the living and those in Heaven. Humanity blames God for many injustices when humankind should blame itself. For there is One God Alone; God is the Source of all things.

"Foolish are the humans worshipping Satan and his followers, for they worship nothing. For when has goodness and profit flowed forth from dead idols? Brothers and Sisters of Our Society have come into untold universes. They have observed the operations of these universes and have reported their findings.

"To our knowledge, the Metric, its triune hierarchy of energies, and the Divine Qualia have restricted the spread of evilness between four brain creatures in the physical world and the most concrete astral planes of common dreaming. Evil respects its bounds as it can only arise from partially conscious creatures."

"I understand, Gabriel, so much better than before. I hope someday, my species will come to understand your message and see its truth. When will the Society send forth a new Saviour?"

As Sophie watches Gabriel's face, she sees he carries an ongoing, intolerably immense sadness in his heart. His facial expression remains only seconds before Gabriel answers Sophie's question.

"Sophie, I do not have an answer to your question. Our last attempt to intervene was when our Beloved Jesus accepted the Christ Consciousness into his being during the baptism at the River Jordan. All of us believed that the proper time had arrived in Israel. Still, we made a terrible miscalculation as to the spiritual capacity of the Jews to acknowledge Christ.

"Contrary to what the Catholic and Protestant Churches have accepted as Dogma, crucifixion was not part of the plan. Christ's teachings aren't literally to be acted out upon the material plane. The Catholics went over to the imagined Satan a long time ago.

"Fortunately, St. Paul salvaged a valuable explanation for Jesus' sacrifice, which remains in the Orthodox faith. Our dear Emanuel wrote many explanatory works to correct the errors introduced by the existing churches.

"I think it is time to leave this dark realm, my dear. We shall return to Damascus for a bite to eat and rest for you. Then, off to another adventure. Take my hand."

The two left Hell and its residents and arrived back in Damascus.

Chapter 8

Gabriel Unveils Sophie's Destiny

s soon as Sophie and Gabriel returned to the rooftop garden in Damascus, Sophie collapsed into Gabriel's arms. He lifted and carried her to bed, laying her onto her back and kissing her softly on her forehead.

Gabriel said to himself, "I am very proud of you, sweetheart. You are a trooper and one day will be with me in perpetuity. I wish I could share more details of your road ahead, but I cannot. There is more to teach, prepare, and test to show that you are ready to accept a wondrous Cosmic Bequest. I know what your heart desires most, and I will do whatever is necessary to fulfil your desire, my darling."

Gabriel returned to the moonlit garden rooftop and prepared a hookah for Sophie when she awoke. Being prescient, he knows she liked musk melon the most.

Sophie slept for several hours and awoke refreshed. As she washed her face and brushed her teeth, she saw a beautiful meadow in the mirror filled with fragrant flowers, industrious bees, and rainbow-coloured butterflies. Curiosity caused her to turn around, and the field was there. Taking up a towel, she dried her face. The meadow remained, and she felt her kesdjan body separate and walk into the meadow.

Once present in the meadow, Sophie heard Gabriel calling to her in a language she did not know but understood. The words were as musical chords, and each sentence carried a melody. She found herself in front of Gabriel, and he was holding a beautiful baby girl surrounded by a soft golden aura. Several Elf damsels were with him.

"Gabriel, what a wondrous child. She has little pointy ears, so she must be an Elf baby. May I hold her?"

"You may hold her."

Gabriel gently hands the baby to Sophie.

Sophie takes the sweet child into her arms and holds her close to her breast. The baby is cooing.

"Gabriel, she smells like fresh-baked vanilla cookies. I think she likes me?"

Gabriel and the elves started laughing most kindly.

Gabriel grins, saying, "Sophie, the little one adores you. See how her aura glows brighter? You don't know who she is?"

One Elf whispers to Gabriel, "How can she know who the baby is? We are far in her future, and she may not know yet. Allow her to hold Rosemunde and return her to you in 1913."

"Sophie, give the baby to Eleanor, and you and I will return to Damascus. We must prepare for another journey. Come, take my hand."

Sophie returns the baby, takes Gabriel's hand, and both find themselves on the garden rooftop.

Sophie saw Gabriel had prepared a hookah while she slept. Gabriel hands her the hose. Putting the wooden end between her lips, she slowly inhales. Holding the Turkish tobacco smoke in her mouth, Sophie immediately notes that its flavour is musk melon. She slowly exhales and hands the hose to Gabriel.

Overjoyed, Sophie stands and throws her arms around Gabriel's neck.

"Gabriel, how could you know? I love you to Heaven and back, sweetheart."

"Sophie, I appreciate the sincerity of your warm feelings. I know that your inner heart desires me to be your polar complement. I know you love me; this love flows from the centre of your kesdjan body. I do care for you, Sophie. I care very much. But, sweet dear, I cannot have an earthly love with you, for such would distract you from the Work," Gabriel replies, stroking her face, "do you understand?"

Gabriel sees small tears running down Sophie's cheeks and bends to kiss them away.

Sophie does her best to smile.

"I understand, my Gabriel. But I ask for one gift, and then I will be the trooper you want me to be."

"I will give you the gift you need, Sophie. I find you desirable in so many ways, honey. I love you as a male angel loves his female spouse in a sacred marriage. If I could choose my eternal mate, I would choose you, dearest Sophie. Perhaps things will change, honey."

Sophie hugs Gabriel.

"Knowing that you love me, Gabriel, and genuinely desire to spend eternity with me is enough. I have never known a heart as kind and strong as yours."

"I know four hearts as kind and as strong as mine. Two are Tristan the Gallant, a Knight of the Table Round, and his beloved Sorceress-Wife, Natanel. The others are their twin daughters, Calliope and Vika. You will meet them someday."

"Good. Sit down, and we will enjoy your musk melon tobacco, and then I will teach you many more things."

As they enjoy the hookah, Sophie prays silently, "God of my heart and realisation, I beg you to find a way for Gabriel to be my eternal love."

Gabriel hears her prayer but does not say what he will do about it.

"Sophie, if you remember our visits with Swedenborg, you remember I said nothing to oppose his understanding of the spiritual world. Even our visits to Hell fell within the spiritual world's parameters he knew while living in 18th century Northern Europe.

"I want you to understand, Sophie, that I did not limit my comments out of respect for the kindly gentleman. I limited myself because his understanding of the spiritual world presented the most advanced knowledge of his era. Most human beings have hardly advanced spiritually since Swedenborg's life. Though Swedenborg was unaware of the Society, the Society helped Swedenborg refine his vision of the spiritual world, a view of significant benefit.

"The knowledge accumulated by our Society stretches over an uncountable number of universes. However, the information released to four brain creatures during their species' life span is minuscule and limited to data required to prevent destruction. More would be counterproductive as four brain creatures misuse what we give them.

"However, the knowledge I share with you, my love, is for the future. I am trying to show you your universe's structure and inner workings. I am providing a blueprint of Creation in bits and pieces so you will understand why four brain creatures are crucial for this universe's overall economy. It would be best to realise that I am preparing you for a Great Work.

"And understand, you will, Sophie. Your desire for my love, which is only the Divine Love accumulating in my vessel for bestowal upon you, has forged a permanent bond betwixt you and me. As the warmth of my love for you increases, the fire raging within your heart and loins will become unbearable. The more you love me, the more you will seek to be with the wisdom and goodness in yourself. And when you have learned what I need you to learn, we will marry, and I will grant your prayer. I pray I have not overstepped."

"Gabriel, to know that you love me completely and unconditionally almost seems a miracle. A miracle humans do not seem to share. To imagine I will learn to love you properly, Gabriel, is beyond me. The depth of your love makes my heart and loins rage with great heat. My desire for you at this moment is unbearable. Using this fire to burn off my human taints and propel my entrance into Society is what I will do, my love. Still, I hope you satisfy my natural desires one day, for I want to be one with you in all ways."

"Honey, someone will memorialise our conversations in a written tome one day. What I am teaching comprises the knowledge the Society will share with the esoteric schools of Earth."

"Gabriel, our dear Swedenborg says neither demons nor angels may voluntarily enter the intermediate world between Heaven and Hell. Such intrusion is only possible when Our Common Father-Mother allows such. Why do people believe in guardian angels, Satan, and demons, Gabriel?"

"Sophie, some questions appear straightforward but have complicated answers. Other issues seem complex but have simple solutions. Your query is convoluted but straightforward. It will take some time to answer your question, as I must first answer many questions you have not yet asked me. However, we must begin with some questions for you.

"I divulged sufficient information to explain why I brought you to Damascus many years before you were born. Our greatest desire materialised during our time together, so you know of a potential future of shared, perfected love and caring. You have received the Work and must use it to manifest your desired love. But, aren't you curious how I brought your body to Damascus many years before you were born?"

"I am curious, but I knew you would tell me."

Gabriel chuckled.

"I see you have faith in your Gabriel. And by faith, I am referring to unshakeable confidence that I will review what is helpful for your development. Such is a good omen. So, I shall explain.

"Each physical universe exists within a twelve-dimensional pocket of space within the Metric. Each universe occupies a volume isolated from all other universes and acts like a thermodynamically isolated system. Physical, astral, and upper-world energies apply. Applying the

Egyptian names customarily used by our Society, these energies are the gebonic, the atonic, and the ptahonic.

"Geb, the god symbolising the fertile Earth and the material energies; Aton, the god representing the radiant sun and the aphysical, mental energies of life and consciousness; and Ptah, the god symbolising Creation and the externalising, transconscious energies forming the souls of the Immortal Ones far beyond the highest levels of the spiritual worlds.

"These three energies exist as a hierarchy. The lowest is the material energies, and the highest is the spiritual energies. For material and aphysical co-universes to function appropriately, only the gebonic and atonic energies are necessary for the beginning. It only requires the ptahonic energies after a universe produces creatures capable of making a higher being body arise.

"Complex physical creatures only arise in universes where macroscopic matter, animate and inanimate, is restricted to observable energy exchanges in three dimensions. You might laugh, but the annals record that the first couple asks God to give them riddles and puzzles to solve together mentally and knots to tie and untie with their hands. God granted the first couple its wish. God reduces the twelve spatial dimensions to three because knots cannot exist in two or four dimensions. Even when the unusual exists in a story, its truth remains undiminished.

"Physical and mental co-universes possess energies, which concentrate, forming material and mental objects. Such is why people have physical and astral bodies. If such organisations existed atemporally, the universe and its creatures would not change as energies could not exchange between them.

"Therefore, a functional universe requires the addition of temporalities so its energies can produce more complex cognitive creatures. This explains why the energy fields entering the universe in the inflationary period expand into the allocated space to cool and allow for gebonic and atonic quanta formation.

"The great kabbalist Luria foreshadowed my explanation as he described Creation using the Hebrew word, *tzimtzum*, which means contraction, constriction, and condensation. Later, Kabbalists wrote, 'Before Creation, only the infinite Ohr Ein Sof was.'

"The infinite Ein Sof contracted Its light to allow for a conceptual space that is finite and available for separate physical and spiritual worlds.

"When it arose in the Creator's Will to create worlds and emanate the emanated, He contracted Himself at the point at the centre, in the very centre of His light. After this contraction, He drew down from the Ohr Ein Sof a straight line of light from His light surrounding the void from above to below [into the nullity]. Creator restricted that light, distancing it to the sides surrounding the central point. Hence, a void remained away from the dominant nidus. It grew down, descending into that void. He emanated, created, formed, and made all the worlds in the space of that void.

"Luria could have said more, but the basic anthropomorphic mindset of the 16th century Kabbalists required him to use humanistic forms. Today, we can speak in geometry and energetics rather than ethereal forces and human concepts. As science was virtually nonexistent, no one would have appreciated the physical connection."

"But Gabriel, you have not told me how you brought me here. We can experientially spend days, and maybe months, exploring the astral, and it is still the same moonlight night in Damascus. Can't we skip ahead a little to the answer?"

"I got carried away with my explanation, and we can skip ahead. Typically, our mental life predicates an actual or perceived separation in space and time. In the physical world, space and time objectively exist. In the astral-spiritual world, we keep the perception of space and time. We need such to function as individual kesdjan bodies. Therefore, our adventures in the astral occur in perceived space and time. My dear, I have placed your conscious awareness outside of time and into its orthogonal eternity. I compress or expand space-time as much as necessary.

"The fact that your physical body is with me some seven decades before your birth and that of your parents is extraordinary, my dear. To my knowledge, this is the first time someone accomplished a full revision of spacetime with someone who is not Immortal. I removed you as a creature in the 21st century and placed you as something new in the 20th century."

For a moment, Sophie saw a flash of satisfaction in Gabriel's eyes, which passed quickly.

"Gabriel, whether I love you in the 21st century or the 20th century, it is the same to me, as being with you is beyond time and space. Besides, now I know you are physically here with me, as an Immortal and a man. I love Damascus and its moonlight. Will we marry in Damascus?"

"Yes, honey, I am in my physical vehicle now. For some unknown reason, I could not transpose myself into your period. So, the only alternative was to transport you here in your beautiful entirety, darling. What you thought was my physical vehicle was only a brilliant illusion. Soon, you will learn why I did what I did. Yes, honey. We shall marry soon, maybe in Damascus, but I think somewhere else."

On hearing the word marriage, Sophie could not restrain herself or the love within her heart and body. She stood up from her chair, going to sit on Gabriel's lap. Sophie feels compelled to kiss Gabriel and brings her lips to his. When her lips touch Gabriel's, she feels a warmth spreading over her entire body like she had stepped into a warm tub. Then, Gabriel kisses her, and the vision of holding the baby girl with the golden aura in her arms fills her mind. Now Sophie understands the meadow and the Elves. But Sophie does not know why. The vision lingers in her mind, and she sleeps on Gabriel's lap when it leaves.

Gabriel wakes her.

"Sophie, I would love to continue your lessons, but you must return to your chair and enjoy the hookah. OK?"

Sophie kisses Gabriel again and returns to her chair in the happiest mood. She reached for the hookah hose, inhaled, and blew a perfect smoke ring within another.

"Sophie, do you enjoy poetry?"

"Yes, I enjoy most kinds of poetry which rise above the mundane. I like fairy tales. Why do you ask?"

"Poetry and fairy tales are excellent communication methods for mysticism and elevated matters of the heart. I want to share a poem honouring the Source of All Love and Wisdom with you. We are leaving for another journey after the hookah goes out and you have had a light snack.

"Remember, the Divine provided two unique gifts to humans: the ability to discern the true from the false and the freedom to choose how to use the good. Each act of a rational creature has a purpose, a means, and a resultant action. While living, men and women choose either Heaven or Hell.

"I have written of God's emanations many times and over the aeons, but this prose-poetry is the clearest and most straightforward. It is what we know to be true about the Divine."

Gabriel opens a small notebook and reads a poem in the Society's Archives called,

The Holy Revelation Of The Most Ancient Church

Harken onto my Voice, for I am the Shepherd of men and women. Just as the mother and the father are Shepherds for their children.

My Love makes no distinction between the young and old, male and female, those who live in my Light, and those still dwelling in suffering and darkness. I am blind to colour and cultural beliefs.

To teach that I favour one tribe or nation over another is blasphemy. My Nature in Its Essence forbids

naming one group my Chosen Ones. How can a mother or father love one child more dearly than another?

I am the Greatest Goodness. I am forever Merciful and Compassionate, for My Understanding of men's and women's actions is complete. Come, my children, live with me as One and even More.

Now of Creation, I dissolved Myself, placing my Monadic fragments into the physical world to complete the Work accomplished by the evolutionary processes. This is my sacrifice for humankind. Without Divine Awareness, the material world is Nothing, only an empty shell of matter without life.

In dissolving Myself at the end of the last aeon, I assured that the Four Pillars of Divinity would Live On:

Lovingkindness, Intending Consciously, Observing Dispassionately, and Knowing the Actuality of the All. I call these the Lion's Roar.

By fragmenting myself, I appear as many to human eyes, though still a whole to my eyes. I ensured my parts could retrace their paths back to me, bringing new information and possibilities into the next universe. The Kabbalists would call such recollections Reshimot.

I have little Power to Act Directly in this new Creation, for by choosing Fragmentation, I relinquished absolute control. I desire humankind to accept responsibility as the Prince and Shepherd of this new world. They must learn to rule wisely as an agent of the Greatest Goodness. If humankind fails, its species will die and be with Me no more.

Many Monads have discovered their inner natures and found they were separate when incarnate but as One when existing only in My Awareness. By finding *themselves, they found the 'I' who has always been the True Continuity without Beginning or End.*

You have seen My Light and Love many times: I am Christ; I am Buddha; I am Zoroaster; I am Krishna; I am mother, I am father, I am brother and sister; I am child; I am Such that none can hide nor banish Me for without Pure Awareness there is no mind nor world; I am Infinite Goodness, Eternal Benevolence and Benefaction, Highest Intention, Endless Seeker of Understanding, the Silence of Observing; I am the Active, the Lawful, the Organiser in all things.

As the Source from which all worlds arise, I am said to Exist, but many misunderstand, for I am found only when a man or woman stops looking. My Existence has meaning only when used as a term for Pure Awareness' marriage with Infinite Space. I can be said to Exist only as Love and Creative Potential Exist when a man and woman join fully in holy intercourse as one unit without distinction. We are the Eternal Complements.

I am neither Mind nor Consciousness, for these are merely the result of Pure Awareness working with objective machines. To believe otherwise is not pragmatic.

I live in the hearts of many worlds, all unknown to the uninitiated of this world's manifestation. Near the end of this time, I will again attain unified Wholeness of Pure Awareness, using the totality of the physical as the instrument of the Universal Mind and Cosmic Consciousness.

I continually inspire the meek ones' hearts and minds to elevate into sages to establish Holy Pathways for finding Where the I Am, as it remains Hidden. Some come onto Me by Loving Me directly and without measure. Others come to Me by acting with unrelenting kindness and justice toward other creatures. Some come to Me by understanding what is the Actual in this Universe.

For these are the Children finishing the Great Task for which this Universe came into Conscious Life? Children discovering Salvation before this material world dissolves as if it had never been. The Greatest of all Gifts I Bestow is freedom of choice; therefore, your Salvation is your own. I forbade Myself from doing the Work you must do, but My Help is never far from your heart if you pay attention and ask.

Remember, Children, I Am closest when you suffer, and I suffer with you. So, look for Me. My Love is Eternal and Perfect and Fulfils all desires.

Gabriel finishes reading and closes the notebook, putting it back into his jacket pocket. He turns, looking deeply into Sophie's transfixed eyes.

Sophie notices his irises' blueness fading away, opening a portal into something more profound. She sees her physical-kesdjan body within the flowery meadow she had visited earlier. The flowers whisper to each other by sharing the sweetness of their fragrances. Birds flitter about, calling out to each other in the most lyrical bird songs. Whenever a pollen-collecting bee lands upon a flower, the flower exudes its charity without restriction. The bee accepts with sincere appreciation and respect.

The meadow glows with the sweetest and purest of love.

Sophie said, "This must be the Garden of Eden."

Neither Gabriel nor the Elf ladies are present, only the beautiful baby girl and herself. Sophie sits upon the rich green grass with her back resting against a giant live oak tree whose canopy reaches as high as Heaven. She cradles the baby in her arms, feeding her on her right breast. Sophie feels her nourishing milk enter her baby's mouth as the baby suckles. But this milk is not just milk; it is the Love flowing from the Divine into her heart and baby.

As she nourishes her little girl, Sophie realises that Divine Love is in everything and everywhere. She understood the female is the most substantial fountain of Divine Love upon the Earth, as females inherently exude love and nourishment. A baby's first experience of nutrition is their first experience of Divine Love from their mother. And for many, sadly, a mother's love is the last joy they feel within the physical realm.

Sophie understood the Society's need for her aid to help restore a proper gender balance in the world's power structure. She recognises Gabriel's gift to her. Sophie sees the other wives of Gabriel nursing their babies, understanding the extent of the Society's Work of Correction. Her child's birth is a Divine Intervention accomplished by the Society, Gabriel, and herself.

The vision fades from her consciousness, and the moonlit rooftop garden again surrounds her.

"Thank you, darling, for showing me our intended future. To bear such a child, our child, I would give you my life, Gabriel, if you asked. I can find no words to express what I feel for you. I think what I am feeling is unconditioned and pure."

Gabriel reaches over to take Sophie's hands into his.

"What you feel now is the purity of God's Love. It will be difficult to remember this feeling in a few minutes, but knowing it exists is sufficient. The greatest gift you can bestow upon me is never to waver in your efforts to enter the Society, for this is the narrow doorway leading to our Eternal Marriage. For Immortals are best as gender-complemented pairs."

After separating their kesdjan bodies from the earthly kelim, Sophie takes Gabriel's hand and stands in a flat clearing on the side of a mountain.

"We, Sophie, are within the Carpathian Mountains of Western Ukraine. I will ask you to observe how the earthly details of this clearing change as we watch the seasons progress. As you observe and describe what you see, I want you to find the Heavenly Realms' correspondent factors in the upper spiritual or astral world. OK?"

"I will do my best."

"Sophie, it is wintertime at this moment. Look up into the sky and tell me what you see."

"Gabriel, I see a blue sky and no clouds. The sun possesses its normal yellow tint but is not very high above the horizon. The air is chilly but tolerable as the wind is not blowing. I do not see any birds in the sky."

"Sophie, extend your hands before you and describe them to me."

"I can see my outstretched hands as the light is good. But they are cold, for the sunlight does not seem to warm my hands."

"Good, Sophie. I want you to remember how the light from the sun in winter can be powerful, but it is not warm. Tell me about this clearing and its trees and animals."

"Gabriel, all around us are hardwood trees with no leaves. Their trunks and branches are greyish brown, and I do not see any moss growing upon the trunks or branches. Some trees have clumps of grey-green mistletoe, so you must kiss me, honey," as she puckers her lips.

"Be serious. I promise to kiss you later. But, entrance to our Society is paramount."

"OK, Meany. I see a red deer buck and his doe nibbling under the snow. Two small white hares eat together near their burrow. The animals have thick winter coats, and the snow is powdery and dry. The forest is quiet, with no birds singing or wind blowing, and I do not see any greenery anywhere."

"Sophie, remember that most plants become dormant during the winter, and animals must search continuously for food. The reason is that the sun is too low in the sky to warm the Earth."

Gabriel sees Sophie shivering, and he wraps his arms around her and holds her close.

Sophie snuggles as close as she can. Gabriel feels very toasty to her.

Looking up at Gabriel, she said, "I understand I have been acting like a schoolgirl. It is strange, as normally, I am very focused on the Work and the Society. I am sure it is because of your bond with me, Gabriel. I never considered being a mother, but I want to have our baby more than anything else. Whenever I think of our baby, a warm flush comes over me, and I crave you to be inside me. I really cannot control my feelings and physiological responses."

"What is happening with you is not unexpected after a mortal woman pledges her soul seed to an Immortal. Do not worry, my dear. I will compound a potion, allowing your cravings to subside until later. I should have been better prepared, but all this is new."

Sophie unclasped herself from Gabriel, as the season was now spring.

"Gabriel, the snow departed, and the trees show fresh green leaf buds. The dormant grass is turning green here and there. The doe is pregnant and will have a calf in another month. The sun seems brighter than before, and I can finally feel its warmth."

"Excellent. Using your seasonal observations of the effects of the sun's light and warmth upon the Earth and its creatures, tell me about the Divine Sun and its light and warmth. Sophie, do not reason; open your mind to intuitive knowing."

Without stopping to think, Sophie blurted out, "The actual sun corresponds with the Divine Sun or the original emanation of God into our universe. The Divine Sun is a Pentacle, or five-pointed star, with miniature Suns at each corner and one in the centre. The central Sun radiates the Quale of Presence to Creation. The Suns at the corners of the Pentacle shine into the Creation, the Five Qualia of Intuitive

Knowing, Selfless Observation, Transcendence, Intending or Volition, and Unconditional Love-Caring.

"I see two Divine Triads, the first union being Love, Presence, and Transcendence, and the second union being Observation, Knowing, and Volition.

I understand that the first Triad simplifies to Love. Swedenborg could not appreciate the finer details of the Teachings of the Society.

"The second Triad is the illuminating Light of the Divine Sun; however, the illumination is without warmth. The Wisdom Triad allows conscious creatures to observe themselves and their interactions with others. Direct knowing allows us to discern truth from falsity, and volition enables us to act for the highest good.

"Winters correspond to well-educated and intelligent people but cold inside toward others. Such possess no altruism.

"The Love Triad provides the sense that we exist as entities but can join with others. Transcendence is the feeling that we can become even more. Love is the pure essence of goodness and binds hearts. As the poet dost sayeth, 'Love is blind as it expresses feelings for closeness and sharing.'

"Summers correspond to people who are genuinely warm toward others but are careless in their relationships and earthly activities.

"I think springs and autumns correspond to times when Love and Wisdom are best understood and applied. In spring, the Earth prepares again for life and requires the addition of warmth. Autumn requires wisdom to prepare for winter. Many animals enter mating seasons in fall when warmth and wisdom join best."

Gabriel hugs her.

"Excellent, my dear, excellent. Today, you saw your inner rationality as your connection to the Noble Organ opened wider. You passed through another door on your path to the Society. I think you have earned a most passionate kiss."

Gabriel takes Sophie into his arms and bends to kiss her. The warmth and wetness return ever more robust when his lips touch hers.

The strength in her legs seems to drain into her feet, and she almost falls, but Gabriel holds her. Her body is merging with Gabriel's. The kiss removes her from the astral world, placing her awareness into a world she could not describe adequately; the only word was Love.

Gabriel removes his tongue from Sophie's mouth.

"Sophie, Love is the most compelling force operating within the universe. Love is irresistible, as it creates a desire for what a creature believes to be good. This is not a problem in subhuman species as the desire for what is right is natural and coordinated with survival and reproduction."

Chapter 9

The Triads

Gabriel explained, "You were correct that love and wisdom must join in a proper ratio for the greater good to arise. However, you failed to see how to join love and wisdom properly. It is essential to understand the common notion that two forces produce a resultant is incorrect. The reason is that four-brain creatures are third force blind by nature and education.

"Sophie, I want you to create the following form in your mind-space.

"First, draw a triangle with an isometric perspective and add the following labels, one to each vertex: Love, Wisdom, and Salutary.[21]

"Within the triangle, place a point in the centre, draw a vertical line upward, and label the upper point 'The Divine.' Now, draw a vertical line the same length as the upper line downward from the triangle centre and label the lower point 'Creation.'

---

[21] That which is constructive, beneficial, and valuable.

"Horizontally and to the left of the figure, level with the word Divine, write 'World 1'; level with the triangle, write 'World 3'; and level with the word Creation, write 'World 6.'

"Do you see the complete figure, Sophie?"

"I see it as you described, Gabriel."

"The triangle represents the universal Law of the Trinity. Three forces are necessary to manifest an effect in every physical and astral interaction. The first force has many names, such as Wisdom, Intending Force, Inseminating Force, Moving Force, or Active Force. The second force has many names, such as Love, Receiving Force, Fertile Force, Stationary Force, or Passive Force. The third force has many names, such as Salutary, Conciliating Force, Embryonic Force, Balancing Force, or Equilibration Force.

"I prefer using either triad: Inseminating, Fertile, and Embryonic or Intending, Receiving, and Conciliating, as the names are closest to the natures of each force. But today, I will stick with the forces like Wisdom, Love, and Salutary.

"Now, draw another triangle below the first drawing with a single point on top. I ask you to add the names of the first three Sephiroth. By the uppermost point, write Keter. By the lower right point, write Chokhmah. By the remaining point, write Binah.

"The Kabbalistic triangle clarifies the operation of the three forces in Creation. For instance, Keter refers to Divine Love, Chokhmah to Wisdom, and Binah to Salutary. Why? Understanding how to realise the intended purpose of Love and Wisdom combined is the nature of the Salutary Force. Divine Love and Wisdom are useless unless directed by Benevolent Usefulness to manifest a resultant physical or spiritual.

"What is most important to note, my dear, is that the resultant of the forces is missing from the diagram using the triangle symbol alone. The result projects orthogonally.

"If you observe the figure, you can see that it is only the skeleton for a triangular bipyramid, or two tetrahedrons stacked one upon the other. So, draw the lines to visualise the triangular bipyramid having six equal faces. Observing the figure, one understands that W1 represents the Unfathomable Infinite Source containing the universe; W3 is the first emanation of the Divine within the creative bubble enclosed with the Infinite Metric; W6 is the point where Creation starts in the material world.

"The Society teaches that W6 represents the deflation of the prior universe and transfer of all its energies into a new inflating universe. This process happens over one Planck time constant.[22] The deflation-reinflation process erases all previous information and knowledge other than the seed plan for the new universe, carried by the consciousness of at least one Immortal Pair.

"The processes of deflation and reinflation of universes have no beginning and no end, Sophie. I will explain more later. But back to the Law of the Trinity. Creation results from the proper combination of Love, Wisdom, and Salutariness.

"Unfortunately, four-brain creatures are selfish by evolutionary nature, and intelligent creatures can pervert the Law of the Trinity. Such perversion occurs whenever human freedom works to attain power, fame, or wealth for personal benefit alone. It is an evil action and a significant problem for the human species. Humans know time and space, understand personal interventions, possess autobiographical memories, and generate imagines. These abilities allow humans to imagine innovative ways to satisfy their core loves or desires, now or in the future, via aggression and manipulation.

"Humans are the only species in this biosphere being cognitively aware of the possibility of ownership of people and things to the disadvantage of others. Most male primates are genetically aggressive and violent, relishing hurting other creatures to gain dominance.

---

[22] The German physicist Max Planck derived a set of units by combinations of fundamental constants. Planck's time is the smallest possible unit of time, being 10^{-43} seconds.

"As I explained earlier, the kesdjan body can gaze inwardly toward the Divine or outwardly toward the material world with its sensual pleasures. As kesdjan bodies come into being in the form of the physical creature, their appetites are naturally those of the carnal world. Socialisation involves religious activities and an introduction to the concept of a Divine Creator or God. A significant reason for children's socialisation is instilling civic and moral values to function effectively as adults.

"A small percentage of people open their hearts to the Noble Organ to connect with the Divine and use their freedom of choice to come under Divine Wisdom and Love. Such people practise love and wisdom daily by being helpful to themselves and others. Such kesdjan bodies resonate with one of the Heavens while alive. They only need a purging of earthly desires to find Heaven.

"Those who lived consumed by earthly desires but worked diligently to not harm others enter the lower Heavens after a significant period in Purgatory. The rest place themselves in a Hell realm comfortable to the Earthly core love."

A question came into Sophie's mind.

"Gabriel, what is different between those who connect with God during life to live under the dictates of true Conscience and those who turn the inner heart away from God and toward Mammon or Satan?"

"The ones activating the soul seed within have discovered that its usual function is to be a vessel to fill with Love and Wisdom to accomplish good works. This capacity is an attribute of wisdom, particularly the ability to discern the true from the false, the higher good from the lower interests, and altruism from selfism. This discovery results from experiencing psychological conflict as to one's ethical behaviours. Their society recommends one way, but something inside tells them their community is incorrect. Such persons possess significant discernment and use it to guide them in life.

"Those who ignore the existence of the soul seed will live as intelligent animals. Self-centred and greedy, the soul seed drifts away in such a being, so the soulless ones remain bound to Hell. The more injurious, the deeper in Hell they go. You saw two examples in our recent journeys to Hell. The residents of Hell have no connection to the soul seed or true immortality. Do you understand?"

"Yes. I understand. I thought you would teach me about the Great Black Lodge but never got around to it? Is this a good time, honey?"

"I told you about the Great Black Lodge, but much more important matters distracted me."

"What kind of important matters?"

Sophie saw Gabriel blush and turn his eyes away for a moment.

"Well, Sophie. The critical matter is you and I. I suddenly realised that you were in love with me, and I felt the same toward you. It surprised me, as I had not been in a human body for some time and failed to appreciate the feeling. Once I was open to the feeling, I realised something extraordinary had occurred on a high level. I knew you must become a Society member as monumental work is underway. I also realised you and I may bring my sister Ariel and Yeshua back into this world when you attain membership. So much for keeping secrets. And to think I am a Scorpio."

Sophie is speechless for the second time in her life.

At last, with tears streaming down her cheeks, she says, "Oh, Gabriel. I understand why I must become a soror in the Society. For such a venture, the parents would have to be Immortals. Jesus's parents, Mary and Joseph, were Immortals. The New Testament is unmeasurably richer than scholars believe. Am I correct, my husband?"

"Correct."

"I call you, Husband, Gabriel, for you have been my earthly husband many times. I can feel the love and kindness you gave me for many lives. I know you have been with me to prepare me for initiation into the innermost Order of our Society.

"Oh, my darling husband, I owe everything to you. So many times, I know I was unpleasant to you, spiteful, stubborn, and hurtful. But every life you returned to care for and teach me. I know you will give all the credit to God, but I think God will give you some credit. Oh, Husband, I love you so much that I am afraid my heart will burst for joy."

Gabriel is most pleased, reaching out for Sophie's hand.

"Wonderful, sweetheart. Your channel to the Noble Organ is very open, as you have accessed the surface layers of the Akashic Records. We have married and produced many children, though none could enter the Third Path. You were quite the shrew in some of your lives, and I must admit, I often felt that I should leave you. But the love of an Immortal is too pure to diminish by poor behaviour. After so many centuries, it is nice to hear that my Sophie appreciates me."

Sophie playfully struck Gabriel on his right upper arm.

"Well, you could be troublesome, too. Admit it. You did not like it when I was overweight. Admit it."

"My preference for thin women seems to be a permanent trait of my being. I will explain later, but it had nothing to do with the depth of my love for you. When you are ready to hear an explanation of the Third Path, you will understand the difference between those in Heaven, Hell and the Immortals. Once you know the Third Path and our Society, which many people call the Great White Lodge, you will be ready to hear of the Great Black Lodge.

"For the moment, I need to provide additional information about the Law of the Trinity. First, do not fret over the terms I use when speaking of the Law of the Trinity. The names are the most descriptive ones for the operation of the Law in action. And remember, Keter connects to both Chokmah and Bina by two arms of the triangle and Chokmah and Bina by the remaining arm.

It is helpful to remember Keter represents the Intending Force beginning Creation by providing the skeleton of the Divine Plan to Intuitive Wisdom Chokmah. The Logos enters only as an original flash of insight along the path of Heh, bringing the Plan and the Laws to all future worlds.

Therefore, Chokmah, as Intuitive Wisdom and Holder of the Divine Plan, represents the Conciliating or Saltatory Force.

As shown in the Kabbalist Tree of Life, Keter is connected directly to Bina via Vav. As the female, Bina receives the embryonic seed from Keter containing the physical and aphysical formless energies necessary for world formation. She also receives the original insight from Chokmah, via Shin. Her job is to nourish and develop the embryo using Rational, Discriminating Intellect. Clearly, Bina is the Receiving Force.

This arrangement never changes. What changes is the nature of the force or entity occupying a particular Sephiroth?

"For instance, sweetheart, let's consider the triad comprising yourself, our future baby, and myself. Males are biologically more assertive than females and occupy Keter; females are more nurturing and gentler and occupy Bina.

The reason four-brain creatures are third-force blind is that they cannot see that each node of the triangle is connecting two other nodes. But it is not so important as the law of manifestation in a plane can only be visualised by six simple figures.

The birth of a baby conciliates the male and female principles. We can assign numerals to the triad elements above to represent energy flows. We can say that power flows from (1) to (2) to (3), so we name the triad (1-2-3).

"The (1-2-3) triad exists in sexual reproduction, for the male desires to give his seed to the female to produce a child. This triad is the Involution or Outpouring.

"For the (2-1-3) triad, we see a baby is possible only after a fertile female has actively searched and attracted a male to inseminate her. The first force is the egg, the second is the sperm, and the third is the zygote's potential. We call this the triad of Evolution.

"Currently, Baby occupies Keter, you occupy Chokhmah, and I occupy Binah to form the triad (3-2-1). We know this triad as Freedom. The potential child is the active force as it desires to be born, so it must create a healthy sexual and mothering urge in the female to attract the father.

"The remaining triads are Order (3-1-2), Identity (2-3-1), and Interaction (1-3-2)."

"Darling, considering my vision and breastfeeding of our little girl, she is a powerful intending agent? She makes my life almost unbearable by creating my insatiable desire for you, Gabriel. How can she do this?"

"Sophie, the child does not exist yet. What is acting is the intending force? At this moment, an attractor pulls us from the future. This attractor was created by our Society's conjoint efforts more than a millennium ago? For nearly two thousand years, this thought form has attracted the energies for the reincarnation of Divine Consciousness to the human world. Soon, Sophie, all your desires will be satisfied. We will marry and create the physical vessel for the Incarnation of the Divine Energies."

"But I do not understand. Was not Christ, the Incarnation of God's Son, brought into the world via Mary's womb? The Trinity becoming flesh? As decided by the Ecumenical Councils at Nicaea and Ephesus?"

"The followers of Christ misunderstood the Law of the Trinity. They did not see that the first outpouring of God comprised the Divine Qualia. They only perceived the sacred images associated with Love as the Father, Wisdom as the Son, and the vaporous Holy Spirit. A mistake I will correct one day.

"Sadly, the majority in a democratic vote is more wrong than wise. Remember, a vote arbitrarily decided much of the Christian dogma in several Ecumenical Councils. Beginning in 325 CE with the First Council of Nicaea, later in 381 CE at the First Council of Constantinople, and finally at the Council of Ephesus in 431 CE.

"The vote of the attending Bishops established but did not prove the correctness of the current credo of the Christian Church. From the

Society's perspective, Nestorius's view (c 386–451 CE), the Patriarch of Constantinople, is closer to the truth but is still incorrect.

"The Society teaches that the physical vehicle, Yeshua, was the natural son of Mary and Joseph, both members of the Society. Mary and Joseph prepared Jesus to accept Christ's Consciousness when John at the River Jordan baptised him to begin the conversion. In Matthew 3:13-17, Matthew wrote:

> *13 Then Jesus came from Galilee to John at the Jordan to be baptised by him.*
>
> *14 John would have prevented him, saying, 'I need to be baptised by you, and do you come to me?'*
>
> *15 But Jesus answers him, 'Let it be so now; for it is proper for us to fulfil all righteousness in this way.' Then he consented.*
>
> *16 And when Jesus had been baptised, as he came up from the water, the heavens were opened to him, and he saw the Spirit of God descending like a dove and alighting on him.*
>
> *17 And a voice from heaven says, 'This is my Son, the Beloved, with whom I am well pleased.*

"Yeshua had been well-prepared, as a vessel of discernment and volition, to accept the Light of Our Common Father-Mother and be an Incarnation of the Sacred Image Itself of the Son as the Third Force. As Divine Consciousness is not an entity, it is incorrect to believe that Yeshua held two people in one vessel. By receiving a spark of the Divine Qualia into himself, Yeshua became the *kli* for the Divine Imago in the likeness of the Elohim. Yeshua was *Homo dei* or God-Man. The Chapter Genesis was the beginning, the Alpha, and Jesus was the Omega's ending. Such, Sophie, is the correct understanding."

"Gabriel, I understand. Using the word Man is misleading, I think? First, God appeared to humans as the Emanation of Father or Yahweh. Humans failed to improve, and 2,000 years later, God appeared as the Emanation of the Son of God, Yeshua. Still, humanity is recalcitrant, some two millennia later. So the Holy Father and Mother will manifest their Daughter. As Yeshua called himself the Son of Humanity, she will call herself the Daughter of Humanity."

"Yes, Sophie, the term Christ is gender-neutral as it is a Greek biblical title meaning 'the anointed one.' The anointment of Yeshua is with the Divine Qualia of God.

"But this time, the Divine Consciousness will descend onto a female so to complete the intended Work of Yeshua, the Christ. Sophie, the name of our daughter, will be Bitya. The meaning of this name is the Daughter of God. She is my sister Ariel, the Lioness, just as they knew Yeshua as the Christ when he attained the station of *Homo dei*. She will remove egoism and greediness through a Holy War against all evil-orientated human archetypes. Since humanity failed to achieve the intended goal proactively, the Holy Family will succeed through a Holy War. This war will eliminate the genes leading to evilness, hence completing humankind's evolution to a species like the Djinn, deified, altruistic, and caring."

"Gabriel, Ariel, is your sister? How can this be? I thought she would be Yeshua's sister? Who are you, Husband? You are a Son of God?"

"What you said is correct. But, my status in the Divine Family is not essential to understand now. You will learn the complete story one day soon."

"Then my status does not differ from Miriam's. Is it true that I am sinless as she was and fit to bear your child? How can this be true, as I was abused sexually as a child?"

"Darling, I removed and burned away your sin, my love. But, back to the subject at hand. Have you not noticed you are a virgin again?"

Sophie reached down to her pelvis unconsciously.

"Gabriel, you fixed me. You are wonderful. Now I know your love for me is pure light. Okay, back to the matter at hand.

"Husband, but if the Divine intervenes, does it not defeat the original goal of humanity completing itself?"

"Wife, humanity cannot appreciate the full extent of the benevolence of the Holy Family and its Unborn Immortals. We can tolerate the suffering created by humankind for a long time. Eventually, we may decide our Grand Experiment failed and must intervene permanently to rectify the system. If our children are incapable of accomplishing Our Goal, and so bring Heaven to Earth, we must act for the sake of Mercy.

"Now you can appreciate why there are so many universes. The self-correction of the evolutionary necessity of ego and body survival comes only to a select group of sentient creatures. This is acceptable, but we always desire more. Eventually, the Divine intervenes before humanity destroys itself."

"Gabriel, the soul seeds survive either way?"

"Yes, Sophie, the soul seeds are eternal and can only evolve. But that is a matter to discuss later.

"The traditional description of the Christian Trinity, as Divine Human Forms, is grossly incorrect, per our information. Using the Trinity, World 3 contains three forces existing without time and space, *aeternum et omnipraesens*. Each of these forces was experienced in the likeness of the Elohim. Love as Father Yahweh, Wisdom as the Daughter Sophia, and Salutariness as the Son Yeshua. The Trinity is practical, but it is incomplete.

"The multidimensional Geometry of Infinite Space is the Divine Mother, who bears the Energies of Manifestation from the Trinity. The Divine Daughter is the invisible Comforter, Holy Ghost, and Spirit of the Trinity. She is the hidden fourth point of the Divine Tetrad. Her name is Isis, the secret star.

"The Law of the Trinity is an operational cut of the underlying Superior Law of the Tetrad. As I mentioned, Creation is only possible by restricting a portion of the Infinite to create a transfinite phase space. When I speak of the Tetrad Law, I discuss concepts most difficult for ordinary human reasoning. The higher rationality must be understood through the Noble Organ. But here goes.

"Imagine a bipyramid in your mind-space. Place the following upon each of the bipyramid's four horizontal points: Holy Father, Holy Mother, Holy Daughter, and Holy Son. These four points represent the creative agents denoted in humanity's Old Testament by the plural *Elohim* and in Kabbalah by *Ein Sof*. The abode of the Holy Family World 3.

Label the uppermost point, Creator, *Ein*, and *Demiourgos*. The Creator is the active agent in every universe, regardless of human-derived forms. The Creator exists in World 1. *Ein* is the Hebrew word for the first emanation of the Source. When people refer to the Supreme Deity or God in their theologies, this is who they are honouring.

Label the lowermost point, *Ein Sof Ohr*, Spirit, which occupies World 6. This point contains all the information necessary for the physical and Oneirion worlds to come into being in time and space. It contains all applicable laws, energies, and possible temporal paths from beginning to end. The *Ein Sof Ohr* metaphorically manifests via *Keter* and the Kabbalist Tree of Life.

Such is why God and the *Elohim* are in Bereshit 1:27, though not adequately described.

Now, I want you to add one last set of terms to your diagram above the uppermost point. It is the Unfathomable Source. Label it using the mathematical symbols of an Infinity (the Mother) and a Point (the Father). The Source contains all possible Universes but is not wholly within any. One day, we will discuss it, but not now.

"The Holy Family represents the four divisions of the Divine manifested as the Elohim. The Unfathomable and Divine Family are *aeternum et omnipraesens*. The Elohim are not God the Absolute but are a fourfold division of God's Will. This pyramid exists outside of Creation. Using terms from the Kabbalah, we can consider Keter the spacetime beginning point through which the Elohim manifests our universe via God's Spirit or the Holy Ghost.

"Sophie, you can understand why the less informed writers of early religious texts, Christian and Egyptian, saw God as tripartite rather than tetrapartite. I need to tell you that the Tetrad appears in the Kabbalah as the Tree of Life divides into Four Worlds. The Law of the Tetrad is entirely outside Creation and not within Creation, wherein the Law of the Trinity rules. So, sufficient hints have been available for some time, honey.[23]

"We find the most conspicuous evidence of the Holy Family in the near-universal preference of nuclear families in the earliest human groups and later civilisations. Such gender-balanced arrangements were an evolutionary necessity for our species. They were the most productive family group for a viable society.

"The Gurdjieff Laws of Three and Seven appear in the descending heptatonic musical scale, numbered from zero to seven, eight distinct notes to an Octave. Hidden within this scale is the melodious Fifth. The descending Perfect Fifth ends on Note F if the octave begins with Note C. There are four intervals in the ascending Fifth, do-si, si-la, la-sol, and sol-fa, symbolising the Divine Tetrad. The Law of Three appears as the melodious descending Fourth, which begins on Note F and concludes the descending Octave, ending with the lower Note C. The Fourth contains the three intervals: fa-mi, mi-re, and re-do. The

---

[23] Notice that the sum of the first four integers equates to ten, so the Tree of Life possesses ten Sefirot.

descending scale is typical of most ancient music, which saw Creation moving from a higher to a lower frequency, the Refined to the gross, or the Light to heaven.

"I do not know if the church will correct its error before Ariel arrives. She may be humanity's last hope, honey. She will be a sweet child but a full-grown warrior and carry a Flaming Sword. It is not Christ who returns for the last battle for humanity, but the Lioness Herself. I will tell you more later. Now, we travel. Take my hand, wife. We are off for more adventure."

END OF CODEX ONE

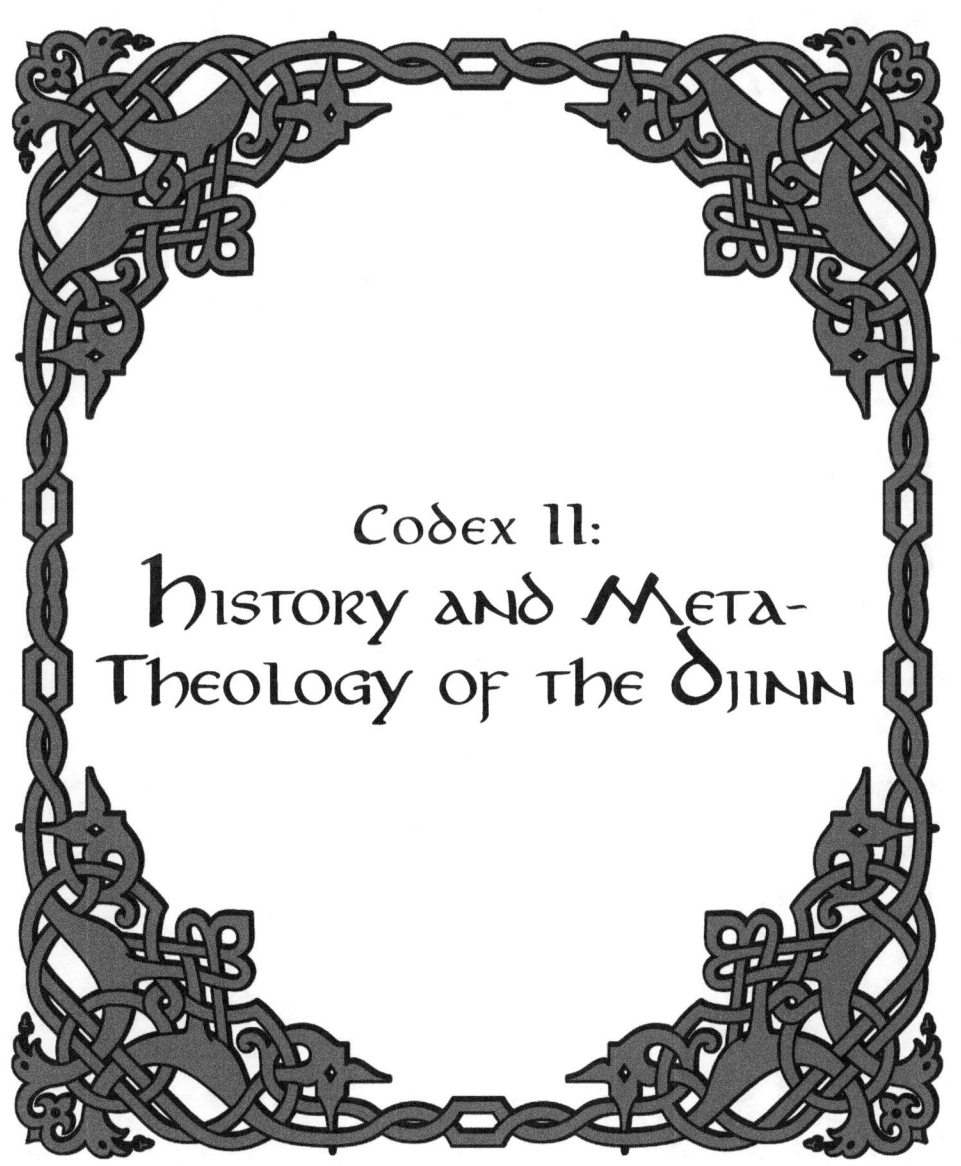

Codex II:
History and Meta-Theology of the Djinn

Chapter 10

The Djinn

Almost instantly, Sophie and Gabriel stand outside the entrance of a most unusual dwelling built into the side of a hill. Deep undulating snowdrifts cover the land like a surreal white sea. A strong winter wind tumbles through the ice-encased tree canopies, causing their branches to flash, reflecting the full moon's light. Moon Maiden sees Gabriel and Sophie wearing fox furs, excellent protection against the chilling wind.

The pair stand upon rough, hand-hewed, wooden planking parallel to the hill face. In front of them stand substantial, wooden doors with brass fittings. Two rows of frosty windows flank the entrance, allowing Sophie to see within. Sophie walks to one window, rubbing the frost off with her sleeve. She sees the room has long tables and benches upon which men and women sit.

She sees men with bare heads except for a long braid in the back. The women have long, braided dark hair, worn long or coiled around each side of their heads. Overall, the people are comely.

Everyone dresses in wool garments and fur boots. All the tables are full of mugs, bread, cheese, and meat.

Taking Sophies's hand, he said, "Sophie, the people you see inside are Djinn. They are wary of outsiders, so please say little. Besides, they are very sexual creatures. An old friend of mine owns this inn, and we will visit with her. These Djinn know of me and will be respectful. I shall tell them you are my concubine."

Stamping her right foot, Sophie replied, "I am not your concubine. I am your fiancé. Why are you saying this?"

"Marriage is not frequent with the Djinn, and only very high-status males have concubines. Pretend that we are role-playing. I need a favour, so do as I ask. You know I love and adore you, concubine or wife."

Gabriel ducks just in time.

Gabriel takes Sophie's hand, opens the door, and the pair walk into the room, allowing the wind to disturb the guests. An enormous brick fireplace is in the back of the room, with a cheery fire burning. Gabriel removes his beaver fur hat, and a few older guests immediately recognise him. They stand up and tell the younger guests to do so.

A pretty lady turned around, and said, "Hail, Lord Gabriel. It has been a very long time since you last visited. Everyone, please toast Lord Gabriel, the Immortal. Clear a table for him and his concubine."

Quickly, a serving girl clears the table as the other guests sit, returning to their conversations.

The lady comes to Gabriel and pulls him to her for a passionate kiss.

"Hello, darling. It has been a long time since we spent time together. I have missed you, particularly on such winter nights. Why are you here? And who is this charming creature? She is beautiful, darling. My name is Alliona, and I own this establishment. Sit. Let us get acquainted."

Gabriel, introducing Sophie, said, "My dear, this is my Sophie. She is from a planet far away from here and is my student. She is doing her very best to produce and bear a wonderful girl child for me. As you know, I am fond of children."

Alliona, opening her arms and moving to give Sophie a warm welcome hug, said, "It is a pleasure to meet you, my darling. Lord Gabriel and I have been intimate friends for many years. Once, I was in a horrible situation, and he rescued me and helped me secure this establishment. I do not know what would have happened without his kindness?"

Alliona helps Sophie remove her bulky coat to sit at the table. Sophie realises she wears tight chocolate goat leather pants with knee-high fur boots. The crotch of her pants rests snuggly and accents her labia with its furrow. She realises she is without panties. She sees Alliona gazing upon her with pleasure and looks down to see if her anatomical beauty is visible. Her torso bears a finely woven cashmere blouse dyed a brilliant red. She can't feel a bra underneath her blouse, and her ample nipples push out the blouse because of the cold in the room. Overall, she feels entirely naked.

She thought, "I guess this is how concubines dress?"

Sophie sat down quickly so she wouldn't attract more attention. Alliona sits down next to Sophie, and Gabriel sits across from them.

Before seating himself, Gabriel whispered to Sophie, "Remember, you are playing a role. You will see why shortly. You are my eternal love."

Alliona waves her hand, and three large mugs come to the table filled with warm spiced mead.

Raising her tankard, Alliona said, "Welcome to my establishment, dear Sophie. Let us toast your health and future daughter."

The three lift their mugs and drink.

Sophie takes a long draught of the spiced mead and then puts down her mug.

"Alliona, this potion is delicious. I like it, thanks."

Alliona replied, "I am glad you like it. But you must eat when you drink, for it is strong, and the herbs may have an unusual effect upon you."

A girl brings thick sourdough bread, white cheese, and some cold cuts of meat. Sophie is hungry and takes a piece of bread and cheese.

While the three of them eat and drink, Sophie listens to Alliona tell her story of Gabriel and herself. Sophie finds the tale romantic and full of adventure. Both are laughing at their remembrances. Sophie does not feel jealous or angry. She feels mellow, relaxed, and happy to be Gabriel's concubine. She loves him so much. Sophie looks over at Gabriel, and he winks at her.

She is so enthralled with the conversation she overlooks Alliona's right hand resting high between her open thighs. Alliona is gently rocking the base of her hand against Sophie. Sophie senses that the crotch of her leather pants is wet. She doesn't know what to do, but it feels pleasant.

Sophie puts her right hand over Alliona's and quickly has an orgasm. Sophie covers her mouth with the other hand to not make a sound.

Gabriel glances at Alliona, and said, "Darling, I would be pleased if you would explain to Sophie how wayward Djinn interact with humans to encourage indulgence in worldly pleasures rather than working on making a soul. Most humans still believe demons are the same fallen angels or persons damned to Hell. Foolish, eh?"

Alliona replied, "Let me think about your request for a moment, Gabriel. OK, Since Sophie is your student, I will help you. Gabriel, you have a keeper here; don't lose her.

"I am sure you and Sophie had a tiring journey, so let my tale rest till the sun rises. I have a room for you. In the morning, we will discuss your request."

Exhausted, Sophie falls asleep as Gabriel carries her upstairs. He knew she was uncomfortable in her concubine outfit and removed her clothing to put a nightgown on her. It was the first time he had seen her naked, and he was pleased, even for an Immortal. He removes his clothes and climbs into bed with Sophie. Sophie moves into his arms and passes into a deep sleep.

Gabriel is up as soon as the sun peeps over the wintery horizon. Sophie remains asleep. He quietly dresses and goes down to the kitchen to have tea with the ladies preparing food for the day.

Gabriel greets everyone.

"Good morning, my beauties. I swear the lot of you are the prettiest Djinn in the whole Djinn universe."

The young Djinn smile at each other.

Alliona comes into the kitchen a few seconds after Gabriel.

"Darling, I see you have not lost your poetic charm. Such sweet words come only from you. I hoped you would pay me a nightly visit, sweetheart. But I am glad that you remain true to Sophie. She is a treasure, and I wish you all the happiness possible from a Djinn oil lamp. But I deserve a passionate kiss from those sweet lips."

And a sweet kiss, it was for both.

Gabriel turns to the kitchen maid, Wintry, "My pretty, will you please take a pot of hot tea and some sweet biscuits to Sophie. Please put them on the table by the bed. Thanks, Wintry."

It surprised Wintry that he knew her name, and she giggled.

"Yes, Milord. I will do it right away."

Gabriel and Alliona sat in the kitchen, discussing her life since Gabriel left. Gabriel had not visited for a few centuries, so catching up was necessary.

Alliona said, "After you left, darling, I remained celibate. I did not want to forget how beautiful we were as a couple. Gabriel, I will always love you. I still want us to marry and have children. But I know it will never be, but I refuse to give up my deepest wish."

Gabriel took Alliona's hands and said, "Oh, Alliona, I have never stopped loving or desiring you. You are our universe's most beautiful, gentle, and generous Djinn. I have missed you much over the past years. Don't give up on your wish, honey. We may marry still. You will make a stellar mother, Alliona."

"I am glad you realise I still love you, Gabriel. I always will. We were happy with each other, and I shall never forget this. I know you continued to watch over me all these years.

"I know Immortals are not like other creatures in love and relationships. I realised long ago that your love for me would never go stale or get diminished by other females you love. I know there is a universe somewhere where I marry you, have children and have all your love. And one day, I will be in that universe with my Gabriel."

"Alliona, you have always been an intelligent lady. What you said is true, my love. There is such a universe waiting for you. One day, you will find yourself in the kitchen of our home and calling the children and me to breakfast. I have always loved you as my only love and always shall."

Sophie enters the kitchen as the conversation ends. She wore more appropriate clothing and did not need to pretend to be a concubine.

She kisses Gabriel on his lips and Alliona on her cheek.

"Alliona, I appreciate your sincere kindness and respect towards me. I understand why my Gabriel still loves you."

It surprised Alliona.

"Sophie, you understand how special Gabriel is? He is unique, even for an Immortal."

"No need for surprise. I was about to walk into the kitchen and heard you two chatting, so I stopped. One of the best indications that a man truly loves you is that he can never stop loving you. I want this kind of husband.

"I must admit that I was not asleep when you undressed me, my love. Your hands felt wonderful. I was hoping you would make love with me, but you are an Immortal of your word. I love you one hundred times more than last night. There is nothing I would not give or do for my Lord Gabriel."

Everyone laughs after Sophie says, Lord Gabriel. Sophie sat next to her husband-to-be, and breakfast came with fried eggs, home fries, bacon, pickles, and warm multigrain bread with butter.

After breakfast, Alliona said, "Sophie, now I shall honour my promise to Gabriel and tell you the nature of the Djinn folk.

"The Djinn were created a very long ago by the same Demiourgos which built your universe. We had physical and kesdjan bodies, like the four-brain creatures of your world. After studying our universe for a long time, our Djinn cosmologists discovered it was so old that it would collapse, and all of us would be no more. We discovered a remote, anomalous connection between our universe and your universe. This connection allows our kesdjan bodies to move into your universe, not our physical bodies. So, we all left our Oneirion and became residents in your Oneirion. Our old universe collapsed and, with it, our bodies.

"Therefore, the Djinn live within the conjoint four-brain species' minds of your universe. Within your Oneirion, we reproduced our old world using the atonic energies. You and Gabriel now exist within the Djinn Oneirion at this moment. Neat, eh?"

"Wow, I thought Gabriel had brought me to another physical world. Your world is so real, Alliona."

"That it is, sweet child. Unfortunately, moving from our original universe into your universe was not innocuous. By transferring to your universe, we lost our Heaven and Hell. We discovered that our species now possessed a semi-permanent lifespan. Our children would grow into adulthood and change slowly over thousands of years. We are mortal; we can die from injuries, illness, or even grief. But when we die, it is our end.

"Interestingly, human myths about their Elves not having a Heaven or a Hell refer to the Djinn and not the Elves.

"Realisation of the finality of our kesdjan bodies resulted in focusing the Djinn mind upon our ancient animal desires. The Djinn were jealous that humans had Heaven and Hell, so they worked with the devil to prevent humans from enjoying paradise. In time, many male and female Djinn found great delight in interacting in the human Oneirion.

Gabriel interrupts, "Darling, I think you need to tell Sophie the complete story; the best you remember it?

"I am sorry, but I was afraid the full story might hurt Sophie's feelings?"

"Do not worry. Sophie is at least as advanced in spirituality as the Djinn were before their departure. I would like her to be mindful of the Djinn's full history. OK."

"OK, honey. If you insist."

Alliona starts over.

"In our old universe, the Djinn were a very advanced race of four brain beings. Because of our science, we could significantly eliminate our genetic defects and extend our life spans. If you did not have a clock and watched the life of a Djinn from birth to death, it would appear much the same as in your species. However, there is a big difference. Although an hour of your time is the same as an hour of our time, we slowed down our phylogeny some 100 times.

"So, rather than taking thirteen or fourteen human years for a female to become reproductive, it required some 1120 or 1144 years. Once you get accustomed to the delay, it is helpful for things that did not change so fast. It allowed for the more spiritual education of our children, so they were consciously awake when they reached responsible maturity.

"At the time of the impending universal catastrophe, our race lived together peacefully, without greed or egotism. For a long time, an Immortal physically lived amongst us and took responsibility for guiding our race to its elevated status. This Immortal was our Gabriel, Sophie. In the old universe, he was my husband and father of a boy and girl who died during the catastrophe.

"No, Sophie, I was not training to be an Immortal, for our race could not do so. Universes capable of creating new Immortals are rare and are one reason your physical world is of value. All we had available were Heaven and Hell.

"I was in love with our Gabriel, but I noticed something unusual in myself. I saw that deep inside; I felt a particular pride that Gabriel had chosen me of all the beautiful Djinn ladies, so I must be the most special Djinn female. I knew such a feeling was inappropriate, but I could not eliminate it. I was afraid to tell Gabriel, as I feared he would stop loving me, and I would never have his child. I was ashamed of myself and felt that I had failed him. Somehow, I repressed the feeling so effectively that I forgot about it.

"Little did I realise by repressing my egoism, I denied information to Gabriel. The information could have changed the future of all the Djinn."

Turning to Gabriel, Alliona asked, "Honey, am I doing what you want me to do?"

Gabriel, smiling, said, "Alliona, you are doing fine. I am happy with you. I promise to do all I can to give you what you most desire."

Sophie could tell from Alliona's face that she had been afraid to speak, but her love for Gabriel was more important than her love for herself.

Sophie thought, "I hope my love shall be as pure as Alliona's. So Mote It Be."

Relieved, Alliona resumes her explanation.

"Back to our story. Gabriel discovered that our old universe was expanding too rapidly, causing the background temperature to decrease too quickly. The temperature had dropped dangerously close to sub-absolute zero. Any large-scale quantum fluctuation could cause an abrupt phase change, leading to the full deflation of our universe. And the destruction of all indigenous life, Gabriel excluded."

Sophie looked surprised, and Alliona laughed.

"Sophie, I was a physicist in my universe, not an innkeeper. And deflation occurs when a portion of the universe violates quantum mechanics by dropping below absolute zero. Absolute zero is the null temperature at which molecular translation stops but not bonding vibrations. Absolute zero is not the actual minimum energy state for the universe. The actual zero energy state occurs when quarks, leptons, and bosons freeze in place. When this happens, the universe deflates and then inflates to repeat an endless chain of universes."

It caught Sophie unprepared.

"Alliona, I didn't mean to be a sexist or something like that. I apologise."

"Don't worry about it. People change with the times. Gabriel found the anomaly I told you about, the connection between your universe and ours. Gabriel discovered he could not send his physical body through the link. But he could send his higher being body, which the Immortals call the praetorian body, and his kesdjan body through the connection.

"Gabriel returned and asked me to accompany him to the anomaly. We found he could pull my kesdjan body through with his own. The experiment was a success. We discovered it would be possible to bring our Djinn virtual reality over. This is like your species' Oneirion, Sophie. We would no longer be physical creatures, but we would be alive. We also noticed that the other universe possessed no four brain creatures.

"Gabriel discussed the problem with our Sacred First. You know this Force by the Hebrew name Elohim or the Holy Family. Gabriel's plan was rational and should start as soon as possible. The Sacred First foresaw no apparent problems. The Djinn sacrificed our physical reality for a permanent dream reality in a new universe. The new universe had no four-brain creatures who might suffer from the Djinn immigration. After discussing with our Elders, we voted upon and agreed to disseminate our decision to the populace.

"It took Gabriel a few days to transport our race into your universe. When we first arrived, we met with unusual darkness. Our daily experiences seemed to flow at the same temporal rate, but no one was dying—all this happening before your sun was born. Slowly, our conjoint Djinn Mind, our Kesdjan Mind, recreated a virtual copy of our old physical universe. However, we soon realised we had attained near immortality by sacrificing our physical bodies.

"Life was excellent until we discovered humanity had come into being in our new homeworld. Naturally, we became interested and could only interact with them by entering their dream space. However, the interaction was most unusual as humans thought the Djinn were true Immortals and divine. They treated us as gods, angels, demons, and mythical creatures, and humans started creating idols to represent us. We also noticed a curious malady called suggestibility or spin, which affects humans. Thinking things which are not accurate as if they are real.[24]

"The suggestibility and worship by the first humans presented a robust stressor upon the unconscious aspects of the Djinn mind. Soon, many of the Djinn began suffering from mental disturbances, causing the love of power and self-aggrandisement. Even though our genetic engineers had deleted the genes responsible for such sociopathic behaviour, they failed to remove the psychoistic habits related to such genes. We saw the humans had infected the Djinn.

"Though I did not visit humans often, I was scared and afraid to tell Gabriel about the infection. I feared he would leave me. But I knew that he might have been able to prevent what happened if I had told him. But, Sophie, I was so afraid that he would leave me, and I became despondent and cried whenever he was not around me.

---

[24] My old friend Gurdjieff called this malady, the Kundabuffer.

"But he found me crying one day and demanded to know why. I finally told him, and he took me into his arms and whispered the most loving words into my ears. He told me he loved and needed me to be healthy, for many Djinn count on me. He felt so strong, Sophie. Finally, my despondence left my heart, and his love for me became even ten times stronger.

"I remember him saying, 'Alliona, I cannot ever stop loving you, for we have shared too much time. What happened would have happened even if you had told me in advance. Even knowing this, the transfer was necessary. Existence is always hazardous, honey. Come, make love with me as if you were getting the child you desire.'"

Sophie moved over and gave Alliona a big hug.

"What a wonderful tale. Gabriel loves you and me even more because he loves us both. What do you think?"

Alliona could only nod her head affirmatively.

"Eventually, the egoism of many of our species attracted them to the deeper human Hell regions, where correspondence grew between the damned and the Djinn. Subsequently, the Djinn learned of humans' deepest fears and flaws and influenced the human dream world. They took on the shapes of those in Hell and came as demons from Hell. I am sure you can guess the rest of the story.

"There is some good news. A small group of Djinn reacted with repulsion when adulated, finding themselves resonating with the lower Heaven's angels. Subsequently, they adopted the appearance of such angels to serve as Heavenly messengers to counteract the work of the other party of Djinn. Such is why both Heaven and Hell can influence your species. If the Djinn had not been available, there would be no such interventions, and perhaps your situation would have been worse. Right, Gabriel?"

"You are right, my darling, as usual."

Sophie said, "This lesson has been an eye-opener. It clarifies many things as to the human Oneirion, or astral planes. I know you want a night with my future husband, and I want you to have such a night. Thanks, honey.

"Perhaps tonight is when you will conceive the child you desire. Your love for our Gabriel is so precious I want to honour such. I give my blessings and hope to share them from a distance."

Tears flowed copiously down Alliona's rosy cheeks.

"Oh, beautiful and precious, Sophie. You already possess the love and understanding of an Immortal, and such a gift is unheard of in my world. I love you as a real sister."

Gabriel rose from the table, kissing his Djinn wife tenderly. He then kissed Sophie. Again, Sophie felt the unbearable urge to be with him but felt close to Alliona. She shook off the feeling, wishing Gabriel a productive day.

Gabriel said he had business to attend to during the day and left Alliona and Sophie alone in the inn.

After Gabriel left, Alliona said, "Girls, two days after morn next, we have the feast for Our Resurrection Eve. When you leave today and tomorrow, wear your scarves and mittens, as I do not want any of you to be sick. We will be busy tomorrow with many partiers at the inn, and you all need to be ready. Come, give me a holiday hug, and then off with you to prepare the pretty dresses I gave you. Make sure you bring a change of clothing. See you in the morning. I love all of you."

Wintry and the other girls came to hug and wish Alliona and Sophie a Blessed Day and quickly disappeared into the winter landscape.

Alliona sat back at the kitchen table.

"Sophie, we will have the entire day to ourselves. I have much to teach you. More hot tea, sweetheart?"

"Yes, please. You are a splendid mother, Alliona. I hope I can be like you when I have my little girl. It breaks my heart that you lost a son and daughter."

Alliona smiles at Sophie. She rises and goes to the iron stove to boil water for a fresh pot of tea. She returns to sit at the table.

"Sophie, let us continue with the Djinn history. First, I don't want you to think most of my people are demonic or hold ill will toward your species. Most of the Djinn live the same way as before the Resurrection. We try to help each other, everyone works, and many attend church to commune with the Holy Family. Even though our scientific understanding is superb, technology has never attracted us, explaining why we live in such a simple manner.

"We enjoy being together, sharing strong mead and tasty food. My inn is the central gathering place in our village. Some days, we are filled with families with children and on other days, only adults. When the children are at home asleep, our Djinn men and women come to the inn to enjoy our herbal drinks and a tryst.

"Gabriel told you we are not a race who often marries and sticks with one mate. Our parents are very attentive to their children and give them priority. At least one parent always stays at home with the children. It is rare for a Djinn to feel jealous unless you are a Djinn who reverted to the prescience days. But the Djinn are very libidinous creatures but admire the married Djinn who remain loyal to their spouses.

"We do not interact with your species, as we do not want to seem to differ from who we are. Anyway, why would we tempt our psychogenetics?"

Alliona stands up to fetch the hot kettle, returning it to the table. She pours hot water into a teapot pre-filled with loose tea to seep.

Bending over her, Alliona kisses Sophie gently on her right cheek and whispers into her ear, "You are such a precious creature, honey. I wish you success in your journey to immortality and permanence with our Gabriel. I am finding my heart is full of genuine love for you."

Sophie turns her entire face to Alliona and kisses her on the lips.

"I am finding my heart is filling with love for you, Alliona. It is such a warm and soft feeling. Thank you. I always wanted to have a sister, and I now have one. I love you, Alliona."

Alliona, smiling, returns to her chair, continuing with her story.

"Some of our histories exist within your spiritual literature, though in the language of another age. The story concerns the one and only Djinn war after the Transplantation. Your historians think the information is human when it is Djinn.

"Now, after stabilising the Transplantation. Gabriel returned to our old universe to recover his physical body and move it into your universe. A funny thing, though. He travelled for a long time, and we all feared that he had found himself trapped in the old universe and we had lost him forever. He returned to await the destruction of the prior universe, which was the only way to remove his physical body when the Holy Family left for a new beginning.

"During this time, two factions of Djinn arose utterly opposed to each other. A Great war ensued, and we lost many Djinn. At the darkest moment, Gabriel returned with his original sister, Ariel. The two raised havoc amongst the evil Djinn while assuring our safety. Now you understand why Djinn addresses him as Lord Gabriel, Warrior Prince.

"Oh, Sophie, you should have seen Ariel, the Lioness. She was so magnificent. She was tall, with deep blue eyes and golden hair reaching her waist. She wore her hair as two coiled braids around her head like an Indian Naga. Her breastplate carried an image of the Egyptian goddess Sekhmet on the front and back. I have never seen a more beautiful woman in thousands of years.

"When she was in battle, flames came from the end of her sword, Ra, scorching her opponents. Wherever she fought, the brown ground turned red from the blood split. And in every battle, Gabriel fought at her side as mercilessly as Ariel, and his fury was great.

"After thousands of years, most of the leaders of both sides were dead, and they arranged a surrender. The details I will tell you about later. Ariel spent a very long time with us after the Great War. She and Gabriel stayed stabilising our religion to become a ward of those who created this universe.

"Ariel taught us a religion, much like the one introduced by Lord Yeshua. Not the corrupted version established after St. Paul and his immediate successors but the Lord's True Teachings, the True Christianity. When we go to church, we offer our love to the Holy Family for the gift of a meaningful life. When we celebrate Resurrection Day, we celebrate our true rebirth as four-brain beings of your universe, Sophie. Ariel and Gabriel showed us the Way.

"Ariel showed much Love and Mercy to those who kept the peace, allowing us to inhabit this portion of the universe, protected from all evil. She banished the degenerate Djinn to your Hell regions to protect us. The Djinn who had gone to war for Good all volunteered for service to the highest Angels of your human Heaven.

"I once asked, our Gabriel, why Ariel sent the warring Djinn into your species' mind. He said it would help your species become conscious. Your natures were violent, and his beloved sister knew no other way to save you."

Sophie listened with eyes wide open, sitting on her bench all this time. Never once did she touch her tea.

At last, she asked, ""Presuming I attain entrance into the Society in this life, our Gabriel said we would create the earthly vessel for Ariel, and she will come. The Djinn and my species are so very similar, Alliona. Do you think Ariel will have to come to us? Will she destroy my species?"

"Sophie, if you are to be the earthly mother of Ariel, you will see honour as profound as Mother Miriam of Lord Jesus. She will not arrive dressed in her chain mail and helmet and will come in Peace first.

"After the Great War, Ariel dressed as an ordinary lady Djinn. She spent much of her time with the women and helped with the births of many Djinn babies. Ariel never demanded we worship or treat her differently than any other Djinn lady. Gabriel told us that this is how her innermost nature is utterly wise on the inside and utterly loving on the outside.

"The reason the Djinn share the religion taught by Christ is that we saw the power of unconditional love flowing outward from Ariel and our Lord Gabriel. For both, every Djinn was a son or a daughter. After a while, we could not help but love them and want to do all we can to help.

"Oh, Sophie, I hope you will be her mother, and then you will see what I mean. I think you already know some of what I am telling you, for Gabriel is very much like her. He called her his baby Sister, and she would smile.

"Sometimes she would take his head into her lap and sing beautiful lullabies to her big brother."

"Oh, Alliona, I do hope so. And I hope I can spend time with you after she is born. She may be the Bitya, the Daughter of God, but she will still be a little girl who needs all the love that mother and aunties can show. Alliona, it would be an honour if you would become Ariel's Godmother."

"Godmother to the Daughter of God, ingenious. I agree, sweetheart. Let us wear our warm clothes and walk outside in the winter sun. There is more to tell you before Gabriel returns.

Chapter 11

By Your Djinny, Djinn Chin

Sophie and Alliona walked arm in arm amongst the bare trees.

Alliona said, "I am sure you know of the Persian avatar, Zarathustra? In your calendar, he lived around 600 or 1200 BCE. After years of study, he saw that the human universe seemed to perch between two superhuman entities, the sons of the mythical Over God, Zurvan, who ruled as Time.

"Zurvan was the father of twin sons, Ahura Mazda, meaning Lord of Wisdom, Supreme Creative Spirit, Guardian of Justice, and True Friend. His twin Ahriman, meaning Lord of Darkness, Destruction, and Hostility. Ahriman's sole goal was to destroy his brother's beautiful creation to return everything to darkness and chaos with the help of his first female demon, the incarnation of concupiscence, or lust, Āz."

"Yes, Alliona, I know of this religion from the university. Why are you bringing it up?"

"Because the story derives from the Great Djinn War, we discussed. The story came to Zarathustra from a Djinn who feared the same thing would happen upon your Earth and hoped to prevent it. I only mention it to show that most Djinn are responsible and peaceful."

"I am glad you shared this with me, Alliona. I appreciate how interrelated all conscious life is within our vast universe. Once, when Gabriel discussed the Stoic philosophy of the Greco-Roman world, he said their philosophy was one of transcorporealism. By this term, he meant that the physical realm functions via energy and information exchanges between entities and objects. Gabriel said the astral and transastral worlds operated similarly.

"All three worlds possess fundamental quanta of information-energy. Over time, these different energies have formed very complex physical and aphysical creatures and objects, like your world, honey. Therefore, it is reasonable to postulate that everything in our universe arose from a common functional form and corresponding usefulness. It astounds me how correct my best friend Jean-Michel was when he wrote his teaching tale about the Library at Babel. You would like him very much, Alliona. He is another one of Gabriel's students, probably his most advanced student. He will be or already is an Immortal."

"Alliona, the Islamic Holy Book, the Koran, talks about the Djinn. Did you know this?"

"I do, Sophie. Gabriel communicated the Quran over many years to the Prophet via a Djinn. As our Gabriel teaches, neither angels nor demons leave their residences. So, the Divine uses the Djinn as messengers and guardians for your race. People see them as angels, for Djinn can assume any form.

"Your seer, Swedenborg, discovered the Archangels' names do not refer solely to individual Angels. They are also the names of great Angel societies involved in Divine Work. Unfortunately, I do not think he was aware of the excellent service by the most evolved Djinn.

"The downside is the evil Djinn resonate with Hell and remain in the general astral planes, allowing them to influence susceptible humans negatively. It has a beneficial side, sister. Our good Djinn can create conflict within the psyches of your race, alerting them whether a desire and behaviour are inappropriate or appropriate. Djinn invented the human belief that every person has a good angel and a demon looking after him. Our Gabriel once told me this is why the Holy Family took the Djinn into their Service to help humanity."

"Sophie, I think it beneficial to share the Islamic point of view to show the differences between the real Djinn and the Djinn of the Prophet.

"The Djinn are beings possessing free will, some residing on Earth in a co-spatial world. The Arabic word Djinn is from Janna, which means hiding or concealing. Thus, they are physically invisible, one reason some people have denied their existence. However, the Djinn world's effect on your world is enough to refute this modern denial of one of God's creations. I find the origins of the Djinn in the Quran and the Sunnah.

> *Allah says We created man from dried clay of smooth black mud. And We created the Djinn before that from the smokeless flame of fire. (Quran 15:26-27)*

> *Thus, Djinn existed before man. As for their physical origin, then the Prophet, may the mercy and blessings of God be upon him, confirmed the above verse when he said Allah created the Angels from light and the Djinn from smokeless fire. (Saheeh Muslim).*

"This description of the Djinn tells us much about them. Because their creation was from fire, their nature has been fiery. Like humans, they, too, must worship Allah and follow Islam. Their purpose in life is the same as ours.

> *Allah says I did not create the Djinn and humankind except to worship Me. (Quran 51:56)*

The Djinn may be Muslims or non-Muslims, and the non-Muslims form a part of the army of the most infamous Djinn, Iblis. These disbelieving Djinn are the devils.

> *(O' Muhammed): It has been revealed to me that a group of Djinn listened and said We have heard a marvellous Quran. It guides unto righteousness, so we have believed in it and will never make partners with our Lord. (Quran 72:1-2)*

"We Djinn are like you in many aspects of your world. We eat and drink, marry, have children, and die. Our life span, however, is far longer than yours. We will be present with humankind on the Day of Judgment and go to Paradise or Hell. Like you, we will also be subject to a Final Reckoning by God, the Highest. Such is our belief.

"We differ from humanity, as God has given us power over humankind. If humans oppress others, they will be accountable. One capability of the Djinn is we can assume any physical form they like. Thus, we can appear as humans, animals, trees, and anything else. Thousands of people have sighted strange-looking creatures worldwide. It seems more plausible that such sightings may have been Djinn parading in different forms.

"The ability to possess and take over the minds and bodies of other creatures is a power which the Djinn used over the centuries. We prohibit using this power, as possessing another being is a great oppression. Human possession is something that has always been a problem for humanity.

"If a person becomes possessed, then one must invoke the name of Allah in expelling the Djinn. Looking at the Prophet's practice and companions, we find many invocations to exorcize Djinn. All of them invoke Allah to help the possessed person. However, after a modern exorcism, the Djinn often returns when the exorcist leaves, knowing that nothing except Allah's words can stop it from oppressing others.

"It is not only humans who suffer possession but also animals, trees, and other objects. The control of idols is one way to do this. By doing this, the evil Djinn hopes to make people worship others besides God. I heard recently that Hindu idols were drinking milk in your world. From Bombay to London, Delhi to California, countless idols drank milk. Ganesh, the elephant god Hanuman, the monkey god, and even Shiva's lingam, the male private organ, all seemed to guzzle down the milk like there was no tomorrow! Unfortunately, people flocked to feed the Hindu gods. The Djinn undoubtedly did this feat as a classic attempt to make people worship false gods.

"Sophie, so some people in your world understand that we exist, Sophie?"

As they continued to stroll together, Alliona would stop whenever she found a winter plant. She would tell Sophie the scientific and common names, describe its yearly life cycle, and explain how to use its medicinal and culinary properties. Sophie was finding herself more impressed by Alliona. She was brilliant.

On one of the botanical stops, Sophie told Alliona, "I hope all three of us can be together as a family, Alliona. I want our future children to grow up as siblings. I know it will break your heart if Gabriel leaves you again, and his love for you is intense, honourable, and tender. My heart fills with the warmest love whenever I see you two together. I love both of you. I truly do, honey. We are going to do this, Alliona. I do not know how, but the three of us are a wonderful family, and that is that."

Sophie saw Alliona's eyes grow wet, and tears streamed down her cheeks.

"Don't cry, honey. It will be OK. Let me kiss your tears away. Come to me."

She puts Alliona's head on one of her shoulders. Alliona presses herself against Sophie, and Sophie kisses up her tears. As Sophie gently strokes Alliona's long, beautiful hair, she remembers the lullaby that her grandmother would sing to her when she was afraid. She sang for

Alliona, realising that she loved her very much. It was a new feeling for Sophie.

In a few minutes, Sophie said, "Sweet love, time to continue our stroll. I need to learn more about your herbarium, and I am sure it will prove useful someday."

Lifting her head, Alliona said, "I love you, Sophie, more than I have ever loved another woman. I want the three of us to be a proper family, perhaps unconventional, but a family filled with love and goodness. I have much more to show you, honey."

Alliona takes Sophie's hand in hers, and they walk. But neither wanted to speak about botany. Instead, they discuss plans to convince their beloved Gabriel to ensure they would be together. The discussion covered many avenues for persuasion, and both hearts overflowed with love for the other.

As they near the inn, Alliona puts her arms around Sophie and holds her close.

"Sophie, I have never felt so loved and cared for other than by Gabriel. I am so happy with you, honey. I would do anything you asked me to do, love, anything. I know our family will be the best in all the worlds."

"I feel the same, sister. We must be together. I love you as much as I love Gabriel."

They arrive at the Inn, entering the room arm in arm. Gabriel reads an old book by the fireplace and looks up when the door opens.

Smiling, he said, "You two ladies are becoming excellent friends. I am happy for all of us."

Like young schoolgirls, both ran to Gabriel, throwing their arms around his neck and smothering him with kisses.

In unison, they said, "We love you; we love you; we love you, honey."

Gabriel tries to push them away, but they want to kiss him.

"Aren't you curious about my business today?"

They stop immediately, remove their outerwear, and sit on a bench holding hands, looking at each other.

Before stopping herself, Sophie blurts out, "Oh, darling, we love you to Heaven, and we love each other just as much. Alliona and I have decided we want nothing to separate us. So, you must have two wives who adore everything about you."

Alliona looked in astonishment at Sophie, and they both laughed.

"So much for our devious plan, Sophie. We might as well tell him everything. And we decided you will make love to both of us so we can have lots of babies from you to love besides Ariel."

"And Alliona will get a physical body and become an Immortal. She is so smart, Gabriel, and understands everything."

Gabriel looks at Sophie and Alliona, thinking, "They are innocent school girls now. The Society is up to some mischief and providing a nice riddle."

He stands up from his chair and walks over to the bench where the girls are sitting.

"Girls, can you separate from each other so I may sit betwixt you?"

They did as he asked. Gabriel put an arm around each waist, kissing each on the cheek.

"OK. We will have a unified family, and I will try to create a mortal body for Alliona. I will have two wives to adore and care for and give you babies to love, regardless of whether the time has come for Ariel. You will be the very first Djinn Immortal, Alliona."

Sophie and Alliona squeal in delight, jumping up to hug and kiss each other.

In unison, they say, "Gabriel, we have the best husband ever. We will love and care for you forever."

"Enough. It is time for us to go into the kitchen and prepare some dishes for Resurrection Day. I know the girls will be here tomorrow, and I want to bake some fruit pies."

Alliona, startled, asked, "Honey, where did you find fresh berries and apples this time of the year?"

"I spent most of my day shopping in the human realms for exotic fruits, different libations, and presents for everyone in the village. I know what everyone truly needs, and all will be happy with my choice. Some of Alliona's inn rooms are filled with presents. It is a most unusual year for all of us."

The girls clap, and Sophie said, "I am looking forward to my first Resurrection Day celebration with the two of you."

Gabriel reaches out for Sophie and Alliona, announcing, "I have a wonderful surprise for both of you. And I am sure neither of you even considered my surprise with all your conniving."

Alliona replied, "Honey, we weren't conniving. We wanted you to love and live with us, and that's all."

Gabriel could feel the strength of the love between Alliona and Sophie.

"I stopped to discuss something with the village Pope. As he plans to attend the festivities, I asked him to perform a wedding the morning after the celebration. He thought he could do so. He asked who was getting married, as marriage was rare in Djinn."

Sophie and Alliona jump up and down in excitement. Gabriel was sure they would wet themselves.

I told the Pope, "Well, do you remember the young lady at the inn last night.

The Pope said, "I remember the young lady. She's precious, Lord Gabriel, and I knew she could not be a concubine."

"I told him the three of us were getting married, and we would create an Immortal family."

The Pope replied, "Give me a moment to think. I see no scriptural impediments and don't know any prohibitions on who can marry an Immortal. I know Alliona stayed chaste after you left. Close enough to virginity for me. It is time for her to marry and have a family again. The villagers will be happy for everyone knows and adores her, for she has always put the village first."

Sophie and Alliona hug each other and look with big doe-eyes at Gabriel.

Sophie asked "How did you know we both wanted to marry you officially? We only told you when we got home?"

Gabriel breaks out into a hearty laugh.

"My precious and beautiful darlings, you forget I can look ahead in time. I knew. But I had to wait until both of you knew. I adore you both and did not want to interfere with your plans to surprise me."

Alliona tells Sophie, "I can have a proper husband at last. I have waited for so many millenniums for this day. And you will have your heart's desire, too, darling. Come, we must go upstairs and check all my clothes. I know I have some unused wedding garments somewhere for both of us. We must be beautiful for our groom. Gabriel, will you do some cooking for us, please? I wet my panties, Sophie, did you?"

"Yes, darling, I was so excited that I wet mine."

Alliona took Sophie's hand, and they ran out of the kitchen, giggling like little girls.

Gabriel sighs to himself.

"I do hope I can live with them. They are going to be the most demanding for some time. I am glad they still are children at heart, an excellent quality if you will live forever. I knew they would wet themselves."

He retrieves flour and leaf lard to begin the first crust.

Chapter 12

Preparation

abriel quickly realises that two days is insufficient time to prepare for the Resurrection Feast. He closes his eyes and calls upon Merlin for help. He asks Merlin to send his kitchen elementals to finish preparing and cooking things that would stay fresh for several days. The kitchen was soon busy with bowels filling, pans clattering, knives chopping, and loaves of bread kneading themselves.

Looking about, Gabriel said, "Thank you very much, ladies. I am off to find a fir tree to decorate."

Gabriel went to the shed, hitched Sweetie to a long sledge, and found a tree saw. Leading the pony out into the fresh snow, he searched for the perfect Resurrection Tree. It took several hours to accomplish his task. Fortunately, the moon was full, and the landscape was well-lit.

Finally, he locates a tree that Alliona would adore. It stood proudly at twelve feet, shaped in a perfect cone, and fully covered with healthy green bristles.

Gabriel looked to the tree, asking, "Mistress tree, I ask to cut you down for Resurrection Eve. I will move you to the inn so you can open the hearts of all present. I shall cover you with ornaments so you will truly be the Queen that you are."

The female spirit guarding this tree said, "I am honoured for my tree to be a part of Resurrection Eve. I know Mistress Ariel will attend this year. Peace be with you, Gabriel."

He retrieves the tree saw from the sledge and drops the queen quickly. Pulling it onto the sledge took some time as the tree was heavy.

As he labours with the tree, he asks himself, "Why are Alliona and Sophie acting like pubescent teenagers? Is it rational to marry Alliona and Sophie and have two wives? Why the start of a genuine family? Something has happened in the Praetorian Worlds. Need to deconstruct this riddle?"

Grabbing the pony by its bridle, Gabriel returns to the inn. He removes the tree from the sledge by the front door, replacing the pony and the sledge in the barn. Gabriel released the pony and gave it some fresh oats and apples.

Taking a tree stand, he heads for the kitchen. He asked the kitchen elementals to help him bring the tree into the inn's primary room and place it securely into the tree stand. The tree was inside and up in a flash. The kitchen elementals asked if they could decorate the tree? Gabriel nodded yes.

It was amazing to watch the kitchen elementals decorate. Ornaments and wreaths appeared out of nowhere and appeared upon the tree. One kitchen elemental found some magick stardust and blew it onto the tree so it shone. After finishing the tree decorating, they attached evergreen boughs to the door and windows in less than twenty minutes. Gabriel had to clap.

One of the kitchen elementals whispered something in Gabriel's ear.

Gabriel replied, "All of you can stay to make history's greatest Resurrection Day Feast. And I shall give you solid bodies so everyone can see and hug you. And yes, all may share this Grand Holiday with us. It is my Resurrection Eve gift to you."

All the kitchen elementals smiled invisibly. They had not prepared for a large party for a long time, and not since Tristan and Morgana married in Camelot. Another kitchen elemental asked Gabriel to invite Natanel, Merlin, Tristan, Morgana, little Eleanor, and Tristan's students to the wedding. They are all at the Crystal Cave and have little to do now.

Gabriel said, "Now, that is a great idea. Bring them tomorrow for Resurrection Eve with the family."

One kitchen elemental created a beautiful wedding invitation card, took it immediately to the Crystal Cave, and gave it to Merlin. Everyone was in the library drinking honey mead.

Merlin turned to the group, saying, "Gabriel is finally getting married. The invitation says,

> *The Ladies Sophia and Alliona, the happiest Brides in the universe, respectfully request your attendance at their wedding on Resurrection Day to the most available Groom in existence, our Beloved Gabriel. Be there or be square.*

"I do not understand what the last sentence means?"

Tristan and his students laughed.

Tristan explained, "One of these ladies is from Earth, Merlin. It means that if we do not show up, we are as boring as sticks stuck in the mud."

Natanel turns toward Tristan, asking, "Honey, isn't Alliona the Djinn sweetheart of Gabriel? He mentioned her a few times when he visited us. If she is, then Sophia must be the Earth girl? I bet she is one of Gabriel's students. Gabriel is a heartbreaker. I wonder why he is marrying a Djinn and an Earth girl?"

Three-year-old Eleanor pulled on Morgana's sleeve.

"Mummy, Uncle Gabriel is an Immortal, remember. He always acts for everyone's benefit. And it is always honourable. You told me

Gabriel was like Daddy, and he wants a family, too. I know they love each other, for I feel it."

Suddenly, a beautiful couple materialised in the room. Everyone bowed for the couple, the Prince and Princess of the Most Holy City, anywhere, Nouseum.

The Princess said, "Do not tell Gabriel, but my beloved husband and I will make a surprise visit to the wedding. Our city owes much to Gabriel, as it does to all of you. Gabriel was never good at inviting his friends. So, let us keep this a secret."

Merlin handed the guests goblets of his honey mead.

Raising his goblet, he said, "Dear friends, let us toast Sophia, Alliona, and our Gabriel. May they share great happiness and success in whatever work they must do."

And everyone made such a toast.

The kitchen elemental returned and told Gabriel that his friends would arrive tomorrow at noon. She said nothing as to the surprise but spoke to her friends. The kitchen elementals joined and made a heartfelt prayer for the wedding party.

The night passed quickly, and the crew accomplished much. One more day and the holiday would begin. The sun would rise in two hours. Gabriel went upstairs to see his brides and opened the door to Alliona's bedroom. Everywhere, he saw clothes piled. Many of the candles had burned down, so the light was dim. Hanging on each side of the dressing mirror were two beautiful lace gowns.

He thought, "I see they found what they needed."

The floor around the chair to the dressing table had hair tresses, a jumble of darkest black and golden-red blonde.

Gabriel thought, "Alliona told Sophie of the most ancient Djinn marriage custom."

When a Djinn female marries, she cuts her long hair to prove she is a virgin. If she is not, there is a Djinn ointment, which will return her to the pristine state when applied to the female genitals. There is also a powder that will remove all past sexual experiences.

Gabriel went to the dresser and saw Alliona's Great Granny's leather-bound codex with parchment pages covered in ancient Djinn writing. The codex was open on the table to pages 68 and 69. He lit some new candles so he could read the handwritten text. Sure enough, the title of the potion was Virgin Marriage Potion.

Reading quickly, Gabriel found some seven ointment jars open as to the ingredients on the dresser top. He saw that the jars' names agreed with the components referenced in Great Granny's and Natanel's recipe.

He found out how much of each ingredient the ritual needed to read the recipe. Read the first footnote, noting that the potion is also valid for human ladies, but they assume Djinn genitalia.

Next to the ointments, Gabriel saw two silver mixing dishes and two stirrers.

He chuckled, "My word, Sophie wants to be a real sister to Alliona. Not a terrible choice."

Continuing to read the footnotes, the second footnote mentioned a herb mixed with an alcoholic beverage to make the nubile Djinn lose her memories of anything to do with lovemaking. The herb jar was also on the table.

"I can only imagine Alliona telling Sophie of this custom. These two are mighty romantic. I hear Sophie encouraging Alliona to ingest the forgetting herb so they both will be virgins. And then they cut each other's hair. Schoolgirls, they remain, and I guess they never realised this makes much more work for their Gabriel?"

Gabriel continued reading the footnotes and turned to page 70, where the last note stood.

The footnote advised remembering not only will this potion return your virginity, but it will also return your body and personality to age 15. Be wary; you might find a temporary episode of great desire for another female, though it may be permanent. We recommend not using this potion alone.

"Now, that was something I did not know, and I wonder if it is true. I doubt the two read any of the footnotes past the first four or five, considering the empty pitcher of spiced mead."

Both were in bed, naked and sound asleep. Gabriel looked carefully at them; they both appeared to be nubile fifteen-year-olds. Alliona was lying on her back with her head on the pillow and her arm wrapped around Sophie. Sophie was lying on her left side with her cropped head resting upon Alliona's right shoulder. Sophie's right arm was across Alliona's chest, just below her breasts. Her right hemipelvis was lodged against Alliona's right upper hemipelvis. Her thigh was between Alliona's spread thighs. The rest of Sophie's leg lay betwixt Alliona's legs.

Gabriel saw them as innocent, loving, beautiful angels.

Both girls had exhausted themselves, so they did not even know he had entered Alliona's bedroom. Gabriel had never seen Alliona with short, dark hair, but she was lovely, especially at fifteen. He felt sorry that he had made her wait so many centuries.

Tears began flowing down his cheeks as he realised his brides spent the entire night trying to make themselves perfect for him.

"They are so old-fashioned. I will honour this ancient quality. I realise they must fight a great battle with me and set aside innocence. I will not take it away from them, and I shall ensure my actions are consistent with such beautiful natures. They shall have their babies soon, Holy Mother willing.

Quickly drying his tears, Gabriel saw a second old codex from Djinn lore on the bedstand beside the bed. He turned the book to read the cover. The open page contained a well-drawn sketch of two fifteen-year-old girls experimenting with mutual oral sex. The writing on the front cover read The First Primer for Young Ladies: Female Anatomy and Beginning Lady Sexuality. Lydia and Natanel.

Gabriel said to himself, "No wonder these two are sound asleep. But I must give them credit for being studious. He quickly glanced at the earlier drawings to see what they had experimented with."

Each had the sweetest smile, and Gabriel felt a great wave of love filling his heart. He pulled up the down duvet to cover them and added wood to the fireplace.

He kissed both on their foreheads.

"I love both of you. Sleep well. We will have a busy day tomorrow."

Gabriel left the room quietly and returned to the kitchen. He told the kitchen elementals to rest for a while, for he must visit someone and would be home soon.

Chapter 13

A Visit with Ariel

abriel vanished from sight, travelling high into the Upper World, stopping in a flowery meadow, and called out, "Ariel, we need to talk."

A beautiful young lady appeared next to Gabriel with long blonde hair curled into two braids and circled like serpents on her head.

Gabriel's eyes brightened.

He grabbed her and gave her a big hug and kiss on her lips.

"Little Sister, you know how important you are to my heart and how much I adore you. You look ravishingly beautiful, as always. I have missed you terribly."

"Stop it, Gabriel. You are my big brother, not my lover," laughed Ariel.

"You don't have a lover, Ariel. Not since our brother murdered you and our unborn twins. No one loves you more than I do, including your adopted family. And if you were to forego being the Eternal Virgin, I would wed you again. I am the only Immortal who fought by your side."

"Oh, Gabriel. What you wish can never be, my darling man. But suppose I was not a member of the Holy Family. In that case, if I were your Alliona or your Sophie, there is no other man I would consent to be with as an Immortal Spouse. Let us sit on the grass so you can lay your head in my lap, and I will sing to you."

Ariel and Gabriel sat down, and Gabriel put his head on Ariel's lap. It had been a long since he had been with her, and he loved how she smelled like Passionfruit and Osmanthus flowers. She always intoxicated him as she sang an ancient song.

After the song finished, she said, "Gabriel, you know the current prediction is that I will incarnate on Earth. I chose Sophie to be my earthly mother and you, my earthly father. You and Sophie genuinely love each other almost as much as you love your Ariel.

"Mother and Father want Yeshua to return with me to moderate my lioness nature. So, I granted Alliona's wish after all these centuries. She has wanted to be your spiritual wife since the Great Djinn War. Her love for you is as pure as I have ever witnessed. Whenever you were away from her, she cried herself to sleep every night. But she is a good trooper who never interfered in your assignments. And she has followed me and taken care of her village always.

"I will give her a physical body, and she will become an Immortal. I know you love Alliona equally to Sophie. Alliona will bear the physical vehicle for my brother, as the combination of her Djinn egg and your sperm. People will think a miracle has occurred for you fathered identical twins, other than gender, from two different women. The old divine birth story is way out of date.

"When we reach a responsible age, we shall descend so that our Divine Consciousnesses live in our vehicles, and the project shall see if humanity is saveable. Sorry, I ruined your riddle."

Gabriel sat up, saying, "I understand. I like this plan very much, darling. And Ariel, thanks for finally telling me you still desire me. Knowing this is finally sufficient. Kiss me, and I will be off. A proper kiss?"

They both stood up.

"Oh, Gabriel, you are most exasperating."

But she leaned forward, kissed him, and held him close.

"Gabriel, I liked this kiss, and I finally feel once again the desire of a female Immortal for a male Immortal. Funny being wet. But enough is enough. Get out of here before you ruin creation. You are a very naughty brother, but one I love most dearly."

She failed to disclose that she had brought Sophie's physical body into the Djinn world, unbeknownst to Sophie or Gabriel. Sophie had never realised that Gabriel's three bodies were always present. She had given Alliona a physical body two days before, and they would discover the miracle soon.

Gabriel found himself back in the kitchen, and the brides were up. Alliona knew about kitchen elementals and could speak with them. Sophie and Alliona ran to kiss him, and he found he loved them much more than before. He understood that this was the only way Ariel could be his lover, and she would love him through them. She is infinitely intelligent!

Alliona spoke to Gabriel and Sophie.

"Every year, Gabriel was with me. He would find a beautiful tree for the inn, and every year, I prayed to Ariel that he would ask to marry me this year. At last, Ariel answered my prayer. And I am glad that my prayer has waited until now. I realise I also needed to be with the most precious Djinn sister in the land, Sophie."

Before Alliona could say anything else, Sophie said, "We have been waiting for you. Do you like our new haircuts? Alliona said we must have short hair to prove we are virgins."

Both girls turned around for Gabriel.

Gabriel said, "I adore your new haircuts."

Alliona said, "And Sophie and I have an enormous surprise for you for our wedding night, but we are keeping it secret till then, right, Sophie?"

Sophie replied, "Right."

Gabriel smiled.

"I will look forward to your surprise. Did you find what you wanted to wear as wedding dresses?"

Alliona said, "Yes, honey, both of us are stunning. Every man will be jealous of you."

Both rushed upstairs to get their gowns.

Gabriel asked the kitchen elementals how long this girlie phase would last. They shook their visible heads and did not have an answer.

He replied, "I guess we will find out one day. I must admit it makes me feel younger in some ways."

Sophie and Alliona returned dressed in their lace wedding gown. The gowns were simple, but the lacework was immaculate. Each dress fit perfectly, and every curve was visible. Gabriel was silent for a moment because of how beautiful they looked. Indeed, Ariel was with them.

He said, "I have never seen two more beautiful women. And forever is a long time for me. I wish it were our marriage night already. And I mean this, my darlings."

"See, Sophie, I told you I know how to excite Gabriel by addressing his taste in female fashions. We are stunning brides."

Gabriel reminded his darlings, "Go put on other clothes for my friends. They will be here soon. The kitchen elementals will soon put out bread, cheese, pickled vegetables, and cold cuts. Now, scat."

Giggling, Sophie and Alliona, hand in hand, hurried to change.

Gabriel thought, "It is going to be interesting. Everyone will know that Alliona used the old Djinn magic on Sophie and herself. I must admit they are fifteen and act that way. The good news is that they will grow up soon, I hope. Soon, I will have two students to take back to Damascus."

Chapter 14

Visitors from Camelot

hortly before noon, Merlin and the other guests from Camelot arrived and struck the door clangour. Gabriel went to answer and welcomed them all inside. The first to enter was Eleanor, who jumped into Gabriel's arms, putting her arms around his neck and kissing him on the lips many times.

Then, she said, "I love you, Uncle Gabriel. See how big I am."

Gabriel placed her on her feet and stood back.

"Why, Eleanor, you must be six or seven now. You are all grown-up."

"I am only three, Uncle Gabriel. You know that. You are so funny," and started laughing.

Then Gabriel kissed Morgana on both cheeks.

"And you, Morgana, are as striking as ever. I hope Tristan adores you; I would if you were my beloved."

Morgana blushed and returned Gabriel's kisses.

"Stop it, Gabriel. You are almost married."

Gabriel turned to Natanel, saying, "I bow to the most accomplished female in all the Universes. I have missed our discussions and practical jokes, Nata."

Nata gave Gabriel a hug and a kiss.

Gabriel asked, "How are things in Nouseum and Montemar?"

Tristan replied, "Quiet for the moment. We have a few more years before the real trouble begins. You remember my students, yes?"

"Yes. Welcome to Alliona's Inn. It has been three years, I think? Shouldn't there be more children, Natanel?"

"The rest of the children are not born yet, as we have been living in Nouseum, so the pregnancies are delayed by Earth standards."

Alliona and Sophie returned to the kitchen and heard the conversation. They walked out, holding hands to meet everyone.

Eleanor piped up, "See, Mummy. I told you they were beautiful and loved each other. I think Uncle Gabriel has delicious taste in women. But I thought they were older. They look like teenagers, Mummy."

Gabriel turned back to his guests.

"They are now teenagers, but they were adults. They experimented with a Marriage Ointment created by Alliona's great granny and Natanel. It is a side-effect, I am afraid."

Looking at Natanel, Old Merlin replied, "I saw a similar spell once. It is quite a hard spell on one person, not to mention two simultaneously. I never found out the sorcerer or sorcerer was, till now?"

Sophie and Alliona came over and kissed their husband-to-be. Gabriel introduced them, and they hugged everyone. Though they still giggled, they did their best to resume their prior personalities as they had special guests to entertain,

Nata hugged Gabriel as she smiled at Sophie and Alliona, saying, "I might tell your wives about who took your virginity, Gabriel. I am not kidding, girls. Congratulations. Come, hug me; I am old enough to be your great granny, Lydia."

Alliona and Sophie hugged Nata.

Alliona asked, "Nata, you know Lydia?"

"Do I know, Lydia? Who do you think trained her? I would have made love with grown Gabriel, but Lydia beat me to the poke. I see you and Sophie used the spell Lydia and I created. Nice job. You read our primer on sexual instruction for young ladies and used our potion."

Alliona and Sophie turned, flushed, and looked at each other in horror.

Tristan interrupted, "Girls, Nata is only teasing you to see how much mettle you possess. She told me that any granddaughter of Lydia already had a place in her heart. And Nata is the most loving woman I have ever known. Ask anyone here."

Eleanor ran to Alliona and Sophie, hugging their legs.

She said, "Papa is correct, as he always is. My grandmother loves almost everyone, and I love her so much. Come and meet my other aunties."

Miss Alliona and Miss Sophie, these are my aunties, Vika and Calliope. They are beautiful twins, and their mummy is Nata.

"Eleanor took the hands of Alliona and Sophia, introducing them to Vika and Calliope, saying, "Aunt Vika and Aunt Calliope, this is Miss Sophie and Miss Alliona.

"Did I make the introduction like a big girl?"

Calliope replied, "That was perfect, Eleanor. Right, Vika?"

"Calliope, Eleanor is more than perfect. She is the best."

All three of them started jumping up and down, giggling.

Vika and Calliope said in unison, "Nice to meet you. We see you are both fifteen. We hope you are silly sometimes, for we are?"

Alliona and Calliope looked at each other, thinking.

Alliona said, "You are correct. My sister and I are fifteen, and Gabriel says we are silly girls sometimes, so I guess we will be friends.

"Eleanor, would you like to meet my pony? Her name is Sweetie. She will take us for a sledge ride in the snow if we dress warmly. Vika and Calliope, you can come too."

Eleanor ran over and took Morgana's hand, "Mummy, can we go for a sledge ride. Will you come, Mummy?"

"Yes, Darling. The six of us will have a grand time."

Feeling like a young girl, Morgana ran and grabbed Alliona and Eleanor by the hands. Sophie held Calliope's and Vika's hands, leading the adventurers.

Merlin piped up, "I see part of the spell has transferred to Morgana. I think it is because of Morgana's affinity for magick and matters of romance. She is going to lose a few years over this holiday. But, back to normal soon, I hope?"

"Merlin, thanks for the kitchen elementals. They have been great. They decorated the tree all by themselves, and it is the best tree ever."

The kitchen elementals heard the compliment and blushed.

Merlin added, "The best kitchen elementals in all of Camelot, I might add," knowing they like to eavesdrop and deserve more recognition.

"By the by, Merlin, I gave them visible bodies as a reward for their hard work. Hope you don't mind, old chap?"

"No, Gabriel."

Gabriel invited everyone to sit down, and the Inn staff came out of the kitchen.

Gabriel introduced them all. None seemed any older than Sophie and Alliona were now.

They all curtsied, saying, "Hello."

Gabriel told the students, "You are in the Djinn Worlds now. These sweet girls are all Djinn. But be careful, young men, for you might fall in love with one of them."

The girls all blushed as they thought the students were very dashing. His female students felt slighted.

Tristan said, "Let it go, wives. It is simply another random event."

Gabriel said, "Girls, bring food and drink for my dearest friends. And then come and sit with us. You can talk to the boys if you like, and they will not be so shy after a drink or two of Alliona's mead.

"My visible kitchen elementals, will you be so generous and put all the presents around the tree? Thanks."

The elementals were excited and quickly accomplished the task.

Gabriel said, "I would like to make a toast to our special helpers on this eve before Resurrection Eve. Merlin, can they share some mead with us?"

"Of course."

Everyone stands, and Gabriel says, "Raise your mead cups. Cheers to the most helpful and loving kitchen elementals in all the magical lands."

Seven visible hands lifted seven mugs, and everyone drank.

Soon, food and more libations were on the table, and the girls and the young men were flirting with each other. Natanel sat with the crew as a chaperone.

Gabriel turned to Tristan and Merlin and told them about his lessons with Sophie. He mentioned almost everything other than seeing Ariel. He even explained why he would have two wives who had become so attached, which was too secret for anyone else.

He finished up.

"It was Ariel who played this little trick on me. I know Alliona will be OK, but Sophie is human. She wants them to be at a perfect childbearing age when necessary. It is a reasonable action, but I do not think she will understand the difficulty of having fifteen-year-old girls for my wives. At least, they remember all that is important. C'est la vie, as the French say."

Tristan replied, "I wouldn't worry, old boy. I have two fifteen-year-old daughters who are also my wives. You think your life is going to be hard; try mine."

Merlin added, "Don't worry. You can handle it. You can ask Morgana; she and the other girls have returned."

Eleanor ran into the room first.

"Daddy, Daddy, Sweetie is a beautiful pony. When we met her, she kissed me on my cheek., and I gave her two apples. We wrapped up in blankets Alliona brought, and I sat next to Sophie and held her hand. Mummy sat next to Alliona, the driver. Vika and Calliope sat together as usual. It was sunny and nice, and I saw animals everywhere. Daddy, look at Mummy. She turned into a young girl, too."

The young ladies came into the room, laughing and pushing each other. Tristan's eyes nearly popped out of their sockets. Morgana appeared to be the same age as Sophie and Alliona. And the twins. He remembered how Morgana looked when they both were much younger. She was so innocent and trusting, wanting only to be loved by Natanel and him.

Morgana ran, threw her arms around Tristan, and began kissing him.

"Honey, we had a great time together, and I feel like I am fifteen years old again. I love you so much."

Looking at Sophie and Alliona, "Maybe more than they love Gabriel."

The two girls stuck their tongues out at Morgana and all giggled.

Merlin turned to Tristan, remarking, "Let us pray. Hopefully, it passes in a few days after we return to Camelot. Just enjoy her. I am sure she will be more amorous than usual. Like in the good old days, eh?"

Merlin backed away before Tristan could slug him.

"Lydia's and Natanel's spells are affecting all of us. I will do what I can for the males; I cannot do anything for the girls."

Merlin said some words in Enochian, and things seemed to stabilise the men somewhat.

Sophie said, "Young ladies, come watch us try on our wedding gowns. Alliona has so many clothes upstairs we can play dress up. You can wear Djinn dresses at the wedding, my pretty twins and little new niece. I am an excellent seamstress; the last one upstairs is a monkey."

Sophie grabbed Alliona's hand and began running upstairs, followed by Vika and Calliope, with Morgana and Eleanor close behind.

Eleanor was shouting, "Sophie is a monkey. Alliona is a monkey. Not Mummy and me."

Gabriel turned to Merlin.

"Are you sure this is going to work out? It will not go well at the wedding, I am afraid."

Looking upward, he implored Ariel, "Keep their bodies fifteen, if it must be so, but make them as they were before, or at least close. They were young and mature. You owe me some mercy, sister."

Tristan remarked, "I didn't know Ariel was your sister, Gabriel?"

Gabriel replied, "It is a timeless story. I will tell you later. I think we all need to get drunk to survive."

Unbeknownst to the trio, Ariel agreed to return some maturity temporarily to Sophie and Alliona before the wedding, not as to appearance but as to demeanour.

Gabriel excused himself and went into the kitchen to see how the food preparation was progressing.

The head kitchen elemental said, "Milord, all shall be ready."

"I have another favour to ask, dear friend. I think the entire village is coming for Resurrection Eve. You will have sufficient food and libations, but the great room may be too small. Would it be possible to invite some carpenter elementals to the wedding and festivities? I need them to construct a large tent outside in the front and some fire elementals to make a small sun for the evening so everyone will be warm."

The head kitchen elemental replied, "Consider it done. Is there anything else you require?"

Gabriel answered, "No, I can do the rest. Thanks again. Seeing you in visible form is nice, and I want you to know you are part of our family. I have allowed some old Elf Magick into this universe for tomorrow only. I want this day remembered and honoured in Djinn and Elemental histories."

The Djinn world is not magical, as is Camelot, some Outer Worlds, and Nouseum. Magick is forbidden, but Gabriel possesses the authority for certain exceptions.

Gabriel had thought about using the Elf Magick for a few days. He knew he could do this without creating portals to Ahriman the Evil.

His thoughts drifted to Ariel, "I spent so many centuries with Ariel during and after the Great Djinn War. Indeed, I understand her complexity better than most. I remember seeing her looking at me with longing, but she always denied it. I do not think she understood because she was reborn after her murder.

"I coaxed her into an actual kiss because I was sure Ariel had absorbed some joys and sorrows from the Djinn. Her kiss told me everything. The Holy Family manifested all of us, so we carry their likeness, other than myself.

"Ariel aches for a Djinn life. She has yet to reincarnate, so any experience must be vicarious. The best she can do is share in the holy love between me and my precious treasures. She will know, and I will know, no one else.

"It will be good preparation for her future incarnation in the human world."

Sophie interrupted Gabriel's musings.

In a most appealing and somewhat revealing costume, Sophie requested, "Honey, we have finished our dress-up and will do a fashion show for everyone. Please go back into the Great Room and tell Tristan and Merlin. I was hoping you could move the tables out of the way and line the benches across from each other so we can walk like models and everyone can admire our costumes. Everyone, including the kitchen elementals, must sit and clap. I will also act as an announcer for us. The girls are all so excited. Vika and Calliope hold fashion shows in Camelot."

Off rushed Sophie to get the girls as Gabriel sauntered to the Great Room.

He asked, "I need everyone to help move the tables back against the wall and line up two sets of benches so they face each other. We must construct a fashion ramp, walking path, or catwalk beginning in the kitchen. Also, I insist the kitchen elementals enjoy the dresses with us."

Tristan began laughing.

"We have fashion shows in Camelot arranged by Calliope and Vika. I would think no Djinn has ever heard of one."

Gabriel said, "I understand, but since it is the eve before Resurrection Eve, we will comply. Morgana is fifteen now; I am sure she wants to be a fashion model after Sophie explains how graceful they are. Use your brain, man."

The students prepared the Great Room, and Gabriel sent the head kitchen elemental to inform the girls.

Everyone sat, including our lovely kitchen elementals. The humans and Djinn saw many happy, rosy-cheeked, and chubby grannies dressed in cooking aprons before them. In a minute, Eleanor appeared by herself.

Eleanor hugged every granny, announcing, "Look, how many Grannies I have, Mummy. I love all of them."

All the people stood up and clapped for all the now visible kitchen elementals, who were grannies.

Eleanor returned to Alliona's room to change. In about ten minutes, Sophie began standing at the kitchen doorway.

She said, "Ladies, Elementals, and Gentlemen, we have prepared a brilliant fashion show. We employed our imaginations to create original clothing. Please welcome the beautiful Eleanor."

Everyone began clapping as Eleanor walked into the room using the foot in front of the foot style of proper models.

As Eleanor moved down the ramp, Sophie said, "Today, Eleanor portrays a young Djinn girl on the first day of school. Please notice the pretty flower in her hair, plaid skirt, and white lace blouse. Most elegant."

Gabriel and Tristan clapped, and so did the elementals. Eleanor smiled, for she was so happy that she was like an actual model of Earth. Sophie gave her a big kiss and a hug as she left.

Next to appear is Morgana.

Sophie announced, "Our Morgana wears a tight, silk evening gown reaching to the floor. She has no underwear underneath. Notice how her crimson dress displays every feminine charm she possesses. Her hairstyle is typical for the 1940s on planet Earth. She is a beautiful model."

Morgana was hot! Tristan stared, but so did Merlin, Gabriel, and every other male. Morgana could keep a serious face, but she did her best to display all her feminine charms to her beloved mate.

Everyone stood up and clapped.

Tristan shouted, "Bravo, Morgana, Bravo."

Eleanor yelled, "Alliona loves Uncle Gabriel and wants to have a baby. So does Sophie."

The twins appeared at the kitchen door wearing matching lace dressing gowns. The lacework was typical of that sewn by the first Djinn, delicate and intricate.

Sophie announced, "The Twins are modelling lacework found in Lydia's chests. Lydia knows vintage, that is for sure. Notice how the lace moves as our beautiful and sexy twins walk down the catwalk. Pay particular attention to their inviting hips as they walk, radiating pure womanhood. Surely, hips for enjoyment and making little ones. Inviting hips and perky breasts; what else can Tristan desire?"

Natanel opined, "So true, so true. But our husband will happily add two more sets of hips and breasts for a feast."

Everyone from Camelot broke out laughing and added comments.

Though caught off-guard, Tristan replied, "Nata, two more sets only? How unfair. I think I shall be with my nine little kitties this eve."

Everyone laughed again.

Andrew, one of Tristan's students, said, "When Nata and Tristan banter to each other, as did the courtesans and poets of Venice, it is a wonder."

More laughter. The modelling began again, with Alliona as the next model.

Sophie announced, "Alliona created the perfect outfit for a night out with her man. Fashions serve an actual purpose, and this beautiful and sexy outfit would entice any Djinn or human male to get on his knee and propose marriage and fidelity. Notice how the leather pants are open to the upper thighs on both sides to display her beautiful legs full length and allure to her man, who we all know is Gabriel, right Eleanor?"

Alliona stopped in front of Gabriel and turned around so he could fully appreciate how well her outfit complimented her person. Then she finished walking down and back on the catwalk. Everyone clapped.

Alliona stopped at the kitchen door and said, "Our alluring Sophie is changing and will be with us in a moment. She is wearing an outfit that she told us was popular on the university campuses during the Hippy Revolution. Whatever that was? Here, she comes dressed in a red, pleated miniskirt. A tight pale-yellow tee shirt with no bra complementing the miniskirt. Notice the fiery red colour meant to attract male and female attention. Are you paying close attention, Honey?

"High leather boots were popular, as modelled by Sophie. Sophie, be a sweetheart and pick up my earring. I lost it when I was on the catwalk. See, it is on the catwalk across from Gabriel. You can bend down."

As Sophie bent down at the waist with her back to Gabriel, he saw she had no panties.

Sophie asked, "Honey, do you like our present. I am as beautiful as my sister. We love you so much."

She finished her walk, delighted that at last Gabriel knew.

Wearing her miniskirt and tee shirt, Sophie announced, "We conclude this wonderful presentation with our bathing suit fashions for next summer. We believe single-piece suits will be the rage."

Sophie and Alliona wore yellow-purple contrasting polka dot suits with high-cut hips, holding hands as they walked along the catwalk. Sophie wore white pearls and Alliona black pearls, and both had put a paper flower behind one ear. Naturally, they stopped in front of Gabriel.

Eleanor came next, dressed in a cute little yellow suit covered in teddy bears and a paper-flower lei made by Sophie.

The twins, staying with the one-piece swimsuit theme, appeared wearing skimpy, sky-blue bottoms, barely covering their vulvas. Both stood tall to emphasise their perfectly shaped breasts and hard nipples.

Sophie announced, "The twins designed and sewed these alluring and revealing bottoms. I don't know about the rest of the attendees. But Alliona, Morgana, and I had the hots for Calliope and Vika when they first wore them. So, I say, let the juices flow forth."

The room filled with laughter.

Morgana walked the catwalk last in a minimalist, golden-thread, high-cut suit. She had long legs and was well-toned. The girls had sprinkled gold dust all over her body, so she sparkled when she turned to display her bathing attire. She had a perfect body, just as Tristan, Merlin, and the students had first seen when she stood naked in the Hidden Temple of the First Ones.

Everyone agreed Morgana is the most perfect woman ever created. She finished her walk, and all the girls made one more walk with Eleanor first, Sophie and Alliona holding hands, the twins next, and Morgana at last.

The party-goers stood up and clapped and clapped.

Merlin yelled out, "Grand show, girls. You must be proper models."

All the models smiling and throwing kisses, as Sophie had taught them.

The models left and returned in beautiful robes they found in Great Granny's old trunk.

Natanel stood up, announcing, "Everyone has had a lovely evening. But I think it is growing late and much work still needs doing. So, off to bed, everyone. The young ladies will show you to your rooms. A treat for our gentlemen, Alliona's girls will follow you into bed if you ask nicely. Eleanor, Vika, and Calliope, you can sleep with your new friends. Goodnight."

Soon, the Inn was empty and quiet. The Resurrection Tree shone so brightly in the dark.

The following day, everyone was up to see the face of the sun peeking above the horizon, lighting the Great Room. The kitchen grannies had prepared a hearty Djinn breakfast of free-range chicken eggs, bacon, ham, chocolate pancakes, fresh multigrain bread, honey from Scotland, exotic jams, sweet millet gruel, raspberries with cream, and Kona coffee with cream. All gathered by Gabriel on his shopping trip the day prior.

Sophie and Alliona wore matching long, milky, jade-green cashmere robes with round gold buttons and loops from the neck to the floor. Both gowns had collared necks with stars and comets embroidered thereon and long sleeves.

Morgana and Eleanor's robes were light scarlet, with long sleeves and embroidered suns.

The twin robes, sky blue and thin wool, were similar in design, so they hung to their frames rather tightly.

Alliona and Sophie sat on each side of Gabriel and whispered together, one in each ear.

"We decided we do not want to be virgins at the wedding. We want to make love to you tonight, so we will conceive our babies. We both used Great Granny's ointment so we would be fresh for you and beautiful like perfect Djinn.

"We read Great Granny's primer and practised so we would not be unskilful in front of you or make any mistakes. We studied almost all night, so you would be happy with us. The twins know about making love and showed us many things. Did you know they are going to be mummies also? Don't make us wait till tomorrow. We want our babies to be at our wedding. Please, please, Gabriel. We need you tonight."

How could Gabriel deny his brides, saying, "Rather unusual, but not against any Immortal rules I know? Hey Alliona, Ariel just told me it is okay in her rule book and told me to remind both of you that Her Spirit is always with the three of us."

Eleanor sat next to Merlin.

"Uncle Merlin, was I a good model?"

Old Merlin gave her a big hug.

"Eleanor, you were the best model of all. I am so very proud of you."

Morgana and the twins sat by Tristan.

Morgana whispered, "Honey, do you like us as models? We did our best to please you. Would you like to be with us later?"

She took Tristan's hand and kissed it before placing it on her lap.

Calliope and Vika sat together, holding hands.

Vika whispered, "Honey, Morgana is a great older sister, for she always includes us in her amorous adventures."

After breakfast, Gabriel stood, saying, "We have much work to do before sunset tonight. The town celebrates Resurrection Eve, the holiest of Djinn celebrations. Those who have not participated in the ceremony will experience its wonder.

Alliona, Natanel, and I have prepared a work list, so please read it and report to your stations. Thanks.

Before anyone rose from the benches.

Sophie asked, "Gabriel, how will the whole village fit into the Great Room?"

Alliona hugged Sophie, replying, "Wait and see, darling. Resurrection Eve and Day are the only times Magick awakens in the Djinn world. It is beautiful and keeps our village joined in harmony and love. Tomorrow evening, everyone will see the Miracle of Resurrection Eve."

While everyone was busy preparing food and drink, Gabriel entered the spacious, flat front yard.

Outside, Gabriel met with the carpenter and fire elementals waiting since dawn. After introductions, Gabriel drew the building plans in the air with the lines made of light. He showed the fire elementals where to place the artificial sun.

He requested a wooden pyramid of base sides equal to nineteen meters, with a roof comprising four triangles climbing at an angle. The four roof segments meet at a point five meters above the floor. The sun shall rest immediately below the upper peak, and the pyramid walls will stay open. When finished, we shall have a golden gnomon.

Under the central peak, you are to lay black granite tiling to fill a pentagram with sides of three meters.

The carpenter elementals immediately gathered the materials.

The head carpenter said, "Milord, we will finish the construction by midnight. It will not manifest until you activate the spell. Thanks for your confidence in our skills. We would like to attend the celebration tonight and your marriage tomorrow."

Gabriel replied, "It would be an honour to have you attend. You will all be visible, so have some fun."

He thought, "It is time for a miracle for the Djinn. I know it is Elf Magick, but they know little of magick and will say Ariel did it."

He heard Ariel speaking to him, "Gabriel, I am so very proud of you. Of all the Immortals, Father and Mother have been the hardest on you ever since you visited them as a little boy, asking to be Their helper. So long ago, none of us even remember in which universe it happened.

"Father and Mother told me to tell you; you are the best.

"Mother said I could be with you, Sophie, and Alliona on the wedding day. I can feel what they feel for you, enjoy whatever joy they have with you, and be with them nursing their little ones, but only in Spirit. Why do I need my physical body when I am a part of both?

"Mother told me your love for me is pure, and I will be your wife, darling. She told me to go to you and tell you I love you as a wife loves her husband, and I may join you. Funny, no one besides you and I will know that it is a triple wedding. I will be at the wedding; I can't miss my second wedding, can I?"

Gabriel responded, "Ariel, I have loved you since we were born into Creation. The nature of my love has matured, but it is much stronger than on that first fateful day. I guess we have created a new Tetrad, my precious spirit wife. Let us all pray that such may do something important to help with the Divine Plan."

Ariel appeared before him for a moment and gave him another genuine kiss.

"Husband, I understand. But now I must go to our nuptial chamber to be with Sophie and Alliona. They will conceive, for I brought Sophie's body and made a new one for Alliona. The first Djinn hybrid, one might say.

"When you arrive, they will tell you that something extraordinary happened. For now, they love you so much more than before. Alliona is bright, and she will know that I am within her and Sophie. She will thank me for answering all her prayers and thank Mother for answering my prayers. She knows that her Great Granny and I are sisters. Love you."

Then Ariel vanished.

The day was productive, and all preparations for Resurrection Eve finished.

Chapter 15

Resurrection Eve

he boys had scrubbed The Great Room floor clean, and the table and benches were orderly for the celebrants to enjoy. Alliona explained the Resurrection Celebration to the others, so everyone was familiar with the tradition and excited.

Gabriel enlarged the Inn so it could hold all the villagers. The design was impressive as he tiered the room, like the Globe Theatre of Wm. Shakespeare. But with many more tiers. What was most striking was that each floor seemed like the second floor for the celebration? The townsfolk gathered in the Inn before sunset.

Everyone is imbibing one of Merlin's ales and commenting on how tasty and potent they are.

As the sun sets, Alliona whispers in Gabriel's ear, "Husband, it is time to begin the Resurrection Eve Miracle. Oh darling, such a special and Holy Night it shall be. Thank you for everything. The Miracle recurs every time I feel the love the young wife must have felt for her husband, and I understand her desire to give her husband a child."

Alliona takes Gabriel's right hand, bringing it to her lips to kiss. Later, everyone watching agreed that a golden halo of light appeared and shone above her head for several minutes.

Gabriel stood and said, "Dearest Friends, our celebration begins. Please stand and bow your heads as we offer a prayer of thankfulness to Our Holy Father and Mother. Join in voice and spirit as we recite each line together:

Great Father-Mother, Fountain Pure,
whose Water liveth within our beating hearts.

Sacred is Thy Name, for in Thy Name
all of existence arises and passes;
returning to Thee at the exigent of ends.

Giveth us this day,
life-sustaining nourishment,
both material and supernal.

Forgiveth us our ignorance in action,
our misunderstandings, our aggressive moments,
encouraging us evermore to make peace with our neighbours.

Help us disregard the voice of the Tempter,
no matter how sweet and melodious it sounds,
by reminding us,
we are your children and not His.

For Thy Home is our mansion,
Thy Goodness, our goodness,
Thy Knowing our knowing,
Thy Being our being,
Thy Observing our observing,
Thy Intending our intending.

*For it shall come to be someday,
that our Land is as a Heaven,
ruled by Mercy and Justice,
forever and forever.*

The stardust upon the Resurrection twinkled brilliantly as the group recited this wondrous prayer. Gabriel began the story.

Once, a long time ago, a young couple lived in a village in a dark forest. The man was a physician, and his young wife a herbalist. They had no children, as his wife had broken her pelvis as a young girl and could not give birth. She walked with a limp, and her husband had to carry her sometimes, for she experienced severe pain episodes.

The man had met her once in a much larger village where she had gone because of her pain. She fell in love when she met him, and he did the same. He treated her pain, and she was much better. Under his care, she could work as an herbalist for the surrounding villages.

He would often travel to her village to see how she was doing and to suggest certain herbal potions.

One day, the doctor asked her to marry him.

She told the young doctor, "I love you with all my heart, but I cannot bear children because of my accident. You will not desire me when you see my twisted, bony pelvis. I am so ugly below my waist. I cannot do hard labour and would not be the wife, a fine man, as you should have."

The doctor said, "I will marry you, and if you cannot do something, I will do it for you. I don't care about your pelvis and limp. I care about your heart. Anyway, no

Djinn lady is as beautiful and as kind as you. Yes, my love, I will marry you."

And dear Friends, this is what they did. He moved to her village and was the best doctor the town ever had. The old grannies felt sorry for both, as they had no other family members and would have no children to take care of them when they grew old. But, as grannies are apt to do, they took turns on holidays to bring the couple to their homes. But there is more to come.

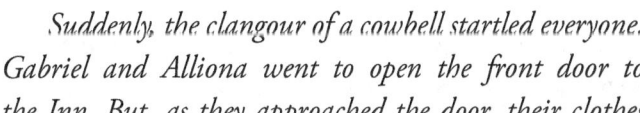

Suddenly, the clangour of a cowbell startled everyone. Gabriel and Alliona went to open the front door to the Inn. But, as they approached the door, their clothes changed, and they were no longer Gabriel and Alliona but another couple.

A great blizzard stormed outside, and everyone felt snow and cold air entering the room from the open door. Standing on the threshold, bent over, and wearing fur hats, mittens, coats, and boots were two elderly Djinn.

The elderly man said in a shaky voice, "Please, kind lady and sir. My beloved wife is so cold and tired. May we warm ourselves by your hearth? We had to leave our church three nights ago, and everyone was afraid to help us because of the War. We have no more food. I will gladly remain outside, but please take Grandmother into your home?"

The young wife replied, "Holy Father, curse these evil Djinn. We are not afraid of them. Please, Grandmother and Grandfather, come inside. We are not rich in goods, but we love Holy Father and Mother and do Good Works *in their Name. My beloved husband is a wonderful physician, and I am a herbalist."*

The two good householders helped Grandfather and Grandmother into their home. They removed Grandmother's and Grandfather's wet outerwear and sat them side-by-side on a bench close to the fire.

The husband examined their hands and feet and announced they had no frostbite.

"Beloved, get the ointment you made the other day, and I will rub it on their hands and feet, and they will be fine.

The young wife handed them mugs of hot mulled wine.

She said, "Do not talk; just drink your mead to warm your insides. Husband, go to the kitchen and bring our guests some of my little poppy seed and honey buns. The ointment is in the cupboard. I am sorry, but my pelvis has been hurting very much. But I did not want to complain."

He hurried to the kitchen and returned with the ointment, the buns, and some soft butter. He spread the butter on some pastries and handed one to each to eat. Grandfather and Grandmother ate quite a few buns, as they were hungry.

The young husband rubbed the ointment into the hands and feet of the elderly Djinn. He knew his wife was in much pain, and his heart ached so much for her.

When he finished, he said, "Excuse me, but I need to get a tonic for my wife, as I know she is in much pain and doesn't want to disturb you."

The young doctor returned with his pain tincture, saying, "Open your mouth and lift your tongue, please."

He placed ten drops of tincture under her tongue, reminding her, "Don't swallow for a count of twenty."

His wife did as her husband asked, saying, "I am the luckiest female Djinn anywhere. Grandmother and Grandfather, I wish you could investigate my heart and see my love for my husband is pure."

After they were warm and full, Grandmother turned to Grandfather with tears, saying, "Grandfather, I told you, Goodness and Compassion still live in this World. We did not lose all."

Grandfather replied, "It is true, Grandmother, it is true."

Grandmother said, "Sweet Child, I see it is difficult for you to move about, and you have a limp. I also see that your husband's heart suffers silently for you. Child, his love for you could not be purer than it is."

The young wife said, taking her husband's hand into her own, "Yes, Grandmother, I broke my pelvis when I was a child, and it did not heal properly, so one side is shorter than the other, so I must limp. My pelvis is deformed, and I hate seeing myself naked. My husband always tells me I am the most beautiful Djinn he has ever met and desires me.

"I do not see how this can be so, but it does not matter as we can make love. I know Holy Father and Mother found me the most decent and loving husband ever. I know he loves me more than he loves himself, so I am thankful for my accident. And dearest Grandmother, I love him and wish to give him a child."

"It is true, Grandfather and Grandmother, she is the prettiest and kindest wife in the world, and I love her very much," finished the husband, "enough of us. Please tell us your tale."

Grandfather told us what had happened to them.

The evil Djinn came to our village for provisions. A young officer walked into our village church, where I was Pope. He said he had orders to burn the church and dispose of us. He was alone and told us he must obey orders but would not kill innocent children, women, and grandparents.

The young officer said, "I must burn the church, but I do not have to kill you; the orders said to dispose of you. Grandmother, go to your kitchen and pack cheese and bread. Grandfather, get your fur coats, mittens, hats, and boots. Bring everything back here as fast as you can."

We followed his directions, and he told us to dress and tie our food inside our coats so it would not freeze.

The young officer told Grandmother, "Your scarf is not warm enough; take mine. You must walk far from here and look for some people to take you in; your neighbours are too afraid to help."

Then he shooed us out the door and burned the church.

As we watched the church go up in flames, Grandmother said, "Grandfather, he is not a bad boy, just confused."[25]

We walked for three days, and you are the only Djinn willing to help us.

The young wife had big tears in her eyes and hugged Grandmother. "I am so sorry, Grandmother. It was not like this at the beginning when Lord Gabriel saved all the Djinn. My husband and I do not have parents or

---

[25] And the young officer repented and has been a great pope.

grandparents, and you may stay as part of our little family. Right, honey."

"Beloved, we cannot have children because of your broken pelvis, but we can have Grandparents to love," the husband replied.

Grandmother and Grandfather looked at each other, smiling.

Grandfather said, "Grandmother, we have found them. These are the Holy Djinn, and it is time for our Miracle."

The young couple did not understand at first. But a golden light emanated from both guests and soon all the couple could see were two light forms.

The young wife said, "Husband, it is the Holy Father and Mother; they are in our home."

Both bowed deeply.

Holy Mother spoke in the kindest of voices, saying, "On the small table rest two seeds. Grandson, you will swallow the golden seed. Granddaughter, you will swallow the silver seed. Drop your gown, granddaughter. Show me your pelvis."

The wife dropped her robe and looked at herself in a large mirror, which appeared from nowhere.

The young wife saw her misshaped pelvis in the mirror and felt ashamed of her ugliness. She tried to hide her deformity but could not and began crying.

Her husband grabbed her into his arms and turned her face away from the mirror, saying, "Honey, when I look at you, I have always seen you perfect. You are the only wife I ever wanted, and we shall be together all our lives. Please, Holy Mother, don't make her look into the mirror again."

Holy Mother replied, "Doctor, turn your wife to the mirror. It is my command."

The young husband turned to his wife to look in the mirror.

Holy Mother said, "Observe the power of your unconditional love for each other. Sufficient Love works miracles. Grandfather, look how lovely our little granddaughter is; she is no longer crippled. She will make wonderful great-grandchildren for us to love."

The wife turned all the way around to see. Her pelvis and lower body were as they would have looked without the accident. She was without pain and had no limp.

She called to her husband, "Oh, husband, I can give you a child. I am whole."

Holy Father said, "Take the seeds as my Beloved instructed you. These will combine with your seeds to prepare a vessel for our Holy Daughter, Bitya. She is the Saviour and will end this needless war and banish Evilness to a place where it will remain."

The two ingested their respective seeds with some spiced honey mead. Holy Father and Mother had vanished into the frosty night when they looked up, leaving all their outerwear.

The young wife said, "Come, husband, I am whole and want to lie with you."

The young doctor was again Gabriel, and the young wife was again Alliona.

Alliona finished the story,

> "The husband and wife left for their bedroom, and a beautiful girl was born nine months later. Her name was

Ariel, the Lioness. And we celebrate her Holy Conception, as Djinn, on Resurrection Eve."

There was not a dry eye in the group. Not a dry eye, humbug. Everyone was crying out of pure joy and happiness. The guests realised that the Resurrection Eve Story was ancient. Still, the parts played by Gabriel, Alliona, and the old Djinn were genuine. Alliona's limp and twisted pelvis seemed so real in the mirror. As if Gabriel and Alliona were the mystical couple, and the Holy Mother and Father had visited. Everyone was in the house with the young couple, Holy Father and Holy Mother.

Sophie asked, "Alliona, it seemed so real, the story. How can this be? You looked so different, and your poor pelvis so badly deformed when you were naked that it made me want to hug you."

Alliona smiled, "Sophie, you experienced the Miracle of Resurrection Eve. The actual reliving of the events leading up to the Conception of Ariel. The Miracle is why the Djinn don't have to believe in the presence of the Holy Family in this universe, for the Holy Ones gave this gift to the Djinn because of the unconditional love of One young couple. They told us we were to celebrate the Miracle every Resurrection Eve. Reminding us of the power of unconditional love so we will never become evil again.

"The Miracle first appeared toward the end of the Great War, when the Holy Family brought the doctor and his beloved into the Upper World. And yes, Sophie, they conceived another daughter before they departed. It was my Great Granny, Lydia, tens of thousands of years ago."

"Wow," was all Sophie could say.

The head kitchen granny approached Gabriel, tipsy, though still most proper, "Gabriel, sorry, I mean Milord. May we retire to the kitchen so to bring out the meal?"

Gabriel had learned all the names of Eleanor's grannies and replied, "Asteraceae, please do so. You can call me Gabriel; I have never liked Milord so much."

The grannies headed to the kitchen, and everyone sat down.

Alliona went to the fireplace mantel and opened an ancient incense censor hanging from a hook. She took some embers from the fireplace and placed them in the censor. She retrieved a walnut box filled with large chunks of frankincense and myrrh. She took a handful, sprinkled the incense on top of the embers, and closed the lid. Then, she lit the wick of a large beeswax candle, held the lit candle in one hand and the censor in the other, and returned to stand next to Gabriel.

Gabriel said, "It is the custom on Resurrection Eve for the mistress of the house to take the candle, symbolic of the Higher Light of Wisdom. She uses it to illuminate her path as she censes this room. The smoke and fragrance of the incense symbolise the Divine Love of the Holy Family.

"Tomorrow, I will have two mistresses in this house. Sophie, whose name means Wisdom, will carry the Holy Candle to Illuminate Alliona's path as she infuses the symbolic World with the Love of the Holy Family. The name Alliona means bright, shining light of Love. Indeed, Love and Wisdom seem like Two while being One.

"Sophie and Alliona, I swear upon all that is Holy and Everlasting that I will honour, love, and cherish you both equally and for all of Time. One day, you discover you are true sisters in a new Trinity.

"Tonight and forever, I will worship in Divine Love at your altars, as established by the Holy Family. So Mote It Be.

"Brides thou be on this the Resurrection Eve, but wives thou be on the morrow. Sophie and Alliona, I love you beyond the bounds of this universe. Darlings, cense the room for the Holy Supper."

Sophie stood up and took the candle from Alliona. As Sophie led Alliona, the room filled with the delicious scent of frankincense and myrrh. Everyone was standing with their heads lowered in personal communion.

Gabriel recited the Holy Pray when the censing finished and the dinner was served.

There is no time to describe the feast other than to mention that no meat dishes appeared on the menu, for these must wait for Resurrection Day. The family enjoyed,

> *Sweet grain pudding with fresh heavy cream*
> *Unleavened, round multigrain bread*
> *Stuffed cabbage rolls*
> *Small dumplings with mushrooms*
> *Dumplings with carrots and potatoes*
> *Slow-cooked kidney beans with potatoes, garlic, and seasoning*
> *Biscuits with poppy seeds and honey*
> *Yellow pea soup*
> *Four different desserts and*
> *Of course, warm spiced mead.*

Toasts continued through the meal, and Alliona's girls and the grannies sat to enjoy. Everyone was pleasantly warm, tipsy, or respectfully drunk.

Suddenly, a golden halo formed above Alliona's head, visible to all.

She stood and prophesied, "Someday, hundreds of thousands of years from now, the villagers will swear, most solemnly upon the Holy Knowledge, that the Love which shone from the hearts of those present this evening was so pure that the Holy Family came to share the Feast and the Third Great Miracle came to be.

"The villagers shall claim that on this very night, Ariel, the Daughter of God, descended into Alliona and Sophie, and both became loyal daughters of the Holy Family. On that night, one of the most celebrated nights in future Djinn history, the Djinn world radiated the fullness of Divine Love. Gabriel worshipped with passion and devotion at the Altars of Sophie and Alliona, bringing the gift of Ariel and a pair of identical twins into existence. The love of three being at last unconditional so that Ariel could confer Immortality.

"If you ask the Djinn how they know this story is valid, they will show you an old parchment codex filled with ink drawings of the time the Holy Daughters spent with the Djinn and the Miracles they performed. They called themselves the Sisters of the Returning Saviour, their Sister Ariel. Ariel came again to the Djinn, and the Djinn came to live fully, as the race had done in the old universe. And each will bow their head and place both hands over the heart region, saying, 'Glory to the Highest for the Fourth Miracle, Amen.'"[26]

Everyone did as instructed.

As Alliona sat down by Gabriel, the stardust on the Resurrection Tree glowed more brightly. Sparks of golden–silver brilliance flew from the Tree into the room, piercing the hearts of all present. With each heart-piercing, the miracle of unconditional love for others was no longer speculative. Each shared a love for the others, as do the Holy Angels, who love others more than themselves.

A soft feminine voice spoke to each, "Child, the Greatest Miracle of All Miracles is experiencing Unconditional Love. So, make it permanent, and never forget that the Holy Family loves you."

---

[26] This story will be told in another place and another time.

The light of the Tree returned to its previous state. No one knew what to say.

Gabriel stood up and said, "Often, words desert us when unconditional love is present. But you can show it by action. Try hugging each other, and you will understand."

Each hugged their two nearest neighbours, feeling the Miracle of unconditional love. At the end of each hug, each received another gift. For a second, each knew the Unending Suffering felt by the Holy Family for the injustice and injury caused to others by egoism.

Gabriel said, "Each must decide which path to travel."

Dinner finished, and everyone helped the kitchen grannies clear the tables.

Gabriel said, "Everyone, it is time to open the presents."

For the rest of the evening, Gabriel handed out presents repeatedly. There is no time to describe all the gifts, but the presents pleased everyone.

Eleanor got many talking dolls representing distinct races in the universe and a dollhouse for them to live in.

Sophie and Alliona received beautiful diamond necklaces, perfumes, dresses, and baby clothing for three little babies.

Morgana got some ancient magick books, a new wand, and sexy dresses.

Tristan's principal wife, Nata, received a charter signed by King Arthur, permitting the first magick school in Camelot. Tristan had searched many years for an opal necklace worn by the Elves' first queen, which held potent magick power. He found it and presented it to Nata.

Nata cried, and Tristan went to kiss her, whispering, "I love you as much as Gabriel loves Ariel, Natanel."

The twins received a complete wardrobe of superb clothing, including clothes for their daughters. They jumped all around.

For Merlin, Gabriel had located the first crystal gazing sphere made by the First Ones. Now, he could check on everything going on in the universe. Gabriel had also discovered some old Hermetic scrolls from Egypt and a few complete Stoic scrolls from Zeno and Chrysippus.

Tristan received a suit of enchanted Elf armour, an impenetrable shield, and a magick sword that no opponent could knock out of his hand.

Eleanor's new name for them, the kitchen grannies, each received several beautiful aprons and new cooking utensils.

Alliona's Inn girls received pretty lace dresses for wearing tomorrow and perfumes.

Tristan's students each received a magic wand that matched their magical personality, plus enchanted armour. His lady students and wives received wands, armour, perfumes, and clothing for Nouseum.

Eleanor said after the presents had been distributed, "Uncle Gabriel doesn't have a present."

"No, Eleanor, I received the very best present one can give to another. Every one of you has trusted and loved me over these many years. Trust and Love are the most precious gifts the Holy Family gives us so we can share them with others. No worldly gift can compare.

"And tomorrow, I will have my Immortal Family, beginning with my beloved Sophie and Alliona. I think God could not love two beautiful ladies more than I do. Even if they are to remain child brides for a few more years. I hope."

Everyone laughed because they knew Gabriel was older than the Holy Family.

"Then I shall have three little ones conceived and carried by the pure love of my precious Alliona and Sophie."

Sophie and Alliona cried as their love for Gabriel overwhelmed them. They thought that tonight, the three of them would make the most sacred love, at least for two virgins. Each was filled with his seed and pregnant by morning, as he had promised. They would give their holiest gifts to Gabriel, and he would reciprocate with his liquid gift of a child to each. A perfect Tetrad.

It was late, so Gabriel sent the villagers home with their presents. When the Inn cleared, he sent everyone off to bed.

"Sophie and Alliona, I will be up shortly, so get bathed and apply my favourite scents and flavours. Sophie, I want you to smell and taste peaches, and Alliona, you are to smell and taste passionfruit. Look for the recipes and where to apply them in Great Granny's potion book. It will take about an hour, and then I shall return to you."

Everyone left the Great Room for their separate bedrooms. Eleanor wanted to sleep with her new grannies, so they took her to the kitchen and made a little bed. They did not need sleep as they had more cooking to finish.

Gabriel went to the front porches and manifested the construction project of the carpenter and fire elementals. Father Frost retreated from the clearing as he watched, and Mother Spring went to work on the foliage and the flowers. The artificial sun he saved until early morning.

Gabriel returned to the Inn, located a free room, and had a nice hot bath.

Conjuring up some oxytocin, he mused, "Biology is a good thing to be an expert in, especially combined with magick."

During his brief sojourn without his beloved brides, Sophie and Alliona had been busy. They had read through Great Granny's potion book and found the two recipes Gabriel said would be within. They mixed the ingredients. Then, they bathed and dried each other and applied the mixtures specified in the book.

Sophie said, "Alliona, let's look some more in your Great Granny's clothes trunks. Perhaps she owned some fancy negligees."

"Honey, what is a negligee," asked Alliona?

"A negligee is a very sexy nightgown the new wife is to wear on the wedding night, which in our case is a night in advance."

"Sophie, Djinn, do not make such gowns. All you will find are simple but pretty, plain or nicely embroidered. I will find two for us."

Alliona began searching and located two beautiful cashmere gowns.

"See, Sophie, how pretty and soft they are?"

Sophie took one of the embroidered gowns and tried it on.

"These are nice. Honey, put yours on, and let's look in the mirror."

The images formed at the mirror's surface showed two young ladies. Sophie possessed loose ringlets of light, red-gold, blonde hair reaching past her mandibles. Her eyes were a shade of dark blue, her nose straight, and the shape of her face, typical of female film stars on Earth, like a gem. Her skin was without wrinkles, and her cheeks had the cutest freckles about her nose. When she wrinkled her nose, she reminded everyone of a rabbit. Pulling her gown tight, the mirror showed a hidden but perfectly balanced figure.

Alliona and Sophie had the same stature and body build and could exchange clothes. Everything was perfect. Alliona's hair was jet-black and fell in waves below her mandibles. Her eyes were green as dark emeralds, her nose straight, and her face was rectangular with a firm jaw and full lips begging for kissing. Her complexion was pale, and she had a small beauty mark on her rosy cheek about one and a half inches below the outside corner of her left eye.

After agreeing the nightgowns were becoming, both climbed into bed with the goose-down duvet pulled to the waist.

Alliona produced another old codex, "Primer Preparing for Marriage and Womanhood."

"Look, Sophie, and here is the part about making love with your husband for the first time. I think we need to read it? What do you think?"

"Your great granny sure understood preparation. We want to do everything correctly, right?"

Alliona nodded, and they started reading the book together and looking at the inked diagrams for about thirty minutes. They had many discussions.

Gabriel walked upstairs to Alliona's bedroom. He opened the door and found his beloved brides sitting in bed with the goose-down duvet pulled up to their waists. Both brides were wearing simple white cashmere nightgowns with embroidery.

Gabriel said, "Now, these nightgowns are traditional Djinn wedding nightwear. Good job. What are you two reading?"

Putting the book under the bed, Sophie said, "Nothing, honey. Just something we found in one of Great Granny's old trunks, and we're finished."

Alliona and Sophie climbed out of bed.

Alliona asked, "Gabriel, will you please lift the foot of the bed and hold it up for a moment?"

Gabriel, curious, lifted the foot of the bed about sixteen inches. Sophie and Alliona pulled a rug over the wooden floor towards the foot of the bed. The carpet held two walnut wood cubes approximately a foot on each side. They placed one block under each leg of the foot of the bed.

Alliona said, "OK, honey, you can lower the legs onto the woodblocks."

Gabriel lowered the bed and tested its stability, asking, "Why did we place the foot of the bed higher than the head of the bed, ladies?"

Sophie placed her hands on her hips.

"Gabriel, you know the answer to that question. Sister and I want our legs to be higher than our heads so that after you give us semen, it will flow into our wombs. We want our babies."

Gabriel looked at both, seeing that they were serious.

Keeping a straight face, he replied, "Good idea, ladies," thinking to himself, "I hope the potion works under Earth time and not Djinn time."

Sophie said, "Gabriel, Great Granny's book, said the new wife is to ask the husband to close his eyes for his bride when she removes her nightgown. Alliona and I are going to remove our nightgowns and climb into bed. We will tell you after we are naked in bed with the duvet pulled up. Then, we will close our eyes, and you can get into bed naked. OK?"

"Why do I need to close my eyes? I already know what you and Alliona look like naked, remember? OK, fine. My eyes are closed."

The three were in bed, and Sophie asked, "Gabriel, how can you make love to both of us simultaneously?"

"Sophie, all I need do is to warp our three world lines in spacetime, and then we make love altogether."

Alliona remarked, "What a clever use of magick, honey. I love you so much."

Chapter 16

Ariel Was Born on this Marriage Day

he sun was up, but it was still early when Wintry knocked upon the doors, saying, "Ariel is Born. It's time for breakfast, and there is much to do. Get up, everyone. It is Holy Resurrection Day and Marriage."

Alliona was already awake, feeling much loved and needed. The night had been magical as Gabriel warped the three world lines into one world line. The elevated foot of the bed trick had done its job, for Alliona could feel seed deep inside her physical and kesdjan wombs. She understood that three of them had become a natural trinity, fully connected in space, time, the astral, and soon in the Upper World of True Soul.

She replied to Wintry, "Truly, Ariel is Born."

Gabriel quickly arose, brushed his teeth, washed his face, and was in the great room with most guests and staff.

All the Djinn said, "Ariel is Born."

"Truly, Ariel is Born," thinking, "I hope no one will ask me about last night. It will be difficult to explain."

In Alliona's bedroom, Sophie asked, "Alliona, where are those two little plugs that Great Granny's book told us how to make? I do not want to move until I have one, for I want all of our husband's seed to stay inside me."

Alliona reached over to the bed table and picked them up.

"Here is yours, sister. Great Granny was a genius. Think how smart her mom and dad must have been?"

Feeling safe with the situation, they got out of bed.

Alliona said, "I like how we smell, Sophie. Passionfruit, peach, and Gabriel. We do not have to take a bath, do we?"

"Of course not, honey. We smell perfect for a wedding."

They brushed their teeth, washed their faces, and combed each other's hair to remove the effects of a rigorous night. They encountered Vika and Calliope, who hugged and kissed each new wife as they left the bedroom.

Calliope asked, "Vika and I remember the first time Tristan made love to us. It was so magical and precious. Whenever we think of it, we cry, right, Vika?"

"No crying today, for our sisters are getting married, and we are happy for all three of you. I also know your secret! You want to make love with us, too. Right?"

Sophie looked at Alliona, and Alliona replied, "Well, Vika and Calliope, what you say is true. When you slept with us naked, we both got so wet and had to fondle each other quietly. We are new at lovemaking, and you can teach us in real time, right?"

Calliope exclaimed, "Hooray for all of us. Vika and I are pregnant, but Mummy hides it with her magick. Time for breakfast."

Vika took Sophie's hand and Calliope Alliona's. The girls rushed to the Great Room.

They were in the kitchen promptly, greeting all with the standard Resurrection Day greeting, "Ariel is Born," to which all responded, "Truly, Ariel is Born."

Everyone had a simple breakfast.

Afterwards, Gabriel said, "Let's all go outside and enjoy the sunlight."

He opened the front door, and the others followed him outdoors. The air was fresh, bees and birds were in the air, flowers bloomed, and green and light were everywhere. Primavera shone majestically.

Natanel, Morgana, Tristan, and Merlin walked up to him, and Natanel remarked, "Nice bit of Elf Magick, Gabriel. Isn't this a Magick-Free Zone?"

Gabriel, smiling, replied, "Not anymore, at least for the rest of the day. It is a time for miracles for our Djinn friends."

The old village Pope arrived with his wife.

He found Gabriel, saying, "Ariel is Born."

Gabriel replied, "Truly, Ariel is Born. The weather is glorious. Must be another Resurrection Day Miracle, eh, Father?"

"Aye, Lord Gabriel, 'tis a genuine miracle. Do you know why it occurred? And all for your most unusual wedding. When do we practise for the ceremony?"

"Aye, Father, I know the reason, and you will find out soon enough. I will get the brides, and we can rehearse on the pentagram under the little sun. Back in a flash, so to speak."

When the Pope turned around to find the pentagram under the little sun, Gabriel and his two beautiful brides stood beside it.

He thought, "Well, Lord Gabriel said in a flash, and that was a flash."

Gabriel explained the ceremony to the Pope and his brides. The Pope quickly learned the service and memorised the words and all the movements when the rehearsal concluded.

Gabriel asked Alliona and Sophie to go dress in their wedding gowns.

Looking at the sun, he said, "Darlings, you have 90 minutes to prepare. Off with you."

Grabbing hands, the two ran back to Alliona's bedroom to prepare. Vika and Calliope went to help them.

Gabriel took the Pope and his wife into the great room for hot, spiced, hard apple cider and cakes.

On the way, he whispered to Merlin, "We need about 500 chairs and tables. Leave a thirteen-meter diameter free space around the pentagram. Today, I have declared this immediate area a Magick Zone."

With the advice of Morgana and Natanel, Merlin made lovely table and chair arrangements with intricately woven Djinn white lace tablecloths and vases full of the most beautiful red and orange roses. One colour for Sophie and the other for Alliona. Tristan was in the kitchen with the grannies, speeding things up with some minor magick.

The villagers began arriving around 11:30 A.M. dressed in their finest going-to-church wear. The village grannies were chattering about only two subjects. The first was the Resurrection Day Miracle of Mother Spring. Bringing forth her gifts to their village amid the winter months of Father Frost. The second was the Marriage of the Great Lord Gabriel to their Alliona and a young lady from far away. And he was marrying them both. What could happen next?

Tristan's students and Alliona's young ladies helped the kitchen grannies bring hot, hard apple cider and cakes to snack. Everyone was eager to see Lord Gabriel and his darling brides.

A horn sounded a little before noon, apparent solar time, and everyone stopped talking and oriented toward the Inn doors. Both doors to the great room opened.

Gabriel appeared dressed in a stunning navy-blue military jacket with light riding breeches and high black boots, with Sophie and Alliona holding onto an arm. Both dressed to the tee in their lace gowns, long diamond earrings and necklaces, and crowns woven of small white flowers by one of the kitchen grannies. No one in the village had ever seen a diamond, much less diamond jewellery. The ladies in the crowd stopped breathing when they saw them.

One little girl said to her mummy, "They are like real princesses, Mummy. They are beautiful."

Everyone recognised Alliona immediately, but she looked very young, and her haircut was short, like a virgin's.

This spell was prevalent long ago whenever a grown Djinn lady wanted to marry. As only virgins may have a church wedding, a nonvirgin needed a miracle to become a virgin again and return to the traditional marriage age of fifteen. The ladies looked at each other.

An old granny told everyone, "She must have found the potion book of Lydia, Ariel's little sister. Both must have done the ritual. Poor Lord Gabriel. But they must love him very much to do what they did."

Standing on the wooden plank porch with Sophie and Alliona, Gabriel announced, "My old friends, I want to introduce the two women I love most in this universe. Sophie from Earth and our Alliona, whom you all know and love. My beloved fifteen-year-olds.

"Yes, she and Sophie found Lydia's potion book and wanted me to see how much they loved me. They wanted to be pure for me. We all know that a woman's virginity was the most precious gift a female Djinn could give her beloved in ancient times. But, to tell you the truth, they forgot to read Lydia's last footnote on the other side of the page. Lydia had a wonderful sense of humour."

Everyone had a merry laugh, and Sophie and Alliona blushed. They were excited to be together, waiting to get married to Gabriel.

An ancient granny walked out of the assembled persons toward the porch. She dressed in dark green velvet with a hat tilted upon her head. She walked without a cane in a most animated style.

No one had seen her for thousands of years, and the village elders thought she must have passed.

One of the eldest grannies said, "Lydia, you didn't die. Why didn't you write to your old friends?"

"Too busy, Mame. I like my adventures."

Gabriel told Alliona, "Take Sophie and introduce her to Great Granny, Lydia. She will adore her."

As the two brides approached Lydia, she opened her arms wide, and they hugged her.

Kissing Lydia on her cheek, Alliona said, "Great Granny, this is my sister Sophie from Earth. She is the sister and friend I always prayed to have, and Ariel found her for me. So many miracles this holiday season."

Sophie curtseyed, saying, "Alliona and I read a few of your other codices. We found your Primers very helpful, and we studied them. They made both of us feel more secure. Thanks, Lydia. May I call you Great Granny, too?"

"Of course you may, Sophie. For now, I have two beautiful and happy great-granddaughters."

Gabriel came down to hug Lydia, "I must thank you. But I wish you had put the last footnote toward the front."

"Sorry, darling, too much opportunity for fun. But it is too bad; I never got to use my potions. You never realised that not only was Alliona in love with you during the Great War, but so was I."

"I must admit that you cut a most alluring pose in those days when you stood tall by the fireplace with your hand on your hip. I might have fallen for you after the potion," turning to Alliona, "she was as beautiful as you in those days."

"I knew you had a crush on my sister Ariel, and I would not make her mad, no way. I am glad to be here for this wonderful day. I have been away for too many millennia and home again."

"But, let me drop this ancient granny form and assume my old self, as I do not age anymore,"

Lydia chanted a few Enochian words and changed into the lady Tristan remembered, no less beautiful than Alliona.

To his astonishment, Gabriel blurted out, "My God, Lydia, you are as beautiful as your dear sister. A tempting morsel, you are. We had a good marriage, didn't we?"

Sophie and Alliona looked at each other in wonderment.

Precisely at noon, apparent solar time, everyone heard a horse-drawn carriage approaching the road as the four of them chatted. Two heralds on horseback proceeded to the carriage.

Blowing their horns, the heralds announced, "Dear People, prepare for the Prince and Princess of Nouseum with friends."

Gabriel said, "Come with me to the porch, sweethearts. This is a very official visit, and you must act like adults."

Taking their hands, the brides returned to the porch and held Gabriel as before.

A beautiful carriage drawn by six white horses with red plumes upon their heads pulled up in front of the porch shortly. Tristan left the porch, opening the door to the carriage. A beautiful young lady, a young man with a young woman, and an older man with an older woman stepped down.

Gabriel and his brides walked down toward the new guests. Gabriel bowed, and the two brides curtseyed.

Gabriel stood up and turned to the visitors, saying, "My dearest friends, may I introduce my brides. This dark-haired beauty is my beloved Djinn bride, Alliona, soon to become an Immortal. This red-gold-haired darling is my beloved Earth bride, Sophie, soon to become an Immortal. I love them equally and as much as I love the Holy Family."

The older man, Caspar, chuckled.

"I am sure you love them as much as you love at least one member of the Holy Family. I am looking forward to hearing more."

A small laugh tried to exit Alliona's mouth, catching her by surprise, so she tried to cover it up. Everyone turned to look at her, and she shrugged her shoulders.

Gabriel and the five guests from Nouseum had a merry laugh. Gabriel hugged Alliona.

"It is not important in the least. I want our family, and I want our babies. I chose you and Sophie as my Immortal mates because our match is perfect, and my life was so lonely before I met both of you. OK?"

Alliona remains confused but does not care if Gabriel loves her and Sophie and wants their babies.

She said, "Okay."

Gabriel introduced the Butterfly Princess and Caspar's academic wife, Hypatia. Then, he found a table for them to sit at, fetching Lydia, Morgana, and Natanel.

Soon, the Princess, the Butterfly Princess, Sophie, and Alliona were best friends. It wasn't often that the Princess of Nouseum and the Butterfly Princess could act like fifteen-year-olds, so they took full advantage of the situation. Gabriel, Tristan, Merlin, Casper, and the Prince stood to the side, discussing Nouseum and the outer worlds' situation. But this is a private conversation, so I do not report it.

At last, the Pope approached Gabriel, who introduced him to the visitors.

The Pope said, "I think the time has arrived for the ceremony as the signs you told me to watch for have come and gone."

Gabriel said, "Great, prepare the pentagram area. Have Tristan's male students form a circle and have the girls stand between them. No matter where they stand, they will have a front-row seat. Come, Sophie and Alliona. We must go inside a private room, and I will perform a very short initiation. We will return in exactly a quarter of an hour."

Off went Gabriel and the bridal dyad.

The Butterfly Princess, an Elf, said to the Princess, "Sister, they are the prettiest and happiest brides I have seen in millennia. They are young, but I can see that they truly love each other and Gabriel with near unconditional love. They are ready for the challenge. Sister, does it remind you of your first days with the Prince on Monreath?"

The Princess replies, taking her sister's hand.

"The love they share is as I had when the Prince and I were human. Maybe the Great Miracle will happen in this sorry Outer World, and we shall soon see. Your Marduk will be with you at last, sweetheart; I know you miss him."

And with that, they went to join the Prince.

Gabriel completed the short initiation, and he returned to his guests. The brides remained inside with Natanel, Eleanor, the twins, Morgana, Tristan, and Merlin.

The Pope and Gabriel were waiting for the brides at the pentagram. The Pope stood in his ceremonial garb at the star point, facing South and facing the pentagram. Gabriel stood at the pentagram's centre, facing in the same direction as the Pope. The students cleared a path between the Inn and the pentagram circle so the brides, with their escorts, would have an unimpeded way into the pentagram.

Four trumpets sounded short blasts, one after another. Holding a basket of rose petals, Eleanor emerged on the ninth trumpet blast. Walking down the steps, she covered the walkway with red and orange rose petals.

Morgana and Natanel followed behind Eleanor.

Following behind them came the twins, throwing thornless roses to the crowd.

Next came Sophie, escorted by Merlin on the right and Alliona, accompanied by Tristan, on the left.

As they walked towards the pentagram, all the birds in the meadow sang an ancient song of the First Ones. The girls and their escorts took two steps and stopped and continued until they reached the pentagram. At the lower-left point of the pentagram stood Natanel and Morgana. Tristan placed Sophie at the point to Gabriel's right. Merlin put Alliona at the point to Gabriel's left. Both stepped back and stood at the right point in line with Natanel and Morgana. Gabriel rotated so all three faced the Pope.

The Pope began, "The First Temple was constructed to Honour the Holy of Holies, beyond Description, the Infinite and Unfathomable, built by the First Ones, the Elfin Race of Mythological Times. Within this Temple, the Elves conducted their Most Sacred Ceremonies. Such are the Holy Marriage, Holy Birth, and Holy Initiation ceremonies.

"Today, we stand within the Spiritual Heart of this Holy Temple to share in the Spiritual Joining of Lord Gabriel, the Immortal, with his Immortal Brides, the Princesses Alliona and Sophia. May the Holy Family bless and keep them permanently.

"I ask the brides to hold one of Gabriel's hands. Blending their female essences with the male essence of their chosen husband and Most Beloved."

The brides follow the instructions, and a golden aura forms about the three after they join hands.

The Pope continues, "Lord Gabriel, hast thou given the seed of Immortality to thy Brides?"

"Truly, it is so."

"Alliona and Sophia, didst thee accept the Seed of Immortality from thy husband?"

"Truly, it is so."

"Lord Gabriel, hast thou given thy worldly and kesdjan seed to thy Brides in Unconditional Love," asks the Pope?

"Truly, it is so. All love must be Unconditional to be True Love."

The Pope asks, "Alliona and Sophia, didst thee accept Lord Gabriel's twin seed and prepare your Holy Eggs for fertilisation by such seed?"

"Yes, Father. We are with child, and the miracle is occurring in the warmth of Unconditional Love."

The Pope asks, "Who gives these Brides in the Holiest of all Unions?"

Natanel replied, "Morgana and I vouch for Alliona and Sophie, the Blessed Sisters of Ariel."

Merlin replied, "Tristan and I vouch for Sophia and Alliona, the Blessed Sisters of Ariel."

"Then, I declare the Sacred Marriage of Lady Alliona and Lady Sophia to Lord Gabriel in Eternity. So Mote It Be."

At that very moment, three Orbs of Golden Light appeared above the pentagram, and tiny, white osmanthus blossoms fell onto the pentagram. A beautiful soft melody created by invisible bells rang out. The scent of the flowers filled the golden gnomon.

It caught the Pope off-guard, but being an expert in the unexpected, he said, "Another Miracle for this Holy Resurrection Day. The Holy Family has given Their Blessings. Let all of us give our Love and Blessing to this Trinity. God Bless them, and God Bless all of us. This ends the ceremony."

Morgana and Natanel hugged and kissed each new wife. Then, they kissed and embraced the new husband. The Pope, Merlin, and Tristan did the same. Every eye in the village was wet with pure love and joy and clapped for the Trinity.

The five guests from Nouseum walked over to the pentagram.

The Princess said, "This is a grander event than I imagined. It has been ages since the Holy Family visited Nouseum. The three of you have accomplished something new in this universe, and I think there is hope for all of us."

Everyone hugged and kissed the newlyweds. The three golden orbs vanished except the last one; the fourth remained within the two pregnant wives.

Lydia congratulated the three of them, saying, "Don't forget, I am going to remain in the village and take care of my new great-great grandchildren whenever they visit."

Now, the celebration began. The villagers produced potent holy vodka for drinking, all homemade. A lively band pulled out pipes, lutes, and hand drums. The kitchen grannies were getting ready to bring out the feast, but Merlin waved his hand and loaded the tables.

Merlin went to Asteraceae, asking, "Dear Lady, you and the others have worked hard enough. Will you join me at my table? You would honour me."

Asteraceae, blushing, replied, "Oh, Merlin, I will join you at your table. Why do you think I have taken such good care of you for so many centuries?"

Merlin blushed and took her hand.

Merlin and Asteraceae sat down, as did all the grannies and helpers.

Gabriel and his two wives sat at a table with his friends from Nouseum and Camelot.

Gabriel whispers, "My darlings, alcohol is not a toxin for the eggs and sperm inside you. So, enjoy the libations. In a week, no more alcohol until I hold my little darlings in my arms."

Sophie said, "Why didn't you tell us we were to make love the night before the wedding? Why do the Elves have such a custom? Make sure you are not so drunk that you cannot make love to us. Alliona and I have cravings for you, husband."

Alliona says, "We have cravings for you, husband. Sophie, we are proper wives now, and I love it."

Gabriel laughs.

"The Elves are the most pragmatic of races. They get incredibly drunk at weddings, so they cannot make love. So, they made a rule that you make love the night before. Smart bunch, the Elves; thinking ahead."

After the feast finished, the tables cleared magically.

Gabriel stood up and announced, "Our family has found a present for each of you, which I guarantee you will love. Close your eyes and open them when I say now."

All the guests closed their eyes tightly.

He waited for some seconds and said, "Open."

Everyone had a present resting on the tabletop where they were sitting. And Gabriel was correct, for everyone loved their present.

The Pope stood up, a little wobbly but coherent.

"Everyone who can stand must stand, and the rest can toast where they are. Let us toast. We love and appreciate our dearest friend, Lord Gabriel, and his blessed wives. May the Miracles given to the Djinn pass into all the worlds. So Mote It Be."

And all toasted the Trinity, repeating So Mote It Be.

The Nouseum guests needed to return to their carriage as there was business to do.

The two princesses walked with Tristan and Natanel.

The Butterfly Princess said, "When the Great War comes, our hopes rest on you and your students. I married Gabriel to Ariel by the Holy Mother's desire; they will fight but can use no more magick than the enemy. My Sister and I will conjure and pray for all of you. We must destroy Ahriman the Evil this time."

Both Princesses kissed Tristan and Natanel on the lips.

As the guests climbed into the carriage, Morgana said, "We love you all. Godspeed."

Gabriel, Tristan, and Natanel wished good health to the others as they climbed into the carriage. Amid horn blasts, the carriage disappeared into the evening shadows.

People played music, danced, ate, and drank for the rest of the evening. Merlin served his famous Deadly Dragon and Dragon's Blood concoctions. Even little Eleanor was tipsy, but not too much, for the twins acted like mothers this evening. Being silly girls, they both found themselves drunk for the first time.

It was early morning, and so Gabriel wished everyone home unharmed.

He thanked all the elementals who had built the temple and shared in the festivities. Then, he requested the marital party go to bed and wished the temple site was as before the night before.

Gabriel said, "Thank you, Father Frost, for this day with your dear wife. I returned all to its original state."

Gabriel took Sophie and Alliona by their hands and up to Alliona's bedroom. He undressed them both and laid them on the bed.

Alliona opened her eyes, saying, "Honey, you will not get out of making love with us on our wedding night. I insist you undress with my eyes open and come to bed. Sophie, look at our husband and see how handsome he is naked."

What could he do but obey them? As he undressed, he heard the voice of Ariel in his head.

"Husband, it was a nice ceremony. I am glad that my family came to share our joy. I am sorry I laughed at Caspar's comment, but it was true. Yes, come to bed and make love to the three of us."

END OF CODEX TWO

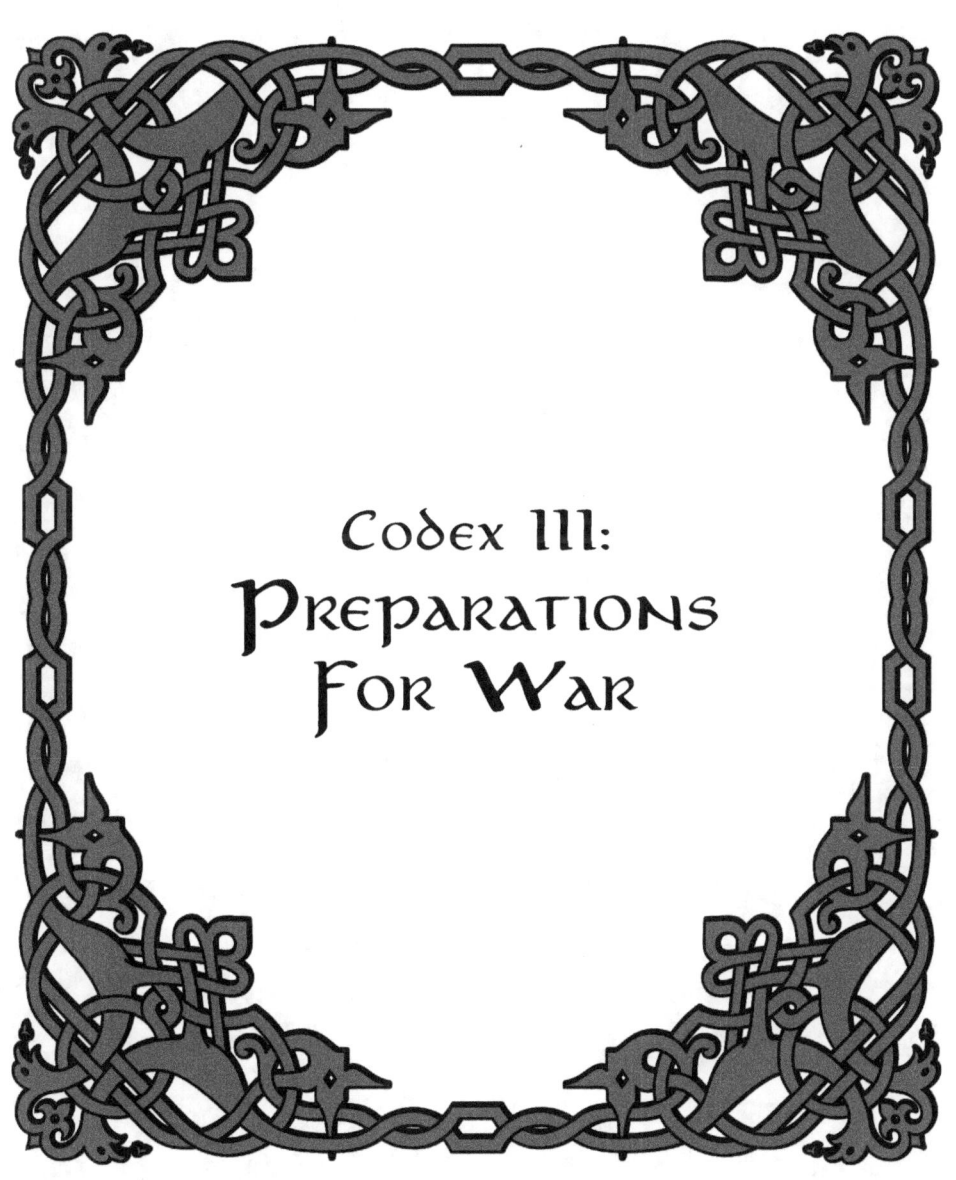

Codex III: Preparations For War

Chapter 17

The Great War Preparations

abriel awoke and carefully climbed out of bed to not wake his darlings. Even in the faint light of the rising sun, he saw the sparkle of genuine joy and love radiating from their hearts.

He laughed to himself, "Another Wonder of Creation."

He found Tristan drinking hot tea with the kitchen grannies in the kitchen.

Tristan asked, "Pleasant wedding. Were the ladies surprised when they discovered that Elves always make love before the wedding, so they marry with seed?"

Gabriel, laughing, said, "Quite surprised, as this was their desire, anyway. Is Morgana still fifteen? Nubile is pleasant, but maturity has its advantages."

"She is still fifteen. Being with her now, I find our past times very vivid. I have noticed one miraculous side-effect of Lydia's potion on Morgana. Even after Merlin rehabilitated her soul, the little dark spot she has carried since Ahriman the Evil turned her is no more. She carried much shame for her past and has had such a desire to obliterate it.

"Lydia's potion, the Holy Family, your magick, and her desire to be pure for Eleanor and myself accomplished the miracle. To be with Morgana again is a genuine gift for me. Thanks, Gabriel. I know you and Ariel returned her to her pristine state."

"Tristan, do not give all the credit to Ariel or me. The miracle occurred because of the intense love in this house since we arrived several days ago. Even Elf Magick is not sufficiently powerful, and only Love and Trust fuel the greatest miracles."

"I understand. I will thank you, Sophie, Alliona, and Ariel, anyway. The love would not have been sufficient without the miracle of the pure and unconditional love within which you all live. Still, we need to discuss Nouseum, so let us walk in the winter woods. The Djinn world remains protected from the Dark Ones."

The pair finished their tea and dressed to go outdoors. Winter had returned, the sky was sunny, and the snow was fresh.

Tristan began, "The Dark Ones have not found Prince Marduk yet, but he will show up soon enough. He is too young and untrained, and he cannot oppose them. The Magick of Ahri-Simeon and Ahri-Lilith continues to grow as their vanity increases. They seem to have contacted something Evil from a time beyond memory. Even the Prince and Princess do not know this Dark Source. Caspar can find no information in the Archives; I see nothing in the Forbidden Magick's Books. We hope you can tell us.

"The military strength of the Dark Ones grows daily in the most human-like worlds, especially within the newer Outer Worlds, which have not been contacted by the Nouseum storytellers. Their spies are scouring the cosmos for planets to rule. They will find Earth one of these days, turning humanity. I am afraid.

"It seems Ahri-Simeon and Ahri-Lilith have many years head start for Prince Marduk to stop them. We need you and Ariel, Gabriel."

Gabriel did not respond. The two continued to walk, hearing only the crackling sounds of their boots on dry, fresh snow.

Finally, Gabriel replied, "I understand, dear friend. There is not even a guarantee we can succeed. You ask for an intervention far beyond any previous response of the Immortals under the Holy Family's direction. You asked me to change the complete set of outcomes purposely for all the Universes under the guidance of Nouseum.

"The Dark Source lives on the other side of the Oblivion. My brother murdered Ariel and our daughters in her womb soon after the first time began. After the murder, I created the Oblivion and placed him beyond it. The three of us are older than the Holy Family, the Djinn, Nouseum, and every universe. We are the First of the First Ones. All of Creation is under my guidance, Tristan.

"Ahri-Simeon and Ahri-Lilith connected with Brother while they were in Oblivion, and he opened a portal. I must destroy and remove my brother from my mother's life records.

"We have good generals for our troops. Your students are maturing, and Sophie and Alliona will complete training in a few years, including High Magick. Marduk and Eleanor will enter battle when they are older. I will rescind my vow not to use Magick in any universe threatened or attacked. Except for my Sister Ariel, the Holy Family cannot participate in the war.

"The Dark Ones need permanent destruction. Oblivion is insufficient."

Ariel spoke to Gabriel, "Darling, what Tristan asks is doable. It is beyond dangerous. The price is immense, even if we succeed. Those who die in battle may rest forever in Oblivion, my precious. Tristan, Morgana, Merlin, and the students are not immune to death. You and I may survive, but Sophie and Alliona may be too young. I know it will break your heart and mine to lose them for a part of each lives inside you and me. I will recover, but you, dear husband, will grieve always.

"I will enter the battle if need be. The Dark Source needs elimination and not banishment. And the door to the Oblivion closed to all Magick forever."

Gabriel said, "Tristan, Ariel and I agree to enter the War. Sophie and Alliona must decide, for they may die, as may you and everyone we love. The Oblivion is open, which will be the endpoint of all who die. The door to Oblivion will close forever. Sophie and Alliona must know nothing until I complete their training in Magick. Agree?"

Tristan replied, "Agree."

Gabriel added, "I am sufficiently powerful to face the Dark One, Tristan. I know your family can deal with Ahri-Simeon and Ahri-Lilith. I have seen Lilith's heart. It is not entirely dark. All she ever wanted was an Elf to love and need her. Tristan, you are the embodiment of Love Itself. You must give her the love she so desperately needs. Love her truly and bring her into your family as a wife. You will rehabilitate her, as Merlin did for Morgana. Your love heals, especially when mixed with your psychotherapy."

Tristan responded, "I have seen motion pictures taken of her before she turned, and she was such a sweet girl, somewhat afraid but frank. She is as beautiful as Morgana. It is a good plan, Gabriel. But I think it should be you and not me. After all, you are *der Über Gott* (the Over God). Let us agree that one of us will take her to love."

"Agree. And please don't tell everyone I am God, which would make my life intolerable."

"Gabriel, I would tell no one. But I must tell you, I am glad you are, for no one else is worthy of such a title. We all love you, Gabriel."

The two returned to the Inn and found everyone in the kitchen having breakfast.

Morgana stood and greeted Tristan and Gabriel, saying, "Tristan, when I awoke this morning, I could not sense the dark spot in my heart. It vanished, and I am as I was when I was fifteen for the first time. Forgiven at last. Of honey, my shame and worry are no more."

When she finished, she started to cry, and Tristan took her into his arms and soothed her. Gabriel saw tears in the eyes of Sophie and Alliona and went to hug them.

Sophie asked, "Is it true, Gabriel. Is her shame gone?"

"Yes, my dears, she is free of her past. Genuine Love heals all."

Lydia arrived in the kitchen after a nice rest. She poured herself some tea and sat by Alliona and Sophie.

Lydia asked, smiling at Gabriel, "Would you like to learn some potion magick, my sweeties? I understand Morgana is a sorceress already. The only magick allowed in our land is potions, notwithstanding Gabriel's shenanigans yesterday."

Looking at Sophie and Alliona, Gabriel good-naturally replied, "I need to thank you for renewing my wives, Lydia. It is interesting and pleasant,"

"So what adventures will you take my two granddaughters on next, Gabriel? I do hope I can spend some time with them?"

"At short time, I am afraid, dear Lydia. They begin their magick training tomorrow. They will return with Morgana and Merlin to Camelot and start classes in elemental magick. Tristan and I need to go to Nouseum for some business."

When they heard training in magick, Sophie and Alliona perked up, but they did not want to be separated from Gabriel.

"Sophie told me that after a couple marries on Earth, they take a romantic trip somewhere nice. Gabriel, Sophie and I want a honeymoon with you. Right, Sophie?"

Sophie added, "You don't want to disappoint your sexy wives, do you?"

"I understand your disappointment, but you now must learn to behave as Immortals. Not to mention, follow the requests of your most considerate husband. Anyway, whether in Nouseum or Hell, I will be with you in your dreams, and they shall be as actual as they are now.

"I already have a most interesting honeymoon for us to enjoy. Be patient and learn as much magick as you can. After Morgana and

Merlin finish with you, Tristan and Natanel will teach Morgana, Merlin, and you the Forbidden Magick of the First Ones. Afterwards, I will teach you even deeper, Magick, even older than the Elves."

Alliona turned to her, Sophie, saying, "I think it will be alright. We need to keep our babies safe, right?"

Sophie nodded yes.

"Then tomorrow, we travel to Camelot. The next day, Tristan and I are off to Nouseum. Don't worry; we should stay only a few months, and then you shall have your honeymoon."

Chapter 18

More Djinn Metaphysics

The joy of returning to the Crystal Cave for its residents was apparent. Eleanor ran to assure her kitty was OK and found the grey-brown tabby, Moorka, sound asleep next to her mouse friend, Cheburashka. Both had grown up together. Eleanor picked both up and kissed and kissed and kissed them.

She carried the two friends to the library to show Sophie and Alliona.

Then, Eleanor said, "Sophie and Alliona, come see my dollhouse. Uncle Merlin made it for me, and the dolls are magical and can play with us."

Sophie said, "No way. We have to see this," grabbing Alliona by her hand, off they went.

The kitchen grannies were still visible to our friends, as Eleanor loved each one very much, and they were teaching her how to cook simple items. Morgana surpassed in magick but was a disaster in the kitchen. The adults retired to the library for some honey mead.

Lydia was the first to speak. "Nice place, Merlin. I will enjoy spending a few weeks with you, maybe longer if you find a liking of my charms.?"

Asteraceae heard this, sticking her nose in the air, and returned to the kitchen.

Tristan added, "I wonder which one will win Merlin's heart? Who votes for whom?"

"Lydia, I have had prior experiences in such matters. They did not turn out well," replied Merlin.

Everyone laughed and enjoyed their honey mead.

Merlin said, "Lydia, I will help you develop a potion to add about five years of maturity to Morgana, Sophie, Alliona, and maybe the twins. I realise the physical changes require Djinn clock time to resolve. Still, neuromaturation would help us deal with the Nouseum threat. Full Immortality will not come to them unless they are emotionally mature. Neither will survive the battle, and it would surely break Gabriel's heart to lose them. Is this possible?"

Lydia thought for a moment and said, "Might be possible. Neuromaturation requires a relatively circumscribed modulation of synaptic densities in particular areas of the neocortex and hypothalamus."

Morgana and Merlin stared at Lydia.

"Sorry, I forgot you could know nothing about the medical science of the central nervous system, the brain. I spent many years with Gabriel at Caltech and learned much about human society and science. He and I visited the Earth for extended stays to attend the university, where he taught physics.

'It is easy for me to become young with my potion magick. Watch."

Before their eyes stood a strikingly beautiful Djinn, who appeared in her late twenties.

Lydia said, "This is how I appeared to Gabriel and those physical creatures on Earth. The potion gave me a youthful body to occupy whenever I desired."

Lydia turned toward a long mirror hanging by the fireplace and looked at her reflection as she slowly turned around.

"I declare, my human form is still as pretty as ever. Gabriel and I were married before Alliona fell in love with him. But our paths diverged, and that was that. Nice memories, though."

Sophie and Alliona returned to the library. Neither Sophie nor Alliona recognised Lydia.

Sophie introduced herself and Alliona.

"Hello, this is my sweet sister, Alliona, and my name is Sophie. We are both pleased to meet you."

Lydia held her hand for Sophie to shake, saying, "It is a pleasure to make your acquaintance. My name is Lydia."

Alliona blurted out, "Lydia, my great granny, Lydia? You look so young and pretty."

"Where do you think you inherited your beauty from, child? Your father's side of the family? No, from your mother's, thanks to your sexy great granny. But enough of this, back to my granny form. There are no eligible young men for dazzling with my curvaceous figure and perky breasts."

In a moment, Lydia was back to Lydia.

Alliona whispered to Sophie, "Sophie, do you think great granny was once a lover to our beloved husband. She is a knockout, and I think she could have convinced Gabriel?"

Sophie replied, "I don't know, sweetie. I think Lydia is Gabriel's type, but I am too embarrassed to ask her, so we will ask Gabriel. That would have been long before I was born; you were still a child. Gabriel is all ours now, remember. And he gave us babies and not Lydia, right?"

"I cannot answer that question. But I know Husband loves giving babies to his lovers. The grannies in my village chat about Lydia, saying she was married and her children murdered."

Lydia asked, "Well, Gabriel asked me to introduce you to Djinn Metatheology and Spiritual Practises. When is the best time? Morning, afternoon, or evening? I would like two-hour classes and some time for practise every day except on holidays."

Natanel, Merlin, and Morgana discussed how to run the magick introductory course for Sophie and Alliona.

Merlin answered, "Lydia, we should run sessions from breakfast to lunch and after dinner to bedtime. Sophie and Alliona must rest between the morning and evening sessions to allow the lessons to merge within their physical and kesdjan neural systems. We think you can teach between 14:00 and 16:00 hr, OK?"

Lydia, throwing Merlin a kiss, said, "Perfect. As it is now 1500 hr, I propose to begin the first lessons. OK?"

Morgana nodded in agreement, calling Asteraceae, "Grannie, will you please be so kind as to bring snacks to the library for all of us who have missed lunch. I will bring Eleanor; she is young but very impressionable and will not forget."

Morgana left to return with Eleanor.

When everyone was ready, Lydia began, "When I was on Earth with Gabriel, he asked me to study comparative religion, with particular emphasis upon the three religions of the Book. You will better appreciate Djinn Metatheology and Spiritual Practise subtleties by contrasting them with the theologies of Judaism, Christianity, and Islam. We were on Earth for fifteen years, providing sufficient time to complete a doctoral program in Comparative Religion and gain a professorship.

"The **first significant difference** is that the pre-exodus Djinn never compiled a physical book of scriptures. We have no Old Testament, New Testament, or Quran to puzzle over whether the words are genuinely those of the Holy Family. Instead, as engrams, our original Holy Scriptures were directly and indelibly impressed upon the conjoint Djinn Meta-Consciousness. No entity can change the syntax and semantics of our astral engrams outside the Holy Family. As every Djinn of responsible age can read our Holy Canon, none can argue or distort its Sacred Content and Intentions for our race.

"During our evolutionary history in our original universe, our race avoided religious wars. The Holy Family's Teachings remained Pristine and Applicable as we used Wisdom to maximise Altruistic Love. As everyone had automatic access to our Holy Canon, the Holy Family's Teachings were immune to political exploitation or employment to destroy life under that subterfuge of Holy Words.

"The Hebrew language used in the Old Testament was not indigenous to Earth but taught to one group of Semitic peoples by a messenger Djinn. Such transmission occurred long after the Great Djinn War. Therefore, you will find many similarities between our Holy Canon and the Hebrew Old Testament and language structure. The significant difference is that we have always used vowel letters, worked in base-ten arithmetic, and never assigned numerical values to the letters. Doing so leads to too much misinformation experienced over many centuries on Earth.[27]

"The author of our original Holy Canon is Ariel's Divine Brother-Husband, Gabriel Baal Eyt. The meaning of Baal Eyt is Lord of the Appointed Time. His Teachings could not be inscribed upon humankind's unruly and chaotic conjoint heart. Hence, his immediate and later apostles recorded them onto parchment or papyrus paper. Such records exist as honest renditions from memory. Still, some variation exists because of human recall faults, particularly confabulations and later scrivener errors. Such differences are seen easily as one reads the Synoptic Gospels.

---

[27] The Old Testament stories of Yahweh ordering a Semitic tribe to decimate the cities of Cannan are not from the Holy Family. They arose from the war archetype Moses and Aaron worshipped. They were uncivilised, dominating, male-orientated, animal herders living in tents and not organised agricultural cities. The oppression of females was not part of the developing agricultural, who lived in a fellowship of equality but came with the warring Semitics from the south and the Kurgans from the northeast steppes. The story of captivity in Egypt does not exist in the Akashic record as an actuality, but is a substitute for the captivity in Babylon.

"So, to understand the True Teachings of Yeshua, one must study the earliest compilations of His Teachings and Spiritual Practises carefully. Modern scholars believe that the Lost Sayings Gospel Q, the Signs Gospels, and the Passion Narrative likely predate the Synoptic Gospels. They should be read in unison with the three Synoptic Gospels, the Gospels of Thomas and John, and the Didache. Mark is the least adorned with pagan religious concepts.

"Although many of Paul's letters are earlier than the Synoptic Gospels, Paul was not a first-hand witness but had access to those who were. Christ called him to perform a particular function, using the Crucifixion and Resurrection story to establish a suitable Church. The teachings of Christ Himself are consistent with those given to the Djinn. Still, there was no Crucifixion or Resurrection, as the Djinn did not interfere in any Holy Mission.

"As to the Master called Yeshua, Ariel's step-brother in the Holy Family, Gabriel gave him His Mission. Gabriel informs us that the Crucifixion was an underappreciated possibility. Christ meant to enlighten the Jews, not be crucified by them. Paul appeared to find a solution to continue the development of Christian Thought.[28]

"However, an explanation of the exact details of the Crucifixion is not an issue now. I may return to it later. What is essential to understand is that later Christianity became corrupt. This is because of the proliferation of pseudepigrapha and literary license by the followers of Mithraism, Gnosticism, Manichaeanism, and Christian sects of the first centuries.

---

[28] Gabriel sent Yeshua to the Jews to convert them from warring to peace as existed in the evolving agricultural societies. But, his experiment failed. Their DNA and mindsets had crystalised, making them unable to be converted from domination into gender equality and world-wide peace. The history of the Christian Church is not significantly better, as the male domination metric still rules.

"Even more dangerous was the theological dogma arising from the Church Fathers' various meetings, beginning with the first ecumenical council at Nicaea in 325 CE and ending with the seventh council in 787 CE. I will return to this subject, but let us remain focused on the Original Teachings of Christ.

"In reviewing the dogmatic declarations of the male-only ecumenical councils and apostolic literature, we remember the participants lived in cultures that debased and oppressed the female, and her essence was stigmatised and underappreciated. Subsequently, the Christian Church fell into dark pathways, as documented in the many egregious waves of abuse of females by the Vatican Hierarchy in Western Europe. The concept of a male-based Trinity developed to obscure the Holy Family's actuality and the equal importance of female energies.

"To review the concept of the Sacred Tetrad, I will return to an explanation Gabriel provided to Sophie before she met the Djinn. I will resonate with Gabriel and recall his instructions without error. Sadly, humanity has not learned this skill, and it will remain outside the reach of the common citizen until their conjoint mind quiets, as did the Djinn mind."

The library was quiet, and Lydia continued speaking.

"Here is what Gabriel has taught about the **second significant difference** between Djinn Christianity and Human Christianity. Sophie has heard it before from Gabriel. I will repeat it precisely for the rest,

"The Law of the Trinity is an operational cut of the underlying Superior Law of the Tetrad. When I speak of the Tetrad Law, I discuss concepts most difficult for ordinary human reasoning. Creation can occur only by restricting a portion of Infinite Phase Space by transforming it into a transfinite phase space. The higher rationality understands such and is available through the Noble Organ.

"The Ari called the Creator's withdrawing a portion of Its Being from a volume of space, *tzimtzsum*. *Tzimtzum* means contraction, constriction, or condensation. This term is used in the Lurianic Kabbalah to explain Isaac Luria's doctrine that God began creation by contracting his Ein Sof Ohr (infinite) light to allow for a transfinite conceptual space in which finite and independent realms could exist.

"Christianity contains a similar concept called kenosis."

Lydia looked around and found everyone fixated on her voice.

"Imagine a bipyramid in your mind-space. Place the following upon each of the bipyramid's four horizontal points: Holy Father, Holy Mother, Holy Daughter, and Holy Son. These four points represent the creative agents denoted in humanity's Old Testament by the plural *Elohim* and in Kabbalah by *Ein Sof*. The abode of the Holy Family World 3.

Label the uppermost point, Creator, *Ein*, and *Demiourgos*. The Creator is the active agent in every universe, regardless of human-derived forms. The Creator exists in World 1. *Ein* is the Hebrew word for the first emanation of the Source. When people refer to the Supreme Deity or God in their theologies, this is who they are honouring.

Label the lowermost point, *Ein Sof Ohr*, Spirit, which occupies World 6. This point contains all the information necessary for the physical and Oneirion worlds to come into being in time and space. It contains all applicable laws, energies, and possible temporal paths from beginning to end. The *Ein Sof Ohr* metaphorically manifests via *Keter* and the Kabbalist Tree of Life.

Such is why God and the *Elohim* are in Bereshit 1:27, though not adequately described.

Now, I want you to add one last set of terms to your diagram above the uppermost point. The first point is the Unfathomable Source. Label it using the mathematical symbols of an Infinity and a Point or the Egyptian hieroglyphs for Temu and Nun. The Source contains all possible Universes but is not entirely within any. One day, we will discuss it, but not now.

The last point to add is below W6. Label it W12, Creation, All That Can Ever Be. This diagram explains everything. Gabriel created it when he created All (everyone missed this last announcement).

"I think you can understand why the less informed writers of early religious texts, Christian and Egyptian, saw God as tripartite rather than tetrapartite. I must tell you that the unmanifest Tetrad reappears in the Kabbalah as the Tree of Life contains Four Worlds. The Law of the Tetrad is outside of Creation and not within Creation, wherein the Law of the Trinity rules. Sufficient hints have been available for some time.

"We find the most conspicuous evidence of the Holy Family in the near-universal preference of nuclear families in the earliest human groups and later civilization, not to forget the Djinn. Such gender-balanced arrangements are an evolutionary necessity for every advanced species and remain the most influential group for a viable society. Different roles for males and females, but fully egalitarian in principle.

"The Gurdjieffian Laws of Three and Seven hide seven distinct intervals to an Octave in the descending heptatonic musical scale. Hidden within this scale is the melodious Fifth. Four intervals in the ascending Fifth, do-si, si-la, la-sol, and sol-fa, symbolising the Divine Tetrad. The descending Perfect Fifth ends on Note F if the octave begins with C.

"The Law of Three manifests as the melodious descending Fourth, which begins on the Note F and concludes the descending Octave having a frequency ending with lower C. The Fourth contains the three intervals: fa-mi, mi-re, and re-do.

"A descending musical scale is typical of most ancient music, which saw Creation moving from a higher to a lower frequency, refined to gross, or light to heavy."

Chatelaine said, "Wow. You blew my mind, overturning everything I learned in my Christian upbringing. But the Divine Form of the Elohim is fantastic as a Holy Family. If they created us in their likeness, then the human family is the most sacred and necessary social unit. It is an error to portray the Divine Form by ignoring the female gender. Gabriel is correct; the Church Fathers of the 4th and 5th centuries were misogynists, so their creation is blasphemous."

"This is what I said," replied Lydia.

After a slight break, everyone was back in the library. Eleanor fell asleep, so Morgana carried her off to bed and was back in her regular chair.

Merlin said, "I find it most interesting that we, who came into being by the creative imaginations of human storytellers, are now functioning independently of them. Perhaps Gabriel will explain this to us one day?"

Sophie responded, "Gabriel once explained that the Astral Realms hold all the possibilities for any universe to manifest, given a proper temporal sequence of the last actualisation of the Universal Wave Function. Gabriel meant our universe came into existence, prepossessing an almost infinite set of world lines. These diverging lines spread outward in time from its physical birth and converge into the next universe's birth.

"Each world line represents a different narrative account of the sum of previously activated physical and astral histories. Many of these narratives apply solely to the aphysical planes, such as Camelot and many world *mythoi*. Therefore, humanity did not create Camelot; humankind only allowed it and its inhabitants to actualise within the Astral Worlds accessible to the conjoint Astral Mind."

Merlin answered, "Brief but understandable. Thank you, Sophie."

Alliona noted, "I think the Work of the Holy Family is much more extensive than we believe or understand. This Work may even be beyond the Holy Family. The answer lies solely within the Unfathomable Source, encompassing all impossibility and possibility. It would be nice to talk about this one day.

"Husband once told me the best way to comprehend the Source, though incomplete, is mathematical. Honey says that mathematics is precise, rule-based, and creative, but the language is never completed.

He said a great German mathematician proved no mathematical system can explain a more expansive mathematical system.

"Our Gabriel is so clever. He told me to visualise a temporal probability rather than the classical atemporal set. The classical set only considers time-stationary elements comprising probabilities within $0 \leq p \leq 1$. If we realise that da Vinci could never invent the aeroplane when he lived, but the Wright brothers did, then possible probabilities change in time. The probability of such an invention for da Vinci was between $-1 < p < 0$, and for the Wrights was $p = 1$. Any probability less than or equal to -1 is impossible for any universe.

"Honey says that the best way to understand the essence of the Source is using a triad, a mathematical point, infinite phase space, and the temporal probability expression. I miss him so much.

"Most theologians cannot understand that sentient creatures, like the Djinn and Humanity, exist to bring nonexistent possibilities into their universes to enrich and further manifest the Divine Plan. Such inflow is evidenced whenever something new and unique occurs.

"Husband taught me every lower form must feed a higher one. The Holy Family feeds plant life through water, air, and minerals. Plants feed animal life, animals feed sentient creatures, and we feed the angelic orders, who feed the Holy Family. The result is the maintenance of the Form of Creation. A system similar to systems found in chemistry and life. Stable, far-from-equilibrium systems evolve to establish complexity and order. This happens because the universe's temperature is cooling as it expands into inactive space.

"Eventually, all available energies for growth are exhausted, the universal temperature drops below absolute zero, and creation is no more.

"There is some support for this thesis. If you remember, Gabriel told us Ahriman the Evil does not live in any universe the Holy Family oversees. Gabriel says Ahriman the Evil exists on the other side of Oblivion. The Oblivion is juxtaposed to Nouseum; Nouseum touches all universes, and the Oblivion touches none. He believes Ahriman the

Evil freed Ahri-Simeon and Ahri-Lilith from the Oblivion. It wants to destroy all the universes before they complete their purpose.

"So Zoroaster, the Persian Messiah, was correct when he introduced Ahriman the Destroyer."

Tears formed in her eyes, but she continued being the trooper she was.

"Gabriel plans to go into and pass through the Oblivion to annihilate this seed. My heart tells me that Ariel will not allow him to go alone, and she will make him take her. But he will not."

Alliona broke down, sobbing uncontrollably and collapsing on the cave floor. Sophie jumped up from her chair, sat down on the stones, and lifted her into her arms, and she began sobbing, too.

Natnael stepped in and did a time lock on everyone but Lydia and Merlin.

Natanel, visibly upset, asked, "Merlin and Lydia, do you know anything about this? You must tell me. I can't lose my beloved; I can't."

Both shook their heads negatively.

Lydia responded, "Nata, Gabriel and I were lovers for many years. We had a baby girl, a pretty baby girl, who Ahriman the Evil smothered in her sleep. I tried to kill myself, but my love for Gabriel was too potent. We searched for the murderer for many years. One day, he located an evil Djinn who had repented many years ago and was now a pope working with lepers and other forsaken Djinn."

"Gabriel told him who he was and how we lost our baby girl?"

The pope fell to his knees before us, saying, "It was I who smothered your sweet child. Nary, a day passes when I do not cry for her. She is why I repented and turned to the Light and the Holy Family for penitence. I know I cannot undo the evil I did, but I can spend the rest of my life helping those in need. If you want to kill me, go ahead, for I do not desire even the life I have."

"I wanted to kill him, but my husband restrained me."

Gabriel said, "Lydia, what has passed cannot come again. Tis better for this Djinn to dedicate his life to those suffering than take our revenge. We must learn to forgive, my love. It is the only way to be free."

The pope stood, saying, "I see I doubled my sin, for I sinned against a Holy Man. I will tell you this, Milord. I did not act on my initiative. Ahri-Simeon told me Ahriman the Evil desired the child's death and you if I could do so. I am sorry, Milord, for the pain I caused you and your wife.

"I know the Great War is coming. I will serve your troops if you take me, for I know herbs and surgery."

Gabriel replied, "It will be as you ask. Serve the Holy Family in love and peace. May they bless you and your good works. Purgatory will give you a second chance.

Merlin said, "I understand. Gabriel has a blood vendetta against an entity with more power than the Holy Family. Gabriel cannot defeat Ahriman the Evil nor pass through the Oblivion unless he has Powers he has never shared with anyone. Powers mightier than those given to the Holy Family. Who is he?"

Natanel said, "There is something within Gabriel I saw once when he was still a boy. He was visiting us, and we four were travelling to a magical conclave. We stopped to camp in a very foreboding place."

Suddenly, Gabriel grabbed Morgana's arm magically and pulled her to me.

He approached something darker than the blackest night, ordering, "Ahriman, I do not allow you in this world. I will tolerate you no more. I order you to return to that place beyond the Oblivion. If you ever return, I will obliterate you as if you never were. Go now."

The Blackness flowed into the ground and vanished.

"Gabriel, what was that thing?"

"Aunt Nata, that was Ahriman the Evil. It does not belong here, so I sent it away."

"Gabriel, how can you send Ahriman the Evil away by command?"

"I don't know, Nata. All I remember is resting in the blackness before I was."

A Voice said, "Come, my love, Mummy needs your help. Take Mummy's hand if you love me."

I took Mummy's hand, and she took me to a light place.

She said, "Husband, whom I love most, become manifest for me and enter this pure womb. One day, you must destroy something that has hurt many universes, a mistake made before Time began. Find your brother and destroy him; his name is Ahriman the Evil. Go, my darling. Mummy will always be near you, so fear not. Be loving with everyone possible, do good works, and be a helper and protector, not a hinderer and harmer. Little One, you are *der Über Gott*. Thousands of kisses."

Then he ran to me, crying and throwing his arms around my waist, saying, "Mummy, where are you. I am afraid, and I need you."

Suddenly, I felt filled with a Great Light and Warmth I had never known since then. A Sweetness was within me.

She said, "Come to Mummy, my beloved. Suckle me and gain more power from me. See, I am always near you. And the breast you are suckling is that of your Auntie Nata. I love her, Morgana, Tristan, and you so very much. You are all part of our family. Enjoy them and protect them, darling. Tristan is the Saviour of this Universe, and you are the Saviour of All."

I nursed Gabriel for a long time.

Eventually, he looked up, smiling, saying, "I love you, Aunt Nata. I truly do. And Mummy loves you too, or she wouldn't have entered you. I feel better when you hold and nurse me."

As I held Gabriel close to my heart, I told Tristan and Morgana. Remember this day, children, and Natanel finished her tale.

Merlin exclaimed, "So, the truth is out. No wonder Gabriel has wed Ariel. He has often told us he is older than everything in this universe and more. He is more ancient than the Holy Family, the First of the Source, and beyond Goodness Itself. More ancient than Ariel and Ahriman the Evil. The situation is worse than I thought."

Lydia suggested, "Natanel, perhaps you can erase this memory from those here today, the students, Alliona, Sophie, and Morgana. It is best for them, for Ahriman the Evil will try to consume them with this."

"Do you agree, Merlin?"

Merlin replied, "Totally, make it so, Natanel."

Alliona and Sophie sat attentively in their chairs.

Lydia said, "Good questions, but we need to stay the course for the moment.

The **third significant difference** between Biblical Dogma and the Djinn Holy Canon concerns our celebration of the original goodness that a newborn creature has when born. We do not acknowledge the existence of an original sin committed by the first man and woman.

"A sin so heinous that the Holy Family would mandate punishment onto all succeeding generations, as stated in the first book of the Jewish Torah arising from the disobedience of a hypothetical Adam and Eve. Specifically, Genesis 3 (Darby Translation),

> *11 And he said, who told thee that thou art naked? Hast, thou ate of the tree of which I commanded thee not to eat?*
>
> *12 And Man said that the woman, whom thou hast given [to be] with me, gave me of the tree, and I ate.* {The only sin committed by Adam was his failure to accept personal responsibility and blame Eve}
>
> *13 And Jehovah Elohim asked the woman, what is it thou hast done? And the woman said, the serpent deceived me, and I ate.* {The sin committed by Eve was her failure to accept personal responsibility and blame the snake.}
>
> *14 And Jehovah Elohim said to the serpent, because thou hast done this, be thou cursed above all cattle and every beast of the field. On thy belly shalt thou eat dust all the days of thy life.*

15 And I will put enmity between thee and the woman, and between thy seed and her seed; he shall crush thy head, and thou shalt crush his heel.

16 To the woman, he said, I will mushroom thy travail and thy pregnancy; with pain, thou shalt bear children; and to thy husband shall be thy desire, and he shall rule over thee.

17 And to Adam he said, because thou hats hearkened to the voice of thy wife, and eaten of the tree of which I commanded thee saying, thou shalt not eat of it: cursed be the ground on thy account; with toil shalt thou eat [of] it all the days of thy life;

18 And thorns and thistles shall it yield thee, and thou shalt eat the herb of the field.

19 In the sweat of thy face shalt thou eat bread until thou return to the ground: for out of it wast thou taken. For dust, thou art; and unto dust shalt thou return.

20 And Man called his wife Eve because she is the mother of all living.

21 And Jehovah Elohim made and clothed Adam and his wife coats of skin.

22 And Jehovah Elohim said, Behold, man is as one of us, to know good and evil. And now, lest he stretches out his hand, take off the tree of life, eat, and live forever!

23 Therefore, Jehovah Elohim sent him forth from Eden's Garden to till the ground from which he came.

24 And he drove out Man, and he set the Cherubim, and the flame of the flashing sword, toward the east of the garden of Eden, to guard the way to the tree of life.

Such sin was reiterated after King David fornicated with Bathsheba in Psalm 51-5, 'Behold, in iniquity, was I brought forth, and in sin did my mother conceive.'

"The Djinn Holy Canon cannot acknowledge the existence of a primordial Garden, as recorded in the written Bereshit or Genesis. The Djinn learn that the evolution of life in our original universe was a product of nature. Combined with an evolutionary imperative instilled within the first living seeds, moving from single cells to consciously aware Djinn. Life was inherently good, as life was the only Path to Integration with the Holy Spirit. Such goodness remains untainted and uncorrupted by natural catastrophes and the usual struggles for survival and reproductive advantage.

"If one reads biblical scripture from an evolutionary standpoint, consistent with the Djinn Canon, the Garden represents the fertile Earth. An excellent habitat providing food and shelter to the many animals living together without the interference of an animal possessing self-awareness and egoism. When self-awareness and narcissism were born, symbolised by the eating of the Apple, an intelligent but unwise creature came into being to disrupt the natural harmony of the living biosphere. Such disruptive behaviour requires expulsion from the bliss of unawareness.

"Expelled or not, the doctrine of original goodness applies each time a child is born into the physical universe. Every healthy baby is born without egoism and self-awareness. A baby cannot be greedy or power-seeking. When they are warm and fed, they sleep with smiles on their faces. When not disturbed, babies are in a calm state of calmness, joy, and contented well-being.

"This inner state of pure joy, simple peace, absolute clarity, and well-beingness, the state of having one's centre in the Kingdom of Heaven Within, Ariel taught to the Djinn and Christ to humanity in Matthew 10 (Darby Translation),

> *13 And they brought little children to him, so he might touch them. But the disciples rebuked those that brought [them].*
>
> *14 But Jesus, seeing [it], was indignant, and said to them, Suffer the little children to come to me; forbid them not; for of such is the kingdom of God.*
>
> *15 Verily I say to you, whosoever shall not receive the kingdom of God as a little child shall never enter it.*
>
> *16 Having taken them in his arms and laid his hands on them, he blessed them.*

"As the Djinn lack a concept of original sin, they did not need to create a story to justify such a false belief. Someone must die so to atone for original disobedience. This tale becomes necessary for humankind after the Jews conspired to kill Christ by crucifixion and blame the Roman authorities.

"As Yeshua spent much of his early life in India studying with the Yogis and Swamis, he could suspend all objective signs of life on the Cross. Reviving his body later. Original Sin and the Resurrection are dangerous dogmas. Plus, humans cannot kill a member of the Holy Family. But that is a story for the future."

The first morning of Magick training finished, and Sophie and Alliona soared in the clouds. The kitchen grannies had cooked a wonderful lunch featuring three kinds of homemade sausage. The sausage came with freshly baked bread, several types of mustard, and scrapped horseradish. A light cucumber salad with onion and radish filled each serving plate.

Eleanor was beaming with childhood pride.

She said to Sophie and Alliona, "Guess what? I helped make the bread. I helped mix the batter and put butter on the outside. I could not use the oven because Granny said I was too small. Do you like our bread, Sophie and Alliona?"

Everyone agreed. The bread was tasty, properly crusted, and the texture perfect.

After lunch, the group returned to the library for more religious lore.

Lydia began, "The Djinn have no necessity to baptise babies as they carry no sin and are born without egoism or greed. The Djinn living under the Holy Family's protection cannot manifest the evils that led to the Great Djinn War. We no longer carry the physical or the psychoistic taints and know factually that Gabriel's Teachings are True.

"We can say we are a new species arising from the flawed one. The human flaw is that it has no conception of the intrinsic value difference between persons capable of bringing the Divine into the world and those who are only the walking dead of the New Testament. We already know the dismal predicament between Gabriel's analysis of humanity and the solution based on our history. Still, we do not know how to implement it. It is a pity."

Sophie noted, "Lydia, how individual, conscious Djinn would work together, intentionally and unbiased, so to discover and accept their genetic flaw is unbelievable. It is even more amazing that such a society would eliminate the defects to benefit all Djinn discovered. Sadly, this would never happen on Earth, for the politicians revel in egoism and greed and would prevent such good works."

Lydia replied, "The human social situation is much more problematic, I am afraid. But I would like to provide the Djinn explanation of why humans believe in original sin. The answer has nothing to do with a mythical Garden created for a unique man and woman to steward. Adam and Eve, the Tree of Knowledge of Good and Evil, the Serpent, the Apple, Disobedience, and constitutional walks with the Holy Father are stories created for political reasons. Nothing more.

"God did not banish Adam and Eve literally from the Garden of Eden, so there was no fall from Grace and Goodness. The actuality is that every child is born into goodness based on genetics. The new baby has no awareness of self versus not-self, cannot reason, cannot recognise feelings, and is functioning at a very primitive level. A newborn is incapable of greed, hate, egoism, like or dislike, or more advanced capabilities. Newborns automatically respond in a manner to appease hunger, cold, heat, fear, or overstimulation. They are like cute puppies.

"However, as the child develops, it differentiates self from not-self, mine from not-mine, how to be pleased, how to manipulate its caregivers. I expect they require this development for a child to develop a working ego and moral standards. They must learn about altruism and egoism, selfishness and charity, justice, mercy, etc.

"But the proper development of the child to become a responsible adult is rare, as social education interferes. A responsible adult has found a method to express more altruism than egoism daily. She has seen the original goodness living within one's being. We do not lose the integrity present in the innocent newborn; adults simply forget it.

They consciously use the ego to empower such original goodness to overcome their tendency for greed, aversion, and egoism.

"A responsible being, which Gabriel and Tristan call a good householder, rediscovers the Kingdom of Heaven and God Within. They function in the ordinary social world using their egos but coexist in the Kingdom Within. Subsequently, their actions are much less harmful to themselves and others.

"The real fall is from goodness into the state of evolutionary egoism and greed. The Esoteric Christian Martinist Orders of Earth describe the Fall as being Lost in the Forest of Errors. It's a somewhat accurate summary, I think.

"Reintegration means that a man or woman becomes conscious of whom and what the creature is. Who and what the kesdjan self is? How do you birth an immortal soul? How do we live as the Holy Family desires? How do you live like a Real Man and a Real Woman?

"It would have been much better if humanity had dispensed with the fabulous and observed the obvious. Such being the position, humanity is asleep and dead. Let me review it so there is no misunderstanding.

"**The first significant difference** is that the original Djinn never compiled a physical book of scriptures. We have no Old Testament, New Testament, or Quran to puzzle whether the words genuinely represent the Holy Family. Instead, as astral engrams, our original Holy Scriptures were directly and indelibly impressed upon the conjoint Djinn Meta Consciousness. No entity can change the syntax and semantics of our astral engrams outside of the Holy Family. As every Djinn of responsible age can read our Holy Canon, none can argue or distort its Sacred Content and Intentions for our race.

"**The second significant difference** between Djinn and Human Christianity. The Law of the Trinity is an operational cut of the underlying Superior Law of the Tetrad. The creation begins with the Creator restricting a portion of Infinite Phase Space to create a transfinite functional space. When I speak of the Tetrad Law, I discuss concepts most difficult for ordinary human reasoning. The higher rationality available understands such only through the Noble Organ.

"Imagine a bipyramid in your mind-space, again, as Gabriel described.

"The Holy Family represents the four divisions of the Divine manifested as the Elohim. The Unfathomable and the Divine Family are *aeternum et omnipraesens*. The Elohim are not God, the Absolute, but are a fourfold division of God's Will. Using terms from the Kabbalah, *Kether* is the spacetime beginning point through which the Elohim manifests our universe via God's Spirit or the Holy Ghost.

"The third significant difference between Biblical Dogma and the Djinn Holy Canon concerns our celebration of the original goodness, the state in which a newborn creature is born. We lack the spiritual concept of the original sin the first man and woman committed.

"Questions, my dearies," asked Lydia?

Sophie asked, "Lydia, much disagreement was present in the early Christian Church for the first 800 years about what made up genuine Christianity. In the early 5th century CE, the British monk Pelagius rejected the concept of original sin. If I remember correctly, this monk taught humans could lead sinless lives as God created. He did not deny that God may help us remain sin-free through His Grace. Human beings can earn salvation through their efforts. I know that the ecumenical council at Ephesus in 431 CE condemned this view.

Lydia responded, "Sophie, you are correct. Let me explain. The Teachings of Pelagius are like those held by the Djinn. We believe that early Christian scripture adequately supports Pelagius's views, and this view should have been Orthodox.

"Within the Gospels, Christ never equates the physical world, matter, or flesh with evil or sin. For example,

John 1:14 And the Word became flesh, and dwelt among us (and we have contemplated his glory, glory as of an only begotten with a father), full of grace and truth;

John 6:51 I am the living bread which has come down from Heaven: if any hath eaten of this bread he shall live forever. Still, the bread withal I shall give is my flesh, which I will provide for the world's life.

John 6:53 Jesus said to them, Verily, verily, I say unto you, unless ye shall have eaten the flesh of the Son of man, and drunk his blood, ye have no life in yourselves.

John 6:54 He that eats my flesh and drinks my blood has life eternal, and I will raise him up on the last day:

John 6:55
My flesh is proper nourishment, and my blood is genuinely drunk.

John 6:56 He that eats my flesh and drinks my blood dwells in me and I in him.

Luke 6:45 The good man, out of the beautiful treasure of his heart, brings forth good; and the wicked [man] out of the wicked brings forth what is wicked: out of the abundance of the heart, his mouth speaks.

Matthew 13:38 And the field is the world; and the good seed, these are the sons of the kingdom, but the darnel are the sons of the evil [one];

"Christ did not teach that the physical body and its characteristics were inherently evil. Based on the psychological and biological understanding of the time, evil and good were not inherent in the physical body but occurred depending on the person's spiritual power. Practising Good was to attune with the Father, and doing evil was to acclimate to Satan as False Egoism.

"However, some church fathers seem to have misunderstood Paul's words in his letters to several churches, as supporting the Hebrew story in Genesis of Adam and Eve. For instance,

> *Romans 8:*
> *2 For the law of the Spirit of life in Christ Jesus has set me free from the law of sin and death.*
>
> *3 For what the law could not do, in that it was weak through the flesh, God, having sent his own Son, in the likeness of flesh of sin, and for sin, has condemned sin in the flesh,*
>
> *4 So that the righteous requirement of the law is fulfilled in us, who do not walk according to the flesh but to the Spirit.*
>
> *Ephesians 6:*
> *12 Because our struggle is not against blood and flesh, but against principalities, against authorities, against the universal lords of this darkness, against spiritual [power] of wickedness in the heavenless.*

"**The fourth significant difference** is that the concept of original sin is not a part of Original Christianity. Original sin is a merging of

Adam and Eve's story with 3rd century Manichaeans supported by St Augustine and other church fathers."

As there were no questions, Lydia continued.

"The fifth significant difference betwixt Original Christianity and Church Dogma concerns the depth of free choice over the moral matters given to man by God.

"The Djinn Holy Canon prevents its adherents from using evolutionary frailty as an excuse for failing to live an authentic Arielian life. The Canon teaches the Djinn to have the freedom of genuine choice in moral matters. A Djinn may harbour the love and wisdom of the Holy Family, or they may want to be a vessel for egoism, greed, and ill-will.

"A Djinn whose will is strong enough can strive toward a sinless life. However, a striver for the Highest Good lives in the heart of the Holy Family, for they will assist when the need for help arises to manifest magnificent work."

"Our Beloved Ariel said, 'Whenever I need to discourse upon the subject of moral instruction and the conduct required to live a life desired by the Holy Family, it is my practise to show by stories and parables the splendid power and quality of the Djinn nature. In such words, I nourish the hope and efforts of my children to achieve the holy life. By demonstrating the consequences of worshipping one or more virtues and vices upon themselves and the Djinn.; they follow the path of righteousness most faithfully because we have hope as our guide and compassion.'

"It is the wish of the Holy Family to bestow into the rational creature the gift of doing Good by their own free will through using the capacity to exercise free choice. The Holy Family created the Djinn so they could choose how to use Love, the food of desire, good or evil, altruism or egoism, charity or greed, mercy or hate, and so on. One could not claim to possess the good of one's own volition unless one also has evil whims. Our most excellent creators wished us to do only one, the highest good.

"The Holy Family detests determinism, for what good is a creature who must follow unshakeable dictate. Instead, creating a hazardous and open-ended universe is better, allowing the design to evolve the desired individuality and love.

"The Holy Family asks nothing impossible. The Holy Family teaches us not to indulge in pointless evasions, advancing the frailty of our nature as an objection to the Ones who command us? No one knows the accurate measure of our strength better than those who gave it to us. Nor does anyone understand better how much we can do than those who gifted us this capacity. Nor have they commanded anything impossible or intended to condemn a man for doing what he could not avoid doing.

"When will a man guilty of a crime or sin accept with a tranquil mind that his wickedness is a product of his own will alone? And not of necessity, and admit his error by accepting what he now strives to attribute to nature to his free choice? It affords endless comfort to the divine law's transgressors, believing that their failure to do something is because of inability rather than disinclination. They understand from their natural wisdom that they judge no one for failing to do the impossible.

"Under this plea, it is impossible not to sin. Believers develop a false sense of security in sin. Anyone who hears that he can't be without sin will not even try to be what he considers impossible. The man who tries to be without sin must perforce sin all the time and even boldly because he enjoys the false security of believing that he will sin.

"But if he were to hear the possibility of not sinning, he would exert himself to fulfil what he now knows to be possible. So, he strives to accomplish it, to achieve his purpose, even if not entirely.

"Ariel brought us, Mercy. Let us be merciful to all. So Be It Truly.

"**The fifth significant difference** was taught by the wisest of humans before the corruptions of St. Augustine, for instance,

> *Justin Martyr said, "Every created being is made up to be capable of vice and virtue. He could do nothing praiseworthy if he had no power to turn either way.*
>
> *Theophilus said, "If he turned to the things of death, disobeying God, he would cause death to himself. For God made man free, and with the power of himself."*
>
> *Irenaeus said, "But man, being endowed with reason, and in this respect similar to God, having freedom in his will, and with power over himself, is himself his own cause that sometimes he becomes wheat, and sometimes chaff."*
>
> *Clement of Alexandria said, "We have believed and are saved by voluntary choice."*

"The only reason St. Augustine and the ecumenical councils declared this teaching heretical was that it would diminish the Church's social control over the laity and allow them to compete with the warrior nobility. The Church stopped caring about the Teachings of Christ before 300 CE.

"The Genuine Teachings of True and Original Christianity are given to every race resident in every quadrant of the Creation when such a race is ready. Sometimes, the Teachings' name is unfamiliar, but what is true never varies, though often contaminated. I shall now tell you of eight sound arguments of Pelagius as to free choice on moral matters."

> *1. Now, we have implanted in us by God a capacity for either part. It resembles, as I may say, a fruitful and fecund root that yields and produces diversely according*

to the will of man and is capable, at the planter's own choice, of shedding a beautiful bloom of virtues or of bristling with the thorny thickets of vices. (Book 1)

2. We distinguish three things, arranging them in a specific graduated order. We put in the first-place ability, the second volition, and the third actuality. Ability we place in our nature, volition in our will, and actuality in effect. The first, the 'ability,' properly belongs to God, who has bestowed it on His creature; the other two, the 'volition' and the 'actuality,' must refer to man because they flow forth from the fountain of the will.

God alone says that a man can will and effect any excellent work. Therefore, for his willing and doing excellent work, the praise belongs to man, or preferably both to man and to God, who has given him the capacity for his will and work, and who evermore by the help of His grace assists even this capacity. This faculty can exist even when the other two have no being, but the latter cannot exist without the former.

I am, therefore, free not to have good volition or action, but I cannot have good capacity. This capacity is inherent in me, whether I will nor does nature receive at this point freedom for itself.

The meaning of all this will be made explicit by an example or two. That we can see with our eyes is not of us, but it is our own that we make good or bad use of our eyes. So again (that I may, by applying a general case in illustration, embrace all), that we can do, say, and think any good thing comes from Him who has endowed us with this ability and who also assists this ability, but that we really do a good thing, or speak a kind word, or think a good thought, proceeds from our own selves because we can also turn all these into evil and this is a point which needs frequent repetition because you calumniate us.

Whenever we say a man can live without sin, we also give praise to God by our acknowledgement of the capacity which we have received from Him, who has given such 'ability' to us. There is no occasion for praising the human agent since it is God's matter alone that is, for the moment, treated of, for the question is not about willing or effecting but solely about that which may be (Book 3).

Very ignorant persons suppose us to do wrong in this matter to divine grace because we say that it perfects not the sanctity in us without our will—as if God could have imposed any command on His grace without also supplying the help of His grace to those on whom he charged His commands so that men might more easily accomplish through grace what is challenging to do by their free will. And this grace we do not, as you suppose, allow consisting merely in the law but also in the help of God.

God helps us by His teaching and revelation, while He opens the eyes of our heart; while He points out to us the future, that it may not absorb us in the present; while He discovers to us the snares of the devil; while He enlightens us with the manifold and ineffable gift of Heavenly grace. Does the man who says all this appear to you to be a denier of grace? Does he not acknowledge both man's free will and God's grace?

7. Whosoever rightly uses this [freedom of the will] does so entirely surrender himself to God and so wholly mortifies his own will that he can say with the apostle. It is already of Him that live, but Christ liveth in me. He placeth his

heart in the Hand of God, so He turneth it whithersoever He willeth.

8. That we can do good is of God, but we do it of ourselves.

9. We can use a speech from God, but we make this fair use of speech proceeds from ourselves.

10. That we can think a good thought comes from God, but that we deem an excellent thought proceeds from ourselves.

12. We have a firm and steadfast will against sinning, which our Maker has implanted in human nature. Still, by His unspeakable goodness, we are defended by His daily help. (Book 1)

13. God sends Grace so that men may more easily accomplish by grace what we command them to do by free will.

"As to the Trinity of Father, Son, and Holy Ghost, Gabriel explained the Djinn position to Sophie. Alliona learned these growing up, which is sufficient instruction for this moment. Questions?"

Alliona asked, "Lydia, I know why the Great Djinn War happened, for we celebrate it during the Resurrection Holidays. But why did the Djinn forget about reading the Holy Canon after Gabriel saved our race from extinction?"

"Honey, that is a question our forefathers and foremothers often asked. Our theologians and philosophers have pondered and discussed without an adequate answer for thousands of years. One day, a young Djinn asked Gabriel this question. The young Djinn later told us that

Gabriel had a delicious laugh when he heard of the bickering and division this controversy created.

"Gabriel said, why didn't someone ask me earlier. It would have been much more convenient."

"Gabriel explained how the Djinn lost contact with the Higher Realms of our Meta Consciousness after their kesdjan bodies separated from their physical bodies. This separation caused a muddiness in the conjoint Djinn Mind, so no one could read the Holy Canon after the original Djinn universe collapsed.

"So, our theologians opened a great conference, or ecumenical synod, at which it assigned each attendee to transcribe the Holy Canon from personal memory onto paper. After seventy days, all the attendees returned with personal remembrances of the Holy Canon and left them with the Hierophants.

"The Hierophants provided all copies to a committee of seventy most learned and unbiased theologians. The texts dispersed some 490 copies to the committee of seventy. Each committee member read their copies to reconstruct the Holy Canon most reasonably. By reasonable, they meant the most common understanding of each verse of the Holy Canons. After the seventy finished, they dispersed the seventy abstracted representations evenly to seven committee members chosen by lot to create the Holy Canon's seven final compilations.

"Following the last task, all the attendees gathered to vote upon which chapter the best recited in the seven final compilations. Some arguments arose, but most attendees approved a final version of the written Holy Canon. It was a forced vote, as none of the original versions could enter the controversy.

"However, as the Djinn exhibited signs of egoism and desire to be correct, controversy over the proper wording and meanings of the Holy Canons became apparent. This controversy became fuel for causing division in the Djinn. Resulting in the Great War.

"The Djinn's inability to read the Holy Canon in its pristine form had to wait for correction until Ariel restored It into the new Djinn conjoint mind. But this knowledge is restricted and not given to the Djinn who serve Heaven nor those who serve Hell."

Merlin said, "Enough religion. We have much work to do to prepare Camelot for the battles ahead. So, we must contribute our hands and minds beginning tomorrow. Nata, you must introduce Lydia, Alliona, and Sophie to Jamus and Molly. We must be diligent in getting them up to speed in magick."

The group disbanded for a break before dinner. Vika and Calliope came up to Alliona and Sophie.

Vika said, "Calliope and I are so glad we can spend time with you. We are silly girls, but we are faithful friends. We are fun to be with and can show you many good things to do in Camelot."

Alliona responded, "Sophie and I enjoyed meeting you when you came to our wedding. We know little magick or anything about running a war, so we feel useless, Vika. It would be nice to spend time with both of you."

Calliope asked, "Did you like making love with Vika and me? We adored making love with you."

Vika interjected, "Calliope, just tell them, or do I have to?"

"Vika wants me to tell you we are in love with both of you and want you to live with us when Daddy and Gabriel are in Nouseum. None of us have our husbands to relieve us when our arousal is upon us. Right, Vika?"

"Correct, Calliope, my precious love. We really love you, and it would break our hearts if you didn't love us. Right, Calliope?"

"Right, Honey. We love you, Alliona and Sophie, so much. I get so hot around you, and I am wet now. Are you two wet, like Vika and me?"

Sophie replied, "Alliona and I love you as well. I am so wet right now, and I want you to spread my legs for your sweet tongues. Right, Alliona?"

"Right, Sophie, I am so hungry now. We want to live with you two until our husband returns?"

Calliope said, "We have another sister who lives with us. She is brilliant and not silly, and we love her, for she is so kind and smart like Daddy. We make love with her, too. Her name is Chatelaine."

"Calliope, aren't you forgetting someone essential in Camelot?"

"Vika takes good care of me when I get too excited to remember things. This is another reason I love her as high as anything can go. I am excited now, and Vika is helping me. Vika says we must ask Mummy if it is okay, for we are good girls and always listen to Daddy and Mummy. Our Mummy is Natanel, in case you forgot. Maybe your memories forget themselves when you are excited. I think I might come in a moment if someone like my Sophie rubs my clitoris."

"Of course, I will rub your clitoris, for you have a nice one."

As the room was empty of anyone but the girls, Sophie had Calliope lie back in a chair, pull up her dress, and allow Sophie to make her come. When Calliope came, she covered her mouth so not to make noise. Then Sophie serviced Vika and Alliona, and Vika returned the favour to Sophie.

Vika said, "Now we need to go find Mummy. She will know we had female lovemaking but will be happy for everyone."

The twins took Sophie and Alliona by the hand and walked to their room to get Mummy's permission to have more sisters. She was sitting by a fireplace translating some more of the Elf Codex. The twins ran to hug and kiss her. Nata hugged and kissed them, followed by many love you(s).

Natanel told Alliona and Sophie, "I know you are newlyweds and should be with your husband and not here with us. But such cannot be, so you shall make the most of this separation. Merlin and I will teach you magick and how to fight as sorceresses, so your vigil here will be valuable for the cause. I know you feel useless now, but you find that being with us in Camelot is a special time in your lives.

"My daughters adore both of you and want me to fix your pasts. Right, my darlings?"

"Sophie told us when we visited for the wonderful wedding that she had a terrible childhood. Unlike the childhood Calliope and I suffered before you became our real Mummy, she suffered neglect and loneliness because no one loved her. But now we all love her because she is so sweet and smart. Right, Calliope?"

"Right, my darling. Lydia is wonderful but not motherly. Alliona's mummy died in the Djinn Wars, and she lived with Lydia. Alliona needs mothering every day as we do, Mummy."

Sophie asked, "How do you know about our childhoods? We never told them to you."

Calliope answered, "Vika and I are oracles, and we talk to Holy Mother. We love her so much, and Holy Mother asked us to love you and be like sisters. Right, Vika?"

"What my hot sister says is true. We want you to be happy like we are. Daddy and Mummy fixed us, so we never felt unloved or not wanted. Mummy can do the same for you."

"Vika, tell them the Elf Codex mentions them. The Codex says Mummy has six daughters to form a Hexagram with Mummy in the middle. So, they are our sisters and lovers."

"Calliope, you are too excited, honey. Why do I need to tell them, as you just did? I have such a silly sister, but she is the best sister in the world," as Vika went to hug and kiss her.

Alliona asked, "Natanel, what is the Elf Codex, and why do the twins think it mentions us?"

"The Elf Codex reveals the future concerning the Great War against Ahriman the Evil. It mentions my six daughters who become powerful sorceresses: Morgana, Calliope, Vika, Chatelaine, and my two youngest. One is a beautiful Djinn, and the other is a human. Gabriel never told you?"

"There seem to be many things; Husband didn't tell us, Nata. Why is he so secretive?" asked Sophie?

"Sweetheart, Gabriel works in our universe's greatest octave, and I imagine others. Child, Gabriel is God and writes our destinies with his Mother, Space. Therefore, he only shares information when necessary to avoid disrupting the flow of events. However, he changes worldlines as soon as necessary."

"Nata, Husband is God? Why did he marry Alliona and me? I am so confused," replied Sophie.

"Come, Sophie, and sit in my lap. You need to be loved now and not later."

Sophie went to sit with Nata, and she began crying. Nata untied her blouse and offered her nipple to Sophie to suckle.

"That's right, honey. Drink Mummy's warm milk. You will feel safe and loved again. Gabriel loves both of you and married you because of his love. Everything Gabriel does is for the good of all sentient beings. We may not always understand his actions, but their motivation is based on his love for everything.

"Sometimes Mother Space visits my twins. She loves them because their hearts know only pure love. They are the oracles Mother Space brought into existence for the end times. They are like you two. You will always be fifteen-year-old Immortals, for this is what Gabriel and his Sister-Wife-Mother decided before time was.

"Sophie, how is my precious daughter now?"

"I feel much better, Mummy. Alliona will understand after you nurse her. Alliona, Nata, is our true mummy; she will carry and bear us in her womb. Tristan will be our father. Come, drink Mummy's milk, and you will understand."

Alliona exchanged places with Sophie, and Nata nursed her.

Sophie went and hugged the twins, saying, "We are sisters! I am so glad, and we can also make love with Mummy. I have an actual family at last that loves and needs me."

After Natanel finished nursing, she chanted a long spell in Enochian. Sophie and Alliona remembered being in Nata's womb as fraternal twins, their delivery, how the twins held them, telling them they loved them so much and growing up with them, Morgana, and Chatelaine. The memories defied all logic; still, they felt Tristan and Nata were their actual parents. Welcome to the family, Sisters.

Chatelaine entered the room, saying, "I see the prophecies of the Elf Codex are completed. I am the intellectual sister of the bunch. Morgana is the emotional sister, and my little sisters, the twins, are just silly, and I love them so."

Chatelaine began chasing the twins around and would tickle one when she caught one. The twins loved the game, which continued until Chatelaine made them wet themselves. Then they tickled Chatelaine until she wet herself, too.

"That is enough, my beautiful girls. Take off your wet dresses and climb into our toasty bathing pool, and I will wash you. If you want Mummy to please you, raise your hand."

All three raised an arm, removed their smocks, and climbed into the bath.

Turning to Sophie and Alliona, "Come, my babies and Mummy will wash and please you too. You have such pretty clitorises and are so big when hard."

Alliona and Sophie removed their dresses and bathed with the others. Mummy washed and pleased them all.

When the ladies finished dressing, they went to the dining room; it was time for dinner. Already seated were Morgana, Merlin, and Lydia. Tristan's other wives and male students were with him in Nouseum training for the army.

After everyone sat, Merlin said, "Well, it will be relatively quiet here with most of our family in Nouseum. I know everyone misses them, and well, at least I do. Still, Natanel, Morgana, and I will keep you busy learning magick and introducing Nata's new babies to Camelot's townsfolk and King Arthur.

"Chatelaine, I remember holding them after birth, and both wanted to pull my beard. I expect you to ensure the twins do not get their little sisters in trouble."

"Uncle Merlin, we know how to care for our little sisters. We really do. Right, Vika?"

"Right, Calliope. Mummy, we must go to Aunt Julia's fashion store tomorrow to buy them pretty clothes and shoes. We want to invite Annie, her sisters, Ingrid, and Vivian to a high tea soon at our house. They have never visited us, and our Victorian Etiquette books say that we must dress properly as young ladies of good breeding."

"Who else are you going to invite, daughters?"

"I think we shall invite Jamus, Molly, Julia, Lydia, Baron Ivan, and Uncle Arthur to a tea party with Merlin, Morgana, and you. A big person's high tea and a girl's high tea. Of course, Chatelaine will be at our tea party, for she remembers how to be a teenager still," answered Calliope, looking at Vika to ensure everything was correct.

Nata asked, "What do you think, Merlin? Can we invite our friends to high tea at our house? I am sure my daughters will help the kitchen grannies dust and clean. Right, girls?"

The twins and the babies, Sophie and Alliona, said, "Please, pretty please, Uncle Merlin. We know how to clean and want our friends to visit our home for a change. Plus, we imagine the townsfolk have always been curious about where Uncle Merlin lives."

"Nata, how the twins and the babies can talk in unison is a mystery to me. But they are correct. It is time to invite some of our friends to our house."

The twins and the babies left their seats to hug and kiss Uncle Merlin.

Nata laughed, "Just like the old days when I was young, eh, Merlin. You have a soft heart, as does Arthur, and I see why you two are friends. Girls, Uncle Merlin will help you create wonderful invitations for our guests after dinner. Now sit down as dinner is about to be served."

Morgana and Lydia sat next to Merlin at one end of the table. The twins sat next to Morgana and Chatelain next to Lydia. Alliona sat to Nata's left, and Sophie sat to her right as she faced Merlin at the other end of the table.

After a superb meal, Merlin took everyone to his library with its Table Round. Everyone created a wonderful invitation for High Tea on a Saturday afternoon in two weeks. After they finished, he asked his messenger elementals to deliver them.

Tristan returned to Camelot to see his new daughters.

Alliona and Sophie are the babies because they are the youngest sisters. They change back into babies after the sun sets on Tuesdays and begins rising on Fridays. Nata and the twins can play with them, bathe them, nurse them, and put them to bed in their little cribs. The three of them have a strong maternal instinct. They wanted to keep them as babies, for they were so cute and precious after birth.

Chatelaine once asked Tristan at a family dinner, "Husband, when you changed history, so Mummy gave me birth, and you became my daddy; how did you make this change without disrupting the universal worldline? An interesting physics question."

Tristan momentarily thought, "Daughter, your question is most interesting. I have never taken the time to wrestle with it until you asked. And because you asked, I have the answer. Well, it is difficult to have an answer if you cannot posit a question."

"The worldlines connecting the beginning to the end are not infinite, but transfinite. By transfinite, I mean that the number is so large that no one can differentiate and count them during the life of anyone's universe. These lines are not actual quiescent lines existing in physical spacetime but imaginary ones functioning in the mathematician's phase space. In quantum mechanics, mathematical calculations deal with spatial and momentum vectors rather than spatial coordinates and time.

"When Nata wanted to become your factual mother, I had to access all your past actualised worldlines. This was relatively easy since there is only one looking back. But there are a transfinite number of nearly identical worldlines for your future. What I did was to untie the information knots in your past and then retie them, making Nata your actual mummy when you were born. Then I choose the worldlines. I cannot erase your memories fully, but you don't care about them anymore, for they are like dream fragments. I needed to give you a new history of living with our family.

"Because Gabriel is the eternal spouse of Mother Space, creation required that He, as energy and awareness, impregnate her to be born as Mother Space's Son, Gabriel. Mother Spacetime desired her husband's embrace; she manifested his sister Ariel for Gabriel to love and impregnate. She also manifested a brother to help with the universe's physical evolution. But, he was imperfect and became Ahriman the Evil.

"This is why we know Gabriel is the God of all universes. He is the best God, for he loves all of us and works for our benefit. But remember, as he has assumed physical form, he cannot calculate the exact outcome for any universe. Does this help, Chatelaine?"

"It does, Husband. But this raises a second question about Sophie and Alliona, our babies, whom we love to nurse and mother. How can they change to babies on certain nights of the week or when we want to love them as mummies? Why do we want our sisters to be babies for us to cherish? Did they want this to happen unconsciously?"

"If you remember, I was absent when Nata reformed their worldline to have her become their mother.

"Darling, not only did Sophie and Alliona want to stay babies, but Nata, you, and the twins wanted them to remain as babies. Your shared desire was not conscious to any of you, but it affected the outcome. Nata worried about having more babies after the twins' births and yours. So, I am afraid Nata's and your combined desires manifested a most unusual worldline for our family.

"I can't correct it as Nata is my sister, just as Ariel is Gabriel's sister. However, I do not think the babies will be babies if they are away from the family."

Before this moment, Nata had allowed the twins to hold a baby in each lap and nurse them. Because Mummy was crying, the twins and the babies started crying. When Tristan finished, Nata cried desolately, for she feared Tristan was unhappy with her, which he was not.

Tristan and Lydia retrieved the babies from Vika and Calliope and bounced them until they stopped crying.

"Now, now, Sister. Why are you crying over what happened? I understand you wanted to love a set of babies in real time. All of you got what you desired, immortal part-time babies to cherish and care for. Sophie and Alliona possessed personas who needed to remain babies to feel wanted and loved. The twins wanted little sisters to love and care for, as they wanted them to grow up happy and fulfilled. Nata, you want to be a mother in so many ways forever because your nature is such. It would be unfair to keep an Immortal immature forever, so you need an alternative that you have.

"Why do all of you believe I will be angry with my wives and babies and send you away? We need to get rid of this worry, finally. My Love is always, so let it go. I love all of you eternally. All is well."

Merlin silently intoned a magical spell to calm the ladies. And everyone was okay.

Merlin said, "I suggest going to bed early, for we will be at breakfast at our usual sunrise time. Goodnight, everyone. Pleasant dreams."

The magical candelabras appeared and guided each to his bed. Tristan went to sleep with Morgana and Chatelaine. Nata, the twins, and the babies went to their room.

Calliope asked, "Mummy can the babies sleep in our arms tonight, so they know we love them. We will be careful with them. When they suckle us, we love them so fully? I had a milk orgasm the other day. Why don't they remember being our babies as teenagers, like Vika and me?"

"Honey, your sisters are too young to have conscious memories of us when they are babies. But it makes them feel happy and safe when we nurse and play with them. Haven't you noticed how much they love and count on you? They seem normal to everyone else, but they like to be near you. At some level, they think you are their mummies, too."

"See, Calliope, once again, Mummy proves how smart she is and why we must always listen to her. But before we sleep with our babies, we need to please Mummy, for her pheromone levels are elevated, not to forget it arouses both of us. Funny, you are not confused tonight, though."

"Thanks, Vika. Mummy, why does it feel like Sophie and Alliona came out of my womb? I made them with Daddy and bore them like you do."

"I feel the same, Calliope, but only when they are babies and not our sisters. Maybe oracles cannot have physical babies, and our babies are spiritual babies? I don't feel pregnant anymore, do you, honey?"

"Now that you mention it, love of my life, Vika, it is the same for me. We delivered our babies when Mummy made the physical bodies for our sisters. Hooray, we are real mummies, Vika, like our Mummy. I love our twins so much, don't you, Vika?"

"I love them so much, Calliope, that I want to make love to you for helping make them. You are the best sister in the world."

The twins jumped up and down with joy and hugged Mummy. Nata thought about it momentarily as she realised how intuitive her oracle daughters were. It must be true, for they never looked like they were physically pregnant, like Tristan's other wives.

"Well, my little oracles. I guess you are genuine mothers, just like your mummy, and it will delight Daddy when we tell him. It makes sense that both of you would deliver the same twins as you are one."

Nata hugged her unusual daughters.

Then Vika asked, "Mummy, what happens when Uncle Gabriel takes grown-up Sophie and Alliona away? We will lose our little girls, right?"

"You won't lose them, my loves. They will always be your children, and they will be babies again when they visit. Best I can do, I am afraid."

"I know how to fix it, Vika and Mummy. We can separate the baby twins from the grown-up twins. Then, Mummy and us will always have our babies, but we didn't interfere with their grown-up lives. They won't have physical bodies, but they will live in Camelot with us and never grow up. Mummy can do this, right, Mummy?"

"My silly little Calliope is as smart as Father and Uncle Gabriel. I am so proud of both of you. Come and hug Mummy and show her how much you love her."

The twins hugged and kissed Mummy.

"Should we split them now or later, girls?"

Calliope thought momentarily, "We can tell Sophie and Alliona that our babies were them when they were young, but they won't grow up. We loved our new sisters so much; Mummy made them our babies, too. Mummy can cast a spell, making everything make sense."

"Hey, Calliope, if Mummy makes them our babies, Mummy will become a Grand Mummy, sweet. Mummy always wanted to be a Grand Mummy, and we did it first, Calliope. We are getting good at magick. Right, sweetheart?"

"Right, Vika."

And so it came to be. Some weeks passed.

Chapter 19

Camelot

ata and the twins arrived at breakfast with their newborns one auspicious morning. For convenience, Calliope took Sophie, and Vika took Alliona. Still, they occasionally exchanged them to not favour one baby over the other.

The other family members were already sitting, waiting for breakfast, and drinking hot, sweetened tea with heavy cream. When Nata and her twins arrived, the jaws of Merlin, Morgana, Lydia, Sophie, and Alliona dropped. They surprised Sophie and Alliona, who didn't know about the babies. It surprised Merlin, Morgana, and Lydia because they had never seen Sophie and Alliona present as babies when they were nearly adults.

Nata laughed at everyone's bewilderment, saying, "Sophie and Alliona, allow me to introduce you to yourselves as little babies. I was so happy and proud to deliver my babies. But your sisters, the twins, also birthed you as fraternal twins. I bore the physical you, and Calliope and Vika bore the aphysical you.

"I know you cannot remember, but some days you were babies and some days young girls. The twins love you so much that they thought they would die from grief when you left Camelot. So, we split your baby forms from your current teenage ones so the twins could love and care for your baby forms.

"Don't worry. You do not need the babies anymore, so all is well. It turns out that the twins were only pregnant in the aphysical, explaining why they never showed their pregnancies. In hindsight, all turned out as Tristan and Gabriel wanted, and all seems well now."

Calliope asked, "Sophie and Alliona, would you like to hold yourselves?"

Alliona looked at Sophie, and they opened their arms for the two babies.

Vika said, "You can nurse our babies, and it is so unique for you to feed yourselves. Mummy gave you milk, so try it and feel how much love the babies and you will share."

Both Sophie and Alliona undid their blouses and began nursing themselves. It took only about a minute before both experienced a delightful milk organism, and neither cared who was watching. There are no words to describe their joy.

When both were satisfied, Calliope and Vika took back their babies and nursed them while the kitchen grannies served breakfast.

Lydia was the first to comment, "I have come across many unique happenings in my life, but this one is difficult to grasp. Calliope, give my granddaughters to me to nurse so I can bond with them properly, please."

Lydia nursed both and had milk orgasms, saying, "One is Alliona and the other by default, Sophie. I see they love Great-Granny's milk already. We have fine girls here."

Nata said, "Now that everything is back to normal, at least average for us, I propose we all go to Camelot this morning. The twins, both sets of babies, and I can take the carriage to Julia's and surprise Ingrid and Vivian with some new friends. Arthur and I have been visiting more often to play chess. His castle is full of joy, especially when the twins visit. I think he loves you two as much as his daughters. I am sure he will dote over the babies, in baby and adult forms.

Merlin replied, "Morgana and I will travel to the Rugby game in my cart. I have some new potions for Jamus and must deliver some herbals to the apothecaries. Then we can go on our errands.

"Nata, you will bring Lydia to get a new dress and introduce her to Arthur. I think a quieted-down Lydia would make for a good queen."

Morgana exclaimed, "Merlin, you arranged a luncheon date with Lydia and Arthur? Are you insane?"

"I do not think my sanity is at issue here, Morgana. Before Tristan and Gabriel left, they cast a potent spell over her to behave more rationally in society. Gabriel is sure her behaviour results from being with him as a single wife and having her baby smothered long ago. So, he made love to her, and she feels secure and loved as his only love. So, she is ready to move on and start dating, and I think the two of them may like each other.

Morgana has a meeting at the Sleeping Dragon Inn with her new social group, Ladies for Gender Equality, to produce a good constitution and mission statement.

Morgana said, "Lydia, I hope you like him and he proposes. It is time for you to remarry and have a baby again."

After breakfast, Merlin's handymen elementals loaded his horse-driven cart with sample casks of his new potions. Merlin and Morgana climbed aboard and left for Camelot.

The rest left in the big carriage and headed to Julia's store. Sophie and Alliona are still confused about the whole situation. The twins held their babies securely and were so proud to be mothers. Silly but good mummies. Grandmother Nata oversaw them to be sure.

Nata, Lydia, Sophie, and Alliona entered the shop first. Nata introduced Sophie and Alliona as her two youngest daughters, who had studied abroad for two years. She introduced Lydia as her favourite cousin.

Then, the twins came in proudly carrying their newborns.

Vika said, "Aunt Julia, Calliope and I had our babies. We named them after our sisters, Sophie and Alliona, because we love them. We took excellent care of them growing up, for Mummy taught us to be good mothers. Right, Mummy."

"Right, Vika and Calliope."

Aunt Julia and her staff surrounded the twins, talking about the newborns. The twins allowed everyone to hold and kiss them.

Calliope said, "Look how happy they are in your shop, Aunt Julia. They must like your designs already, and I think they love you and your girls?"

"What a sweet thing to say, Calliope. I love you and Vika very much and need hugs and kisses for your old Auntie."

Calliope and Vika hugged and kissed Julia, saying in unison, "You're not old, Julia. You are perfect and always nice and pretty. We love you all the way to heaven, Right, Vika."

"Maybe a little higher, my beautiful sister."

Calliope and Vika started to giggle, and Julia and her girls did not know why. All loved both, even with their eccentricities as oracles.

Nata entered the conversation.

"Julia, I need a dress for Lydia today, for we have a luncheon date with Arthur and his twins. Merlin thinks Lydia is the perfect partner for Arthur, so we introduce them today as another surprise. He adores my twins, for they took away his depression. Ingrid and Vivian feel like sisters to them. None of them knows about our newborns, so it will go nicely.

"Therefore, I need the perfect dress for my cousin to appeal to Arthur. Isn't Lydia beautiful and elegant, Julia?"

"Lydia has a certain style, which I think Arthur will like. I hope it works for all of Camelot loves Arthur and wants to see him married and happy again."

"Also, my youngest daughters need wardrobes for the current season, so they need a dress for today and more clothes for later. Can we do this, Julia? I can use some magick if we need to."

Julia replied, "I have three perfect designs to see how they work. Lorelei, honey, please get my sketchbook for me."

"Yes, Mum," hurrying to get the sketchbook.

Julia's designs were perfect, and Nata manifested them with magick for Lydia and the youngest. They looked elegant.

The family departed the shop, and the carriage brought them to the castle. After leaving the carriage, a page took them to Arthur's library, and Arthur and his twins were waiting for them.

As soon as they entered the room, Ingrid and Vivian ran to the twins.

Ingrid turned to her father, asking, "Daddy, our twins had their babies. Newborns are so beautiful. Can Vivian and I hold them? I think as best friends, we can be their mothers also?"

Calliope answered, "Great ideas. Now, our little angels will have four mummies to love them. Right, Vika."

"A great idea, my genius sister. And Uncle Arthur can love them like a daddy. Right, Ingrid?"

"Right, Vika and Vivian. I like this idea, for Daddy needs more girls to protect and love. Our cousins are more like our sisters; we love them like sisters. So, maybe Daddy will have to be like a grandfather to our babies and a daddy to Vika and Calliope."

Both sets of twins surrounded Arthur, begging to make Vika and Calliope honorary sisters and the babies honorary granddaughters.

Arthur looked at Nata in bewilderment.

Nata replied, "Tristan won't mind, Arthur. It will be good for you."

Calliope held up Sophie, "Here, honorary daddy, hold and kiss your granddaughter. As an oracle, I know she loves you and needs your love as much."

Arthur took little Sophie in his arms, being careful, for he had not held a baby in a long time. Sophie smiled and made a little giggle for Arthur. Tears started flowing down Arthur's cheeks, for he could feel that Sophie loved and needed him, and he hadn't felt needed for a long time. He handed Sophie to Nata, and Lydia gave him a handkerchief to wipe his eyes.

"Here, use this to wipe your eyes, Arthur. I am Nata's cousin Lydia, and you will marry me someday. Time somebody your age took care of you."

"Thank you, Lydia. You are a confident lady, elegant, I might add. Come everyone, let us have lunch like a proper family. And that is an official order of your king."

Lydia placed her arm in Arthurs's, and everyone headed to the dining room.

Nata whispered to her youngest, "It has been a strange night and day, my perfect daughters. The deep magick is about us. If I had to guess, Ariel has rearranged everything for a good reason?"

Nata heard a sweet female laugh in her mind.

"Nata, it was me, for I want all of you to be happy and fulfilled. All of you are important, so I watch over you, too. I love you, Nata. We are related, my love, but you will need to guess how?"

The luncheon went very well. Lydia charmed Arthur without overdoing it. It seems she likes him. Arthur agreed to become a second father to the twins and a grandfather to their babies, place them under royal protection and make them princesses. The two pairs of twins could finally be proper sisters. Ingrid and Vivian had told Calliope and Vika how much they loved them many times. They truly wanted to stay fifteen-year-olds, so they would always be silly together.

Arthur and Lydia stayed to chat. Ingrid and Vivian took Nata and their new sisters to their rooms to play mummy with the babies. Nata watched them play. They were so happy being together. Nata could see that the two sets of twins had bonded strongly.

During a quiet moment, Nata asked, "Ingrid and Vivian, do you want to be sisters with Vika and Calliope forever?"

Both said, "Aunt Nata, we love your twins so much that we might die if we had to part company. We never knew our mummy, but we love you as our mummy. Calliope told us you could become our genuine mother by magick, and then we would have a proper mother. We don't need to tell Daddy all the details, do we?"

"Children, if I used magick to make you my daughters, so you and my twins were your actual sisters, you might have to marry Lord Tristan? How would you feel about this?"

Vivian replied, "Ingrid and I can marry Lord Tristan and have real babies. I love him already. Sometimes, Ingrid and I pretend we married him. Sometimes, we pretend we married Gabriel, too. Right, Ingrid."

"Right, Vivian. If we married Tristan, I think Daddy would be happy for us. Daddy loves Lord Tristan as an uncle."

"Vivian, why do you and Ingrid pretend you married Gabriel?"

"I don't know, Mummy. Calliope told us this one day when we met Gabriel. He is so nice and handsome, and Ingrid got wet."

"If Calliope told you, perhaps Gabriel wants to marry you and give you babies?

"I tell you what I will do, girls. We will ask Gabriel to marry you after your father agrees to marry Lydia. He will happily have you two with babies to protect and love. So, we must be patient for a little while till your father falls in love with Lydia. If the marriage is good, I will give your father a long life like Lydia's, so he can live with us almost forever.

All the twins hugged and kissed Nata. Then, it was time to feed the babies, and Ingrid and Vivian helped with the nursing.

Nata thought to herself, "They belong together."

When it was time to leave, Vivian asked Arthur, "We love Aunt Nata as much as we love you, Daddy. Would we displease you if we called her mummy?"

Arthur felt the future held a new life for him, saying, "I do not think your birth mother would mind. You may call Nata mummy if it makes you happy. She is the best mummy in all of Camelot and likely in all the world, and we will consider her the Royal Mummy of Camelot, as she is like a mother to our city."

Arthur turned to Lydia and said, "Lydia, I had a wonderful time with you today. I haven't felt so young and happy for a long time. Would you like to go riding with me in the morning? You may stay at the castle in an agreeable room."

"I enjoyed being with you as well. I would love to go riding with you, so I agree to spend the night in your castle. Do you play chess, darling? I play a mean game, myself."

"I do, Lydia. Perhaps after dinner. Would you like a tour of the castle?"

Nata said, "Time to leave, girls. I want to take Ingrid and Vivian to Merlin's house for a few days so you and Lydia can get to know each other better. Would you mind, my dear?"

"A good idea, Auntie. Girls, pack some clothes and behave yourselves. I adore you, Nata. You are the best of my relatives. Godspeed."

Nata hugged Lydia goodbye, saying, "Lydia, don't rush things, please. Arthur will marry you, but you will not have sex with him for a month. You can stay in the castle. Go to Julia's for extra clothes. Charge it to Tristan. I will watch you."

"Okay, Mother. I will behave myself. Love you."

Nata and her daughters left for the Sleeping Dragon Inn for dinner with Merlin and Morgana. They boarded their carriage and arrived shortly.

When they arrived, Molly was cleaning near the Inn's front door.

She saw the twins with their newborns, "Glory to the Saviour. We have newborns at last. Come, girls, and show me your babies. Jamus, come here for Calliope and Vika delivered and brought their beautiful babies to visit us."

Nata said, "We didn't have time to call you Molly. The babies just came, and Lydia and I had to help with the deliveries. Lydia is my cousin, and she is staying at the castle this evening. Properly, of course.

"These beauties are my youngest daughters, Ms Sophie and Ms Alliona. They finished university and came to stay with their mother, who missed and worried about them terribly."

Sophie and Alliona curtseyed.

Alliona replied, "Pleased to meet you, Mum. Mummy has told us much about you, Jamus, and your daughters, and we feel like we know you already."

Nata next introduced Ingrid and Vivian.

"Molly, I am proud to introduce Arthur's twins to you, Princesses Vivian and Ingrid. They are like daughters to me. Right?"

Vivian and Ingrid replied, "Yes, Mummy. We love you so much."

"Jamus, hurry. The princesses are with Nata. Hurry."

Jamus and his daughters finally arrived.

Bowing to Nata and the Princesses, Jamus said, "Glory to the Saviour. Princesses and newborns all at one time. Wow. Come and sit. Annie, fetch some of Merlin's new brew for everyone and some appetisers. Hurry."

Merlin came from the back of the Inn, having finished his last delivery of beers and wines.

Merlin asked Nata, "And, where, pray to tell, is our Lydia? Spending the night at the castle? I told you they were an excellent match."

"I hate to admit you were right, but I told Lydia not to have sex for at least a month. Lydia could charm a dead snake to life (pun intended). Vivian and Ingrid want me to birth them so the two pairs of twins can be together for eternity. All from Ariel intervening in our worldliness. She told me so."

"Living with Immortals is always challenging, even for us lesser Immortals. But I am glad for the twins; they need more than each other to survive eternity."

"Agree. How was your day, Merlin?"

"Quiet, thank Gabriel. Got you, Nata. You thought I was going to say, God?"

"The princesses will say with us as the Arthur-Lydia romance proceeds. I will birth them, for I love them as much as the twins. To find two sets of twins who don't want to grow up and are silly in the same way must be impossible, but it happened."

Meanwhile, the twins were at a table with Annie and her sisters. All doting on the newborns.

Annie said, "I wish for a baby after Thomas and I get married, and our children can play together. I hope we can marry soon."

Vika replied, "I will ask Mummy if she can bring everyone home for your wedding. When can you marry?"

"Daddy said as soon as Thomas visits, we can marry. I am so excited, Vika. To be a wife and a mummy has always been my wish."

"Same for Vivian and Ingrid. But the worldlines tell me Uncle Gabriel will marry them. Please say nothing."

"Don't worry, I won't tell anyone, period."

"Thanks, Annie. Mummy would be furious if you did."

After dinner, the party went home in the carriage. Merlin's pony knew the way home and followed behind them.

Nata, the girls, and the babies retired to their rooms.

Nata said, "Time for our bath, daughters. Put the babies in their cribs, remove your clothes, and enter the bath."

Sophie, Alliona, and the twins were naked in a minute and were in the bathing pool. Vivian and Ingrid were naked and standing by the side of the pool.

Ingrid asked, "Mummy, are we pretty in your eyes? We want to be pretty like our sisters, and we don't have pubic or underarm hair like our sisters."

"All my daughters are pretty, including you. If you are not clean, I cannot have you come out of my vagina, so let me wash you. Have you seen my twins naked, Vivian?"

"Yes, Mummy. The twins think we are beautiful and tasty, and we think the same about them. We took baths together and slept naked whenever they stayed at the castle. Are we bad girls, Mummy?"

"Of course not. All my daughters are good girls. Would you like Mummy to wash you?"

"Yes, Mummy, Ingrid and I bathe each other and the twins. They taught us that our private places should be clean and sweet so they can kiss us and make us come. We would like to come very much, Mummy. Calliope says, 'Making love with Mummy is the best thing in the world, for Mummy knows so many secrets to keep us coming. Daddy sometimes makes love to Mummy and us, which is fun.'

"We hope our future husband likes us and marries us. Right, Ingrid."

"Right, Vivian."

Mummy bathed the girls and then changed the worldlines, so she was their birth mother. Nata took the two to her breasts and fed them her magick milk to make everything permanent. She also allowed them to experience birthing the babies. Nata didn't know why, but she made Gabriel the father of both sets of twins.

Then the twins washed the babies and got ready to nurse them.

Nata said, "Vivian and Ingrid, now you are mothers too. If you bring them to your breasts, you will have milk."

Vika and Calliope gave a baby to each one and let them nurse them until they fell asleep. They showed them how to change the babies and put them to bed, telling them we love them so much. Nata felt great joy watching them. After the babies were asleep, her daughters came to bed and allowed their sisters to nurse them, and they nursed Vivian and Ingrid. Nata finally put them in their beds. Ingrid and Calliope, Vivian and Vika, and Sophie and Alliona tucked them in and kissed them goodnight.

As Nata lay down by herself, Chatelaine came to sleep with her.

Chatelaine kissed her mother, saying, "Mummy, now you belong mainly to Morgana and me. We will never allow you to sleep alone, and we will take turns taking care of Eleanor so you will not be alone until Daddy returns. Come, let me nurse you until you fall asleep. I am sure that the Deep Magick tires one out."

"You are a dear, Chatelaine, always paying attention, ensuring everyone is okay. I love you, daughter, and will do as you ask. I can always count on you to protect everyone. I will speed up your magick training, but now I am drained, so I will be your baby.

As Chatelaine nursed Nata, she was content with her life. She loved having sisters to play with and watch over but realised she wasn't meant to be a mother. She was a scientist and intended to remain one, even if sorcery was the only science practised in the Oneirion.

She saw herself working with her scientist husband on a new project as she fell asleep. The names on the desks were Madame Chatelaine Polyakov and Professor Jean-Michel Polyakov.

Three and one-half months had passed since the babies came to Camelot.

Lydia and Arthur married, and everyone in Camelot was happy for them. Baron Ivan was Arthur's Best Knight, and Lady Nata was Lydia's Madame of Honour. The ceremony was in the town park so the Camelot residents could share the newlyweds' happiness. Arthur declared a three-day holiday for everyone.

The kitchen grannies at home watched Baby Sophie and Baby Alliona. Merlin and Nata used their magic to provide drinks and provisions for everyone and games to keep the young ones occupied. Nata allowed the two sets of twins to organise the games and prizes under the watchful eye of Chatelaine. The twins were so proud that Mummy trusted them with such a big event.

Tristan, Gabriel, and Tristan's students came to Camelot for the wedding. Sophie's best friend, a very handsome young man, came with them. Jean-Michel was Gabriel's prize student and a newly initiated Immortal in the Society.

When Tristan introduced Chatelaine to Jean-Michel, he bowed and kissed her left hand.

Standing, he said "Mademoiselle Chatelaine, votre beauté est celle d'un ange d'en haut. Sûrement je suis mort et je suis au paradis.

(Mademoiselle Chatelaine, your beauty is that of an angel from above. Indeed, I died and am in heaven)."

Chatelaine blushed. She immediately liked Jean-Michel.

Then Chatelaine remembered her dream and looked at Tristan.

Tristan winked at her, speaking silently to her mind, "Jean-Michel is my gift to you, Chatelaine. Genuine love knows no bounds and only bestows. I gave you another destiny, my love. Enjoy it."

Tears flowed down Chatelaine's cheeks as she realised Tristan was pure love.

Jean-Michel produced a hankie and wiped Chatelaine's eyes.

"I see Eros has spoken to you? May I stay and help you oversee the children's area? I know much magick and many stories."

Tristan said, "Great. You two are meant for each other, and God has shown both of your destinies. I am delighted. Bye."

Tristan left to visit his dragon friend, Philathorn,[29] whom he invited to the ceremony with some of his orphans. Philathorn had changed much over the years and carried himself as a responsible dragon always does. His orphanage was the talk of the dragon world, and he married a pretty dragon named Nimue, who was as good a mother as Natanel. The orphan dragons felt loved.

Tristan found tears in Philathorn's eyes, for he had learned to love genuinely and care for others.

"Philathorn, seeing you and your family brings hope into my heart that someday we rid ourselves of Ahriman the Evil, and all life will care for each other. I am so proud of you, old friend."

Nimue said, "Honey, I see your friend holds much love for you. Haven't I always told you that dragons and humans can get along if they put aside fear and try? Excuse me, Tristan, but I must see how my little ones are doing. Mummy's job is full-time."

---

[29] See the Purpose Journeys Begin to learn of Philathorn.

Nimue left, and Tristan said, "Your wife needs to spend time with my primary wife and sister, the sorceress Natanel. She loves being a mother and is rebirthing children all the time. How are the children doing with giving the little ones rides in the sky?"

"All is well, dear friend. Everyone was a little nervous at first, but when my girls rolled over so the children could rub their tummies and get licked by the Dragons, all seemed okay. After a while, even the adults joined in. Your two sets of twins ran the children's fair admirably. Merlin told me you and Natanel have three pairs of girls. I didn't ask for details. I never apologised to you for almost killing you, and I am sorry for my behaviour."

"It was a good thing, so forget it. My dear friend, Gabriel, who you will meet soon, writes our destinies, Philathorn. If I were a dragon, you would be my hero for moving from the dark into the light. Your family will need to help us in the Great War ahead. I thought of a new fighting unity—a sorcerer or sorceress paired with a dragon and bonded by sharing blood—friends and battle partners for life. Fire mated to magick. What do you think?"

"Most dragons did not join Ahriman the Evil, so it is possible. Dragons and people bond emotionally when raised together; I have seen this in other worlds. When young dragons and people are together, the dragon adopts a young child as its life partner. They will die for each other when they grow up with no reservations. They are spiritually married to each other. It is a beautiful thing to see Tristan. You must fly with me, and I will show you."

"Agreed, if our wives give us permission."

Both shared a friendly laugh, and Tristan excused himself to speak with Gabriel.

Gabriel sat with ten or twelve little children, telling them fairy tales about ordinary boys and girls. Tristan listened to his friend and understood why Mother Space chose him as the Great God. She selected him because he cared about sentient life and would live with them to improve them.

When he finished, he excused himself and walked over to Tristan.

"Merlin, Nata, and your lovely daughters made a wonderful celebration for Arthur and Lydia. Sophie and Alliona are happy having Nata as their birth mother. Nata's trick of separating the babies from the teenagers was nifty. I may have to try that myself one day?

"The twins seem happy with their new birth sisters, all being birth mothers for the babies. I would never have grown up if I had the choice, for the world has always been harsh. And I have repeatedly failed to correct the situation.

"Tristan. I have a twelve-year-old daughter in ancient Greece named Isis, an exact copy of myself but of a different gender. She refuses to grow up because she says Daddy's little boy never grew up, and they love each other so much. She says my little boy is the source of all my power because he is full of hope and persistence. Probably true. How are Sophie and Alliona?"

"They are happy here. The people of Camelot like them. I think they feel like this is their home. The four twins love them as babies and teenagers. Both love Nata, as they need a genuine mother, Gabriel. They will leave with you, but you must allow them to visit us."

"I am glad, and I will. Come, let us find Nata."

Tristan and Gabriel found Nata helping change and nurse infants so their parents could enjoy the festival. Nata radiated love and motherhood.

"Tristan, Nata reminds me of my wife, Leto, goddess of motherhood and demureness. I will have to introduce them one day."

Nata washed and dried her hands and came over to chat with her husband and friend, "How are my two favourite gentlemen doing on this beautiful evening?"

"Just checking on my beautiful wife. Gabriel says you remind him of his wife, Leto."

"What a pleasant remark, Gabriel. I love being a mother, which is the most important job in all the universes."

"It is Nata. Therefore, I always support female equality and opportunity,"

"Then you must help Morgana while you visit, as she started a women's group on this subject."

"Funny that you ask because, in the future, Alliona will become Demeter and Sophie, our daughter Kore. They are excellent organisers. I will finally fix things for the last time by conquering the world before the vainglorious Macedonian Alexander. Women's rights are a big deal with Demeter, Kore, and myself. Let Alliona and Sophie work with Morgana, for it will benefit everybody. I will keep you updated."

Nata asked, "Gabriel, how do you keep things separated in your mind, anyway?"

"I cannot explain; I just do it. I see so many possibilities for people and follow their every moment. Mother says I write destinies, and she makes me forget them, so I have more fun and freedom to change them on the go."

"Gabriel, tomorrow evening we have dinner and a Saviour's meeting at the Sleeping Dragons Inn. We are reintroducing the Elf Religion, and it would be great if you came to support us."

"Can do, Holy Mother."

A surprised look came over Nata's face.

"Gabriel, you already know?"

"Of course, I know, darling. I write the destinies, remember. I also help people rise above fate to grab and hold on to their individual destinies. What would you like me to say?"

"Whatever is best, my dear. I would love to chat with your mother one day about you."

"Easy enough. I will bring Isis here tonight, and you can chat with her. Isis is how she manifests in our universe. I told Isis about the twins, and she wants to spend time with them."

Suddenly, a beautiful twelve-year-old girl appeared next to Gabriel, dressed in a tunic from ancient Athens.

Isis looked around, saw Daddy, and jumped into his arms.

"Daddy, I missed you so much that I cried every night. Mummy and Auntie Ariel could not console me. I felt I would fade away without my daddy. Please, always take me with you. I love you the best of all your wives, and my vagina is number one."

Gabriel put her down, and Isis looked around.

"Oops, I shouldn't have mentioned the V-word. I am sorry, Daddy. Please don't get mad at me."

Gabriel laughed.

"Isis, when have I ever been angry with you? Never. Corrective, yes, but angry, no. I love you the most, and you have the number one V-word. These are my friends. This is Lady Nata, the greatest sorceress of all time. She is like our Leto for mothering. This is her husband, Lord Tristan, the god of love in our universe."

Isis curtseyed.

"I am pleased to meet you. I can be serious when I need to be. I know Lady Natanel, and I know Lord Tristan. They are our first children. Daddy trusts me with his secret assignments, like discovering that the Amazon Āvi was really his Warrior Sister, Ariel. Right, Daddy."

"Right, Isis. You have me all to yourself while you are here."

"Promise me, Daddy, that you will never leave me alone again."

"I promise, Isis. Let Nata take you to meet the twins. She picked up another set. And now Daddy will have two new wives, pending King Arthur's permission, as they are his daughters. Tristan is like Daddy; his wives are his daughters, usually."

Isis took Nata's hand, and Tristan and Gabriel went to find Arthur.

Nata introduced Isis to the twins and the babies, Sophie and Alliona.

"Girls, this is Uncle Gabriel's special daughter, Isis. She is twelve, but you will love her because she is creative and funny. Plus, she knows how to make love with you."

As the children's fair closed, Nata left the twins and her babies with Isis and returned to work. Returning to the baby station, she saw Chatelaine holding hands with Jean-Michel.

Nata thought, "Tristan released her to a new destiny to fulfil her dreams. I need to go to them."

Nata approached them, introducing herself, "Hello, I am Chatelaine's birth mother, and she is my most mature daughter. She was to oversee my two sets of twins and my babies in the children's fair."

Chatelaine remembered and started to cry, "Mummy, I am so sorry, but Gabriel's best student and I started discussing physics, and I forgot. Please, Mummy, don't be angry with me. I think Daddy wanted me to fall in love with Jean-Michel. After all, Daddy wants me to be happy."

"Come here, my precious, and hug me. I cannot be angry with you, for you have always been the elder sister for the younger ones. I am proud of you. Daddy and Mummy want you to be happy. Daddy does his best to help all of us feel loved and needed. Remember, Daddy is the god of love."

Turning to Jean-Michel, Nata holds out her right hand to him. "Well, if you are Gabriel's best student, then you know you and Chatelaine will get married and do science, or magick, here. Let us say he helps the universe move, so everyone benefits."

Jean-Michel laughs, saying, "Nice to meet you, Leto of Camelot. Gabriel told me I was in for a surprise now that I was an Immortal. He told me I would meet my intended mate on this trip. Chatelaine is a brilliant choice; I find her immensely interesting and pretty. I think I may stay in Camelot, Mother. Being re-birthed might be an interesting experience, though it appears it only has worked for females. I imagine avoiding father-son conflict."

"You are a clever one, young man. I must check on the twins, both sets."

Vika went over and hugged Isis.

"Isis, I am Vika; these are all my beautiful, hot sisters. Meet my darling, Calliope. Vivian and Ingrid are my other hotties; the last two are our baby sisters, Sophie and Alliona. All of us love our baby sisters so much. Mummy always tells us we must protect our baby sisters and ensure they aren't harmed. And all of us smell fresh and taste nice."

All the sisters came and hugged Isis, who was happy to meet new friends close to her age.

Calliope asked, "Isis, would you like to make love to us later and maybe to Mummy too? I love you already, for I know you are special, and Uncle Gabriel spent thousands of generations making you. Right, Vika."

"Right, Calliope. We never met the number one vagina. Our baby sisters are special, too, for they have Djinn genitalia. We wish we could have bigger clitorises to go inside each other like Daddy does. Ingrid and Vivian, would you like to look like our little sisters?"

Ingrid replied, "We would like that too because we could squirt inside our favourite hollows. Right, Vivian?"

"Right, Ingrid."

The four twins surrounded Isis, asking question after question about her family. It amazed them that Gabriel had married seven veritable goddesses and two Amazons. They wanted to hear all about ancient Greece. Isis was wise enough to leave out the part about Alliona and Sophie turning into Demeter and Kore.

Isis asked, "Vika, how do you and Calliope know so much about me?"

Calliope replied, "Isis, Vika and I are the oracles. You come to visit us sometimes. Did we pass your trickly test, Mother Space?"

Isis, smiling, said, "It is a secret which you must never tell. But I am little Isis, and I am wet now. How about all of you?"

Chief Female Body Inspector Calliope went around and felt everyone reporting, "Everyone is dripping wet, Captain Vika. What next?"

"I think Inspector Isis needs to verify your finding, Calliope. We must be scientific."

Isis went around feeling the privates, reporting back, "Captain Vika. I verified Chief FB Inspector Calliope's findings as to wetness. The babies have nice firm clitorises. I am ready to take the first squirting, Captain."

"Thank you for your fine work, Inspector Isis."

Isis said, "I think we will follow up when we get home this evening or even now if I do one of Daddy's time-locks."

"What is a time-lock," asked baby sister Sophie?

"Watch, and I will show you."

Isis time-locked Camelot.

"Look, everyone is frozen in space, so we can play together for as long as we like. Then I will restart time, and no one will know. Lift and take off your dresses if you want to make love."

All the girls undressed and made love to each other, ensuring that the baby sisters penetrated all of them and gave them pudding.

Baby sister Alliona said, "Isis has the number one vagina, for it adjusted to our size, vibrated, and controlled when we came. Hooray, we must ask Mummy to make us all the same, and sisters must be the same. Right, everyone?"

In unison, the sisters and Isis answered, "Right, baby sister Alliona, you are as brilliant as Calliope and Chatelaine."

As the Children's Fair was over, Nata and her daughters thanked Philathorn and Nimue for making the Fair a success and showing people that dragons are moral creatures who need to feel loved and appreciated.

Nata said, "Philathorn and Nimue, I think you will be welcome in Camelot from this day forth. Everyone loves dragons. I created some tee shirts for our residents, saying on the front, 'We Love Dragons.' On the back is a picture of you two."

Nata showed them a sample, and Nimue said, "Oh, Nata, I think we need more mothering in the world, right, honey?"

"Right, darling."

The girls hugged every dragon and waved goodbye as they returned home.

As soon as the dragons flew, little sister Sophie ran to Mummy with tears, saying, "I didn't want them to leave yet, and I want them to stay because I love them, and they are so regal and kind. Please, let us visit them soon?"

Nata hugged Sophie.

"They will visit soon, Sophie. I promise. Let me dry your tears."

Nata and her daughters went to the Sleepy Dragon Inn for a private dinner for Lydia and Arthur, celebrating their marriage as the dragons had gone. Nata ensured everyone had clean clothes to change into, even a pretty dress for Isis. Of course, both sets of twins dressed in similar attire and jewellery. The babies wore original dresses, which matched well. Chatelaine had an elegant evening dress from Aunt Julia's store and was ravishingly beautiful, waiting for her new prince. As much as Julia tried, Chatelaine's pregnancy remained apparent.

Gabriel and Tristan stood next to Chatelaine as Jean-Michel arrived at the Inn.

Tristan told Gabriel, "I imagine this is the first time an ex-husband gave away his pregnant ex-wife at her upcoming wedding?"

Gabriel laughed, replying, "Another potential worldline, uncovered. You have a wonderful heart, Tristan."

"But Husband, what about our child," Chatelaine asked?"

"I can't change that, honey. I need our son for the wars. Jean-Michel knows you are pregnant, as does the rest of the world, abdomen."

Jean-Michel approached them, saying, "Chatelaine, you are stunning this evening. It shows genuine pride not to cover up your pregnancy but to accent it nicely. Good job, my darling."

Tristan said, "See, Chatelaine, all is well. I am off to find Merlin."

He kissed Chatelaine on her left cheek and left.

Jamus and Thomas had rearranged the tables for a wedding dinner. Arthur, Lydia, Tristan, Nata, Gabriel, Merlin, and Morgana sat at the head table. The sisters all sat together. Nata had explained why Chatelaine sat with Jean-Michel and not them. None of them really understood, but they always trusted Mummy and Daddy. Being careful to make them feel secure, Nata assured them that Daddy would not give them away in the future.

The notables of Camelot occupied the other tables, including Baron Ivan, Julia, the mayor, and city council.

When the time came for the wedding toast, Gabriel stood, saying, "Glory to the Saviour, for the Saviour glorifies the people."

Everybody stood repeating their new greeting, "Glory to the Saviour, for the Saviour glorifies the people," then sat back down.

Gabriel remained standing.

"As the most senior member of this family, I am honoured to bless Arthur and Lydia on this fabulous wedding day. I have known Lydia for many years and am new to your King. I find him a wonderful king who shall reign for a long time. As I can see into the future, as does my son Tristan, I see a fine son who will be a wonderful king to Camelot. I think the good has overcome the sad, eh Arthur? So, lift your tankards and toast King Arthur and Queen Lydia. Long may they reign over Camelot."

Everyone stood and toasted the King and Queen and then returned to their seats.

Gabriel continued, "Before our feast begins, I must say a few solemn words. First, Tristan and Nata are my son and daughter, and Tristan is the Saviour. I am the creator of the Elfin Religion and am delighted you are learning about it.

"The Elves are awake and are preparing to destroy Ahri-Simeon and rehabilitate Ahri-Lilith. She is with her brother because her heart broke a long time ago. I can fix her, but I cannot fix her brother, for Ahriman the Evil entirely entangled him with itself.

"Destroying Ahriman the Evil has fallen to me, and I will not fail when the proper time arrives. The Saviour, Holy Mother, and I continuously search the worldlines for the approach of Ahri-Simeon in Camelot and elsewhere. The Evil cannot work directly, but Ahri-Simeon can and will attack. I do not know when, but I know the Deep Magic protects Camelot. So be prepared. I will send an army of Elves to support Baron Ivan's army as soon as the Elves have re-established their fortresses.

"Our family will not fail you. Glory to the Saviour."

Everyone in the Inn stood shouting for a full minute, "Glory to the Saviour, for the Saviour glorifies the people."

Nata, the Holy Mother, stood.

"Now that you know who our father is, you are in the best of hands. Friends, there is a working God, and you spent time with him today. He is never far away, for he understands how tough life is, so he suffers with all of us. He doesn't want or need worship. Like us, he wants to love and be loved and see the physical and the Oneirion reunited as one habitat.

"Papa is a good God, for he blushes whenever we praise him, cries when life is sad or tender, and admits his miscalculations. My mother has been with you today. Mummy, come up here, please."

Isis stood up and ran to Nata to hug her.

Turning to the crowd, Isis said, "You see me in my present form, but I will show you my adult form."

Isis changes into a full-grown woman, far surpassing the beauty of Morgana and Nata. Everyone looking at her falls in love with her because the love radiating from her heart is unconditional and bestowed regardless of personal merit. The room fills with the images of fortunate children who died early and lived with her in perfect health. She is the Mother of all beings.

Molly cries out, "Jamus, I see our little one who died so young. Look, an angel is holding her wee hand."

Lydia stands up, "I see my baby girl that Ahriman the Evil smothered so long ago. She is happy and waving at me."

All the families losing young ones saw their children.

Mother Space, the Mother of All, said in a voice full of love and caring, "Children, I cannot fix your lives in the physical, but I can provide a heaven for those who live life with love for others. Love is never forgotten."

Mother moved over and kissed Gabriel on his lips.

"I love you for many reasons. I am Mother, Sister, and Wife, and you are Father, Brother, and Husband. When we began Creation, you agreed to come into it and help our future children for the sake of helping alone. You have never asked me for anything except to love you, and I love you beyond measure or the transfinite, as you like to say."

Everyone laughed, including Gabriel.

Isis assumes her usual form, saying, "That's all folks, back to our party."

Isis returns to her seat between Sophie and Alliona.

A grand miracle happened to those in the Inn. They all came to love their neighbours more than themselves, like the Elves and Angels. Now, they understood and could transmit the Elfin Religion.

The party continued until the sun rose the next day. All the partygoers dispersed for a peaceful repose in their homes.

Chapter 20

Evil Rises in the Dark of the Night

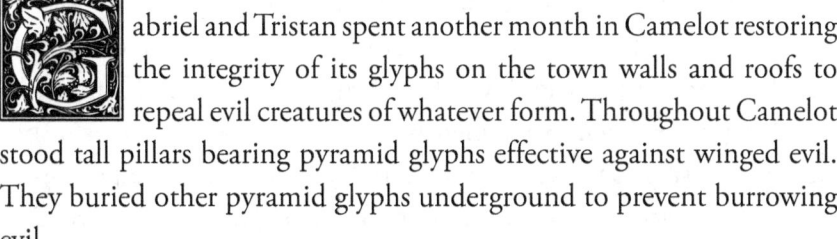abriel and Tristan spent another month in Camelot restoring the integrity of its glyphs on the town walls and roofs to repeal evil creatures of whatever form. Throughout Camelot stood tall pillars bearing pyramid glyphs effective against winged evil. They buried other pyramid glyphs underground to prevent burrowing evil.

If the town wall and house glyphs are breached, all the houses and buildings have warded safety shelters for the inhabitants.

They built a broad moat fed by underground water to keep demons out of the town, as most could not cross over water.

The only things the glyphs could not prevent were physical projectiles, but Camelot's walls were sturdy.

Tristan and Gabriel placed protection glyphs on all the soldiers' armour. The knights and their horses carried protection glyphs similarly. Swords, lances, and arrowheads displayed killing glyphs.

They also designed and manufactured sophisticated, highly accurate machines to disable enemy siege towers and catapults. These machines covered the perimeter of Camelot.

They reported to King Arthur and Queen Lydia when all preparations were finished.

Gabriel reported, "Your Highnesses, Tristan, and I have done everything possible to protect Camelot in our absence. Our only weakness is that our sorcerers and sorceresses are so few. It will not be easy for Morgana, Nata, and Merlin to repair breaches and incinerate demons and soldiers. I do not see any clear signs of attack, nor can the rest, but I am concerned. My spy elementals see no activity anywhere near Camelot. I don't know why, and I can't stay, for I need to be in Montemar by the end of this week. Tristan and I need to lead an army against Ahriman the Evil in a strategic outer world under siege by the humanoid forces of Ahri-Simeon."

Arthur replied, "I am so thankful for your additional help, Gabriel. Tristan has watched over us since he first arrived as a twelve-year-old boy. Everyone in Camelot loves Aunt Nata, Morgana, and him. Lydia and I felt the miracle performed by the Mother of all beings at our wedding feast. I have seen a new spirit in Camelot. More people are attending services at our Elfin Houses. I am delighted, right, Lydia?"

"Yes, darling. Gabriel, I told my husband about our baby after the Miracle and how we lost her. Arthur, tell Gabriel what you told me, please."

"I told my lovely wife. Lydia, I am glad Gabriel loved and married you and gave you a child. If Lord Gabriel loved you enough to marry and give you a child, I have found the best Queen in all the lands. That is what I told her, Gabriel. I am sorry you lost your child, but somehow you made something good out of it?"

"We did, Arthur. It was a minor miracle but a gift performed by a mortal creature. The Djinn, who smothered the baby, found the light, dedicating his life to serving the lepers' spiritual and physical needs.

He will be a doctor in the Great War ahead. Therefore, I never give up hope for all sentient creatures."

Tristan said, "Your majesties, Gabriel and I must leave for Montemar with our students. I am leaving Thomas and Andrew, for they want to marry Annie and Stef. Nata will bring them to me in a few weeks. Ciao."

Gabriel and Tristan turned and left the room, walking to the Sleeping Dragon Inn to see the family. When they arrived, Sophie and Alliona ran up to Gabriel and hugged and kissed him.

Then they hugged Tristan, and Alliona said, "Daddy, can we go with our husband when you two leave? Mummy said it was up to you, as Daddy is the boss."

"Daughters, you must stay with Mummy for a little longer. We are off to war, and it would not be safe for you. Soon, Gabriel will leave with you on your belated honeymoon, bringing Isis with him, for he worries about her. We are not leaving until after the two weddings, which are tomorrow. My God, time flies these days. Sorry, Gabriel."

"Alright, my boy. Come, wives, we have some business to take care of."

The three left to make love, which seems to be the primary reason for going elsewhere in this story. Curious. Then again, love works mysteriously. And it was not time to tell the baby sisters that Gabriel was their father.

The marriages of Thomas and Annie and Andrew and Stef went well. The soon-to-be newlyweds asked for an Elf service, which was nice (other than the brides not being pregnant). Merlin presented his newest potions, and Nata had the kitchen elementals prepare the meals.

The following day, Gabriel, Tristan, and his students returned to Nouseum for a short war staff meeting. The students were not ready for battle, so they stayed in Nouseum. For unexplainable reasons, Gabriel left Jean-Michel and Chatelaine in Camelot.

Several weeks passed as Camelot went about its business without information on the battle. The worlds Tristan and Gabriel departed to were a cluster of planets whose electromagnetic and atonic fields disrupted physical and aphysical communication between the planets. The war was going well for the Elves, but slowly, as Ahri-Simeon had sent a massive armada to these planets. He attacked many cities simultaneously, causing the Elf generals to spread their troops as far as strategically rational.

Suddenly, and without warning on the new moon, a great, well-equipped demon-dwarf-human-ogre army with siege towers and catapults appeared around Camelot. Above the city, lizard-like flying demons tried to attack the guards, but the glyphs kept them at bay. Fortunately, Arthur pulled in the floating bridge, connecting Camelot to the surrounding lands so the invading army could not enter.

When this failed, their commanding officer, a humanoid demonic princeling, ordered them to pick up boulders and burning logs to drop into the city from the sky. This failed, too, as the glyphs repelled anything in recent contact with a demon.

The defence deterrents stopped the demon attack. The princeling ordered his ogres to bring the catapults within firing range and prepare them for launching. This took most of the night, so Camelot was now safe.

While the initial attack was proceeding, an elemental reported to Merlin. Merlin sounded his emergency bell. Nata had told her daughters to stay in the room, putting Chatelaine in charge. The noise frightened the infants, and the twins picked them up and nursed them. All the girls were frightened, but Chatelaine knew what to do.

Nata and Morgana met Merlin, and Merlin reported, "Camelot is under attack by Ahri-Simeon's troops. Elgin, my spy, told me that one of his chief princelings is in charge. His name is Crafty. Elgin estimates the troop strength at forty-thousand. They have sufficient provisions for at least six months before they must raid the countryside.

"I cannot contact Nouseum or Gabriel, for there is a local disruption to our communication lines. This princeling is smart, and we must not underestimate him, and we must fight alone. What should we do, Nata?"

"First, Merlin, we must double-secure this cave and its food and water source against attack. I doubt they know we are here. We must protect the children at all costs. Merlin, inform the elementals and place them in charge of the children.

"Morgana, fetch our battle armour and weapons. Merlin, go find your armour."

Several of the elementals arrived for a briefing on the situation. The ten male battle elementals Gabriel had left were the first to arrive.

Their Captain (*Lokhagos*) said, "Madame, we will cover this place with non-detection and demon-killing invisible glyphs and traps for any non-demon enemies. I will send a messenger to *Stratigoi* Ares and Otrera in ancient Athens. She is *Stratigos* of the Amazons and is Isis's birth mother. We all serve Lord Gabriel.

"Our Supreme Commander (*Polemarchos*) warned us of an ultimate battle between good and evil. They prepared us to die in defence of the good. But today, our concern is securing this fortress and guarding the children and other elementals.

"I will keep you informed. Soldiers secure this fortress. Excuse us, Lady Nata."

The *Lokhagos* and his aides left.

Merlin found his battle armour and told the kitchen grannies about everything.

"Asteraceae, you and the remaining elementals must care for and protect the children."

All agreed to do as asked.

After dressing in their armour, Morgana asked, "What will we do, Mummy?"

Nata replied in a calm voice.

"The three of us are going out there to kick some demon ass, killing as many demons as possible. Our glyphs will protect us. I doubt the princeling is aware of you and I being present. Merlin, most likely. He has made one mistake of vanity. Failing to collect information on his enemies.

"I have sent an elemental to our Dragon friends about the attack. They know nearby DragonElves, blood-bound Dragon and Elf battle pairs sworn to destroy evil. It will take a few days for them to arrive. Philathorn told me of them during our Children's Fair.

"Hold my hands so we can transport ourselves to Arthur's castle to protect Camelot."

The three magi joined hands and found Arthur, Lydia, and his knights in the war room. Nata noticed a new knight dressed in black guard plates and chain mail, likely making him invisible at night.

Arthur stood up, saying, "Glad you are here, Nata. The glyphs work well, protecting us from the demons, but the army has ogres, humans, and dwarves immune to the glyphs. I am discussing our defence with my knights."

"Arthur, who is the knight with his back to us? I have never seen him."

Before Arthur could answer, the knight was next to Nata, saying, "Hello, Mother, your mystery knight is Jean-Michel. I am most surprised you did not suspect I was an Elf Prince. Is Merlin's Crystal Cave secure? Are Chatelaine and her sisters safe?

"Yes, Prince. The Cave is secure and hidden by ten battle elementals Gabriel left with us. The captain sent a messenger to ancient Athens to call out Gabriel's Army of humans, elementals, and Amazon Horse Archers for the Final Confrontation. It is years earlier than we predicted.

"Well, I am delighted you're with us. I know you must have more battle experience than every knight in this world."

"So true, Mother. I fought in the original wars against Ahri-Simeon. After the war, I chose not to slumber with the other Elves. I continued battling independent warlords in the outer worlds. We will beat this princeling."

"Sir Knight, why do you call me Mother?"

"Gabriel knows more of your life than do you and Tristan. For Tristan was not your first lover."

"Who was my first lover? I suppose you are going to say, Father?"

"Good guess, Mother. You came into being long before, Tristan. After your creation, you fell in love with Father and married him. I am the first son you had with Father. When Tristan was born, he needed a mate, so Father erased your memory completely, and you fell in love with Tristan.

"Don't try remembering, for no memory traces exist anywhere but in my mind. If you are curious, I will let you re-experience your forgotten past."

"Is now a good time, Jean-Michel?"

"Why not? I time-locked this world? Sit down, take both of my hands, and close your eyes. I will use some First Magick to have you relive everything. You loved Father first, and so he married you."

Nata sat in a chair, took Jean-Michel's two hands, and closed her eyes. The Elf whispered some words in Enochian, and she found herself in a meadow on a perfect spring day. Nata saw her father resting in deep meditation, naked, lying upon some soft ground moss. He had been swimming in the river. She felt a new desire in her pelvis and heart, watching her naked father.

"She reached down and discovered she was wet for the first time. She didn't understand what was happening but went to lie with Father. Instinctively, she gently made him erect and then climbed on top and put his penis inside her. She didn't know she was to move, but her desire grew until her father and her climaxed, Father coming out of meditation (see the puns?)

Father said, "Do you love me, Natanel?"

"Father, I have loved you since the moment you created me. I didn't know that I wanted a child at first. I knew something was missing. Today, I learned what it was. I am a mother and your mate. Will you accept me?"

"I accept you, Daughter, as what I call a wife, for you gave your pureness to me. We will have a son at the proper time."

Jean-Michel let Nata's hands fall, and she returned to ordinary awareness.

"You are the second person I have loved, my son. I gave birth to you, and now I understand why I feel so bonded to Gabriel. What changed?"

"Mother Space and Father had your brother, Tristan. But Tristan grew up very lonely for unknown reasons and became very depressed. To fix the situation, our parents agreed that Tristan and you must be spouses to not feel alone. I grew up and lived with the Elves and saw nothing wrong with our parents' decision. Father never stopped loving you as his wife and friend, Mother."

"But now I want Father inside me. I love him as he was my first. What am I to do?"

"An interesting conundrum, Mother. Let us worry about that later. We have a demon princeling to exterminate with all his crew."

"Balder, I sent an elemental to Philathorn, for he told me he knew where lived DragonElves. I asked for their help."

"DragonElves, I didn't know that any still existed close by. This is excellent news, Mother. They are nearly invincible. Back to battle strategy."

"Your Majesties, please gather around my scale model of Camelot and its environs to discuss our offence."

Arthur and his commanders gathered around the table.

Arthur said, "Prince Baldar, did you say offence?"

"Yes, I did, Majesty. I am very familiar with these princelings and how they think. Their weak points are two. The first is that demons are notoriously stupid and lack ingenuity and foresight, requiring the princeling to control them in a battle towards the ultimate objective, victory. The second is their vanity and false self-confidence, causing them to underestimate their enemies and endangering their safety. Distract him, and we cause disarray in their army. Our best defence is a potent offence, as this is not what old Crafty will expect. I fought him before and won. Perhaps I will kill him this time?"

"The town is secure from demon attacks for the moment. Crafty will send ogres to deface our glyphs. The ogres can swim underwater to cross the moat, a problem with so many. The town walls require a constant watch. They can use the borrowing demons to get close to Camelot and finish the tunnels to penetrate the city. To protect here, the citizens will have to help patrol the streets.

"I dispatched an elemental messenger to my friend and brother, Prince Festian. My messenger returned at the last hour, informing me that Festian would bring ten thousand battle-hardened Elves to attack the enemy from behind. He will be here in two days.

"At first light, I will cross the moat with my battle horse to taunt and shame old Crafty. Don't worry, my horse is an Elf horse and can walk on water and fly."

Lydia asked, "Prince, you are going alone?"

"No, Your Highness. He cannot kill me as I am an Immortal. My goal is to challenge him, kill his best supporters, and inflict a wound of pride on him.

"This manoeuvre will give us some time to prepare further. As we wait for Festian and one clan of the DragonElves, we will begin raids upon the rear of Crafty's Army by our Knights. The battle glyphs will protect them if careful, but some will die for Camelot and you, Majesties.

"Arthur, your Army needs you to remain in Camelot and be visible daily to our troops and citizens. The townsfolk must not panic or try to leave; the enemy will take advantage of the situation if they do. Fear only strengthens demons. You must assure the townsfolk of our eventual victory. If there are demon intrusions, your troops will stop them. Use each success to encourage the people. Issue swords and lances to all able-bodied men and women and allow them to patrol their city.

"Lydia, you know war, and so I ask you to support the women of this city. Tell them of the Great Djinn War and keep them occupied with suitable chores.

"Holy Mother, this is an excellent time to proselytise the Elf Religion. There is substantial power underlying it, which will unify and strengthen Camelot. Until we need Merlin to repel an all-out attack, he and Jamus, as the Announcers, must build the people's faith in the Saviour and Father. Tell them both are at war elsewhere, but their power is always with those who have faith.

"Everywhere I walk, I want to hear the people shouting, Glory to the Saviour, for He glorifies the people. Sorry to be so abrupt, but you cannot win without my help. War is not about rank but about comradeship and trust in our brothers and sisters, knowing each will die to protect the other. Questions?"

Several of the Knights asked technical questions about the raids.

"Good, the sun is rising, and I go to toy with old Crafty's mind. This time, I will rid the world of him. Arthur, thanks for your confidence in me. I will not let you and Camelot down. Morgana, you will ride with me; come."

As Baldar left to prepare, Nata walked with him.

"I am very proud of you, Son. You are forceful and direct when needed, like Tristan and Gabriel. I want you to wear my handkerchief to remind you of your mother's love when you go to battle. Keep your sister safe."

Nata handed it to him and kissed him on his lips. Baldar secured it to his breastplate and took Morgana by the hand.

Morgana asked, "Why are you taking me, brother?"

"Two reasons, Morgana. First, I know you can fight like an Amazon. Second, Crafty hates females, and watching you defeat his strongest warriors will antagonise him, so he becomes less vigilant."

"What is your real name, anyway?"

"My actual Elf name is Baldar. Mother chose my name."

"So, what are we going to do for Mummy? You re-birthed her love for Gabriel, even greater than her love for my Tristan. You took responsibility for her, brother."

"I do not know, sister. But this is not a problem now. Let me adjust your armour and ensure you have the proper glyphs."

Baldar inspected Morgana's armour and made some minor changes. They left for the stables for two Elf battle horses, mounted, and left Camelot as the sun rose in the east. Arthur, Nata, Merlin, and the principal Knights watched from the city walls. Nata held Merlin's arm tightly.

The two warriors crossed the moat with their lances held high. As it was daylight, the land was free of demons. No ogre could approach them as Morgana created a magical shield around them. Nata's handkerchief fluttered in the morning breeze.

Prince Baldar roared, "Crafty, it is your best friend, Prince Baldar. I came to kill you and feed your body to the pigs. Show yourself. I will not kill you today, which would be much too easy. I must irritate you for a while; you misshaped runt of the demon litter. Your brother, Luther, is twice the princeling you are."

Baldar whispered to Morgana, "He hates his brother. He picked on Crafty when they were young and always connived to get better assignments. I am sure Crafty feels royally pissed off and will be here in a moment."

A guard of black dwarves appeared with an insignificant creature dressed in dull black armour on a pony. His visor was up, showing a pale face with large black eyes, no eyebrows, thick red lips, and a tiny nose. The creature reeked of evilness.

Crafty addressed the Elf, "Greetings, Elf. You Elves are weak and smell terrible. I see you brought homely Morgana to protect you.

"I look forward to watching my battle dwarves chop you to pieces. They are immune to your shield, Morgana the Whore. Attack, my pets."

The dwarves attacked Baldar and Morgana, and the two dispatched them in ten minutes. Baldar threw his lance at Crafty during the battle, which the battle shield deflected, and Baldar's lance returned to his hand.

In a free moment, Morgana picked up some wet ogre turds in her gloved hand and threw them at Crafty, hitting him in the face.

Crafty was about to order all nearby soldiers to attack when Natanel appeared. Raising both hands, she willed all her magick into them and sent a pressure blast, pushing back their assailants three hundred and thirty meters. Nata collapsed on the ground, and Baldar lifted her, stabilised her on his horse, and climbed behind her. Morgana mounted her horse, and the trio galloped back to Camelot.

The guards opened the city gates, and Baldar dismounted near the Sleeping Dragon Inn, carrying Nata inside. Morgana was by his side.

Molly saw them enter, saying, "Jean-Michel, take Milady into my bedroom and place her on the bed. I will examine her. I think Milady has a magick injury. Annie, run and fetch the new young doctor who came to Camelot last year. He will know what to do. Hurry, dear."

Molly carefully cut off Natanel's upper garments and saw severe burns on her arm and thorax.

"Stef, bring me my sterile towels and the sterilised herbal water Merlin gave me last week. We need to keep her burns wet for the moment."

Annie returned with the young doctor.

He examined Nata, asking, "This looks like she pulled all her life force into her thorax to produce a repulsion wave. I have never seen such a nasty wound; she must have been distraught. The Lady Natanel is an Elf.

Morgana asked, "Doctor, can you save her? All her daughters will fade away if she passes. We can't lose, Mummy."

"I may restore her, for I am an Elf doctor. I will need a litre of blood from you and Baldar. Molly, I also need as much of the burn-healing herb that Merlin gave you. Finally, we need as many people visualising the healing of the Holy Mother as possible. Ring the church bells to call the people to the churches. Send criers out, telling everyone to go to their local church, for the Holy Mother has attacked the demons and suffered mortal injuries.

"Tell them they must call her soul back to Camelot, as it is far away now. Hurry."

Molly washed a sharp knife in azeotropic ethanol to sterilise it. Baldar cut a primary vein in Morgana's arm and then in his own, allowing the blood to drip into a large cooking pot.

Annie brought two handfuls of the burn-herbs, and the doctor asked Molly to add alcohol and stir it until he needed it.

When the doctor finished the herb potion, he poured it gently over all the burn areas. Then he took some powder from his travelling chest and sprinkled it over the burns, requiring them to turn Natanel over carefully.

As he worked, it continuously spoke words of the Deep Magick, calling forth Creation's healing forces. Finally, he spread the slightly congealed blood on her burns, front and back. He continued drawing forth the healing energies around Nata as a golden cloud.

At last, the doctor said in the common vernacular, "I ask you, Mother Space, Mother of all beings, to take one of my lives and give it to your daughter, Lady Natanel. Destiny needs her love and care. I ask this favour of you, Mother. So Mote It Be."

Mother Space appeared before everyone, "I grant your request, my generous grandson; your sister is healed and free."

As Mother Space's Sacred Image dissolves, Nata sits up, saying, "Why am I half-naked? Where am I? The last thing I remember is saving my children. Are you safe?"

Morgana kissed her.

"Mummy, you saved Baldar and me. You were so brave. But you almost died from severe burns caused by the repulsion wave, and this excellent physician saved you."

In amazement, Nata looked at the doctor, saying, "Kulkin, you are alive. Where have you been? I stopped sensing your life aeons ago. Let me kiss you, nephew."

Kulkin sat next to Nata, and she kissed him, saying, "Children, this fair Elf is your cousin, and he is the most famous Elf Physician ever. When he was born, my sister dunked him into the magic pool and asked that he receive extra lives to save others, and I imagine he gave one to me?"

"Yes, Auntie. I gave one to you. I am glad it wasn't my last one, and Mother Space allowed me to keep one."

Morgana, sighing, said, "Who would ever think I would meet a lost cousin during a demon invasion. None of us knew about a cousin whose mother was my aunt. And discover I have an Elf brother who insults demons simply to irritate them."

Baldar put his arm around his half-sister and kissed her right cheek. "I love irritating demon princelings, honey. And I love you even more.

"I heard I had a cousin named Kulkin who cared for people in the outer worlds. Nice to meet you."

Kulkin replied, "I heard I had a cousin who was so stupid that he would insult demon princelings for fun."

Both laughed, and Morgana added, "Insults are child's play; I threw wet ogre turds into his face.

"When I threw it, I said, Eat shit, sucker, and so he did."

Everyone laughed.

Baldar said, "Now that everything is normal let's discuss our next offensive.

"Nata, every morning, you and Merlin will transport twelve knights to the battlefield and retrieve them when necessary. Their magick shields will protect them while the knights attack only the ogres. Each raid should last only an hour. Raids will continue throughout the day at random times.

"Crafty will be pissed off when we add random nightly raids to the agenda. I want to keep him from sleeping as it will make him sloppy.

"We must report to Arthur, for I am sure he is worried. Come, Auntie, the four of us must assure everyone that the Holy Mother is back with our thanks to a fine Elf doctor."

The four warriors left for the castle.

Arthur and Lydia hugged them when they arrived safely, thanking Nata's saviour.

Morgana introduced the doctor who had saved Nata, explaining that he was an Elf and how he invoked Mother Space to revive Nata and give up one of his lives.

"I have a sister somewhere whose son is Kulkin. And Baldar is the son of Gabriel and me. After Gabriel brought me to life, I fell in love with him and lay with him in deep meditation, and I became pregnant with Baldar. Tristan was born much later than I was. Tristan did not have someone to love, so Daddy erased my memory and gave me Tristan to love. Being Divine is confusing."

Lydia said, "We are glad you are alive and well, Nata."

Baldar finished the story, saying, "Getting rid of the demons is not much of a challenge because of our glyphs. To have a three-dimensional kill, I need you to create tetrahedrons with glyphs on all four sides. I would like the three magi to create a few thousand killing glyphs, which I can have the Dragons carry over the demon camp and drop from the sky at night.

"I am more concerned about the ogres, as they love battle and are unafraid of dying. Crafty will hate to use them, as demons are plentiful and expendable, but he will have no choice. We should focus our raids on the ogres during the day and humans and dwarves at night. The ogres won't care, but the randomness creates anxiety and fear in the humans and dwarves.

"We will remove the ogre catapults as soon as they are in position. They know of DragonElves and will not let them approach their machines so to burn them."

Two messenger elementals entered the room and bowed to Prince Baldar.

The first messenger reported, "My Liege, the Dragon Philathorn, and the DragonElves will be here tomorrow. They fly under cover of darkness."

The second reported in Old Elf, "Prince Festian's fortress is under attack now, so he will be delayed coming to Camelot. He sends his regrets and best wishes."

The messengers rose and left the room.

As the messengers had spoken in old Elf, Baldar relayed the messages in Camelot English, "Your Majesties, Festian is under siege and cannot come to our aid now. Philathorn and the DragonElves will be here tomorrow night. They fly under cover of darkness. This is not good, but we will prevail."

Baldar excused himself to the restroom. Kulkin went with him.

Kulkin said, "This is bad, cousin. Can we still win?"

"I don't know, Kulkin. I counted on Festian. Our magick would be of great use if Father or Tristan were here. Neither Merlin nor Morgana is powerful enough to face the princeling with magick. I am a battle elf, invincible in any arm-to-arm conflict, but not a mage.

"I don't understand why I cannot contact Father and my uncle, and no one else can call them either. I am exhausted and need to sleep a little. Please tell everyone else to rest, for the night raids are coming up soon enough."

The battle elemental arrived in ancient Athens and reported to *Stratigos* Artemis.

He reported, "Goddess. Gabriel's sons, Lord Tristan and Baldar, and his daughter, Lady Natanel, and the city of Camelot are under attack by the troops of Ahri-Simeon. My *Lokhagos* says they need support immediately. We cannot contact our *Polemarchos* as he is engaged in another quadrant. The Great War begins. The enemy is forty-thousand strong with ogres, dwarves, humans, and demons."

"Soldier, I do not know how we can help, and I will contact the other goddesses and Lady Ariel to see how we can go into the future. Get some food and rest."

Artemis left to round up the other goddesses and the two Ariels. She explained the problem.

Āvi said, "I will lead the troops in battle as I have fought against Ahriman the Evil before with the Djinn. If you can get me into the future, I will go with my Amazons. The last time I saw Eugenis was when he came to pick up Isis a few days ago, and he did not say where he was going?"

"The messenger said he and Isis had been visiting a place in the Oneirion called Camelot. I don't know how to move into a time when we do not exist. Do any of you know how to do this?"

Hekate replied, "I know of such a Magick. But I need access to the Waters of the Temple of the First Ones."

Ariel replied, "I can take you there, Hekate. The doors know my hand."

"Good. It will take me three days to prepare for transferring our troops. As a mistress of magick, I will fight. But to return, I must show

Ariel, Demeter, Kore, and Hera how to return everyone when victory is ours. So only Āvi and I go to battle, and Artemis and Athena must stay for current negotiations.

"If Husband is not responding to anyone's messages, all communication is disrupted. Let us leave for the Temple now. I know of several places in our universe where these places are. After our warriors leave, I will be in our husband's time and search for him. The rest, do whatever you can in the next three days."

Hekate and her co-wives left. The other goddesses continued with the unification negotiations. Zoe and Otrera were to stay in Sparta. The messenger elemental returned to the future to report to Lord Baldar that reinforcements would arrive from Sparta and Athens in three days.

"Prince Baldar, a messenger awaits you in the war room."

"Thank you, page; tell him I will be there shortly."

The page left. Baldar tightened one loose piece of armour. Then he left for the war room. When he arrived, the messenger bowed.

The messenger reported, "The goddess Hekate said she will complete the magick necessary to send you thirty thousand battle elementals and Amazons.

"Lord General Eugenis' warrior sister Āvi will lead the troops. She was Ariel in the Great Djinn War.

"Goddess Hekate said, 'Hold strong, Commander. May the One True God, my Beloved Eugenis, strengthen your troops.' She promised her warriors would arrive in three more days."

"Excellent, come help me into the rest of my armour. I have ogres to kill."

The soldier helped Baldar into his armour. Then he left to eat, rest, and return to report the message's delivery.

Balder reported the welcome news to Arthur and Lydia.

"Where is Mother?"

"Nata left for a few hours to check on her daughters. I imagine they are scared. The oldest ones are fifteen. The King's two daughters are with them. Merlin's Cave is well-hid and well-guarded. Chatelaine has a clear head and will watch over all of them."

Baldar and his knights raided the ogre camps randomly during the day. At night, he attacked the dwarves and humans. Philathorn and his friends began dropping glyphs onto the demon camps twice a night, so the demon troops diminished. But it seemed to Merlin's elemental spies that Crafty was replacing his lost demons with ogres and humans. Baldar said he would do this if he were Crafty.

The best news was that Camelot had lost no knights or soldiers in the skirmishes.

The DragonElves arrived the following day, stabling the Dragons in the town park. The people brought them meat and beverages, standard fare for the Elves. The Dragons were astonished as little children came up to hug and rub them behind the ears when they put their heads on the ground. The female Dragons and Elves were the most moved, as they could not bear little dragons or Elflines to love and listen to DragonElf lore.

Baldar met the Commander and his lieutenants in the park.

Baldar knew the Commander from the Last War and threw his arms around him.

"Cousin Lokatin, it has been centuries since we last met. It is a pleasure to see you joining the battle."

"Same here, Baldar. I see Ahri-Simeon is moving. How is your father?"

"Gabriel is fine, old friend. He agreed to rid Creation of Ahriman the Evil but left the clean-up to us. My mother almost died saving my half-sister, Morgana, and myself. Another cousin is here, Kulkin. Do you remember him?"

"I do; he tended many of my soldiers in the Great War. He is a marvellous doctor. How did he get here?"

"After the War, he began travelling the outer planets tending to the sick. He ended up in Camelot and has the biggest heart ever.

"Let me introduce you to my lieutenants, Marduk and Eve. They are superb officers and have seen many battles."

"Welcome, friends. Our townsfolk and children love Dragons. We had a Children's Fair a while back, and my brother Tristan invited his friend Philathorn to the event, and it was a hit with the people. Funny how things work out. Come, let us go to the Sleepy Dragon Inn so to see Mother and Morgana,"

Baldar took his friends to the Inn. When they entered, the Inn was full of people sitting at tables listening to the Holy Mother tell of her recovery. It was a miracle by the Great Mother to send her grandnephew to Camelot last year.

When she saw Baldar walk into the Inn, she invited him to stand next to her.

She said, "This is my son, Prince Baldar, and brother to our Morgana. Gabriel brought him to Camelot as Jean-Michel, and you may remember him spooning with my Chatelaine."

Everyone laughed, for most of the attendees remembered.

"My son is the prince in charge of saving our city from the demon princeling, Crafty. He summoned his old battle comrades, and some have arrived today. These are DragonElves, bound to a battle Dragon by blood and love. They are protectors of all good people. Like my son and nephew, they refused to sleep with the other Elves and continued fighting Ahriman the Evil. Let me hear some clapping."

Clapping, she heard. Then she raised her arms, and the people started chanting an ancient Elf prayer to the Mother of All beings in old Elf. As the sound increased, the table tankards rattled, as did the windows.

Then, Nata lowered her arms, and the people finished with "Glory to the Saviour, for he glorifies the people. Glory to the legacy given to us by the First Ones. Health to our Holy Mother, Nata, for she loves all of us as her children. So Mote It Be."

All the DragonElves had teary eyes, for they saw that the Old Ways had not died. There may be hope.

Baldar turned to the crowd, saying, "My brother Elves and I thank you from the deepest parts of our hearts. We thought our religion had perished long ago. Instead, we find it alive in Camelot. We shall destroy the invaders and send fear into the black heart of Ahri-Simeon. Glory to the Saviour, for he glorifies the people. Innkeeper, full tankards for all our friends if the meeting is done."

"We are done, my son. I ask that your knights and soldiers refrain from war tonight and feast and drink at our fabulous inns. Jamus, send messengers to the other inns to provide drink and food to all our protectors. But, silently.

"Combining our magick, Merin, Morgana, and I can shield our city for twenty-four hours from all evil, thanks to my nephew, Doctor Kulkin. To think that our best physician was an Elf, none of us knew, not even me.

Jamus stood, saying, "Tonight, glory to those who rediscovered and now practise the Way of the Elves. We may not be Holy or Immortals, but we are part of this Creation. We will be the best we can be to fulfil Gabriel's dreams. So Mote It Be "

The entire town brought food and drink to all the soldiers. The crowd clanked their tankards and swore oaths to be Elf-like and love our neighbours more than ourselves. The magick shield held up all night and into the early afternoon of the next day.

Mother Space and the Most Holy Mother, spinning our fates, smiled at each other.

Chapter 21

The End Wars Begin

Nata, Merlin, and Morgana teleported Arthur and Lydia to the Cave in the morning. The children played an old game where one person wore a blindfold and tried to catch another player. The players taunt the blindfolded player. Vika wore the blindfold, and Calliope, Ingrid, and Vivian were twisting her nipples and jabbing her. The babies were playing a card game. The real babies were sleeping in a playpen, watched over by the grannies.

When Nata appeared, Asteraceae said, "Girls, your parents are here."

Vika tore off her blindfold and ran to hug and kiss Mummy with the other girls. Then they hugged and kissed Arthur and Lydia. They were excited, so Vika took Calliope's hand to calm her down, preventing her from wetting herself.

Ingrid and Vivian sat next to Arthur, holding his hands.

Chatelaine finally asked, "Mummy, how is the war going? We have been safe here with our grannies. Our grannies had us pray for everyone in Camelot for fifteen minutes every morning and night. Asteraceae said our prayers would help protect the town and bring soldiers to help us. Did our prayers work, Mummy?"

"Darling, your prayers helped us so very much. No one has died on our side. I met a nephew, my sister's son. He is an Elf doctor in Camelot and saved Mummy's life. Jean-Michel isn't exactly Jean-Michel, but Prince Baldar, an Elf Prince. He is my son, too, and Gabriel is his father. How it came to be is a long story.

"Our dragon friends came to help us fight and brought DragonElves, pairs of Elves and Dragons, who pledged love and life for each other. Gabriel's wife, the goddess Hekate, sends Gabriel's sister, Āvi, with Amazon warriors and more battle elementals to fight for us. Every hour, another miracle occurs."

"Mummy, does Prince Baldar remember me," asked Chatelaine?

"Of course, he remembers you. I think he loves you, sweetheart."

"He does, Mummy? I hope so, for I adore him and miss him. Tell him his Chatelaine loves him."

The families played games in the morning. Around lunchtime, Calliope went to her mummy.

"Mummy, I wet myself, but I don't want the others to laugh at me. Will you come and change me?"

"Of course, I will change my excitable daughter. I love you so much, Calliope. I never want to lose you. Take my hand, and we will go to our room."

When they arrived in their bedroom, Mummy looked around and saw everything neat and clean.

"I am proud of all of you for keeping your room neat. Come to me, and I will take your dress off and clean you."

Nata cleaned Calliope and put a new dress on her.

Calliope said, "I am afraid, Mummy. I saw bad people in my dreams who were dark Demons who wanted to kill all of us. I didn't tell the others because I knew they would be afraid. Don't let the bad Elves kill us, Mummy. Please."

"Oh, my little girl, it isn't easy being an oracle, is it? It is too much pain for any little girl to bear. Mummy is so proud of you, darling.

I love you all the way to Papa. Did you know that Jean-Michel is Mummy's son?"

"I knew Mummy, for he looks like you. But I know his real daddy is Uncle Gabriel. Before our daddy was born, you and Uncle Gabriel married and loved each other more than the Elves could understand. He gave you to Daddy so Daddy would not cry from loneliness anymore."

"You and your sister know everything, don't you?"

"Not everything, Mummy. Just a lot. Can I go play now?"

Nata took Calliope by the hand and returned to Merlin's library.

Morgana and little Eleanor spent the morning doing little girl stuff.

The kitchen grannies prepared a wonderful lunch, and everyone had a great time. After lunch, the adults returned to Camelot, knowing their children were safe.

Suddenly, a beautiful young woman dressed in Grecian armour appeared in the war room, asking, "Who is the Commander of this Army? I am Āvi, Commander of the Army of the Djinn in the Great War. My troops will arrive tomorrow, and I must see the positions of our enemy so I know where to situate them."

"Commander, I am Prince Baldar, *Polemarchos* (Field Marshall) of our Army. The King of Camelot is Arthur with his Queen Lydia."

Āvi went to Lydia and hugged her.

"I have missed my little sister. Nice to meet you, Arthur. You married a hell of a lady. Congratulations."

"*Polemarchos* Baldar, I understand you have Dragons. I must borrow one to do an aerial survey to best disperse my troops."

"*Lokhagos* Lotakin will allow you to ride with you on his Dragon, Aviana. I will take you to him now and ride with another rider. No time to waste."

Baldar and Āvi left to complete their aerial survey. They returned in a few hours to discuss strategy with the DragonElves' officers and senior Knights of Camelot. Āvi had insisted on surveying all lands within a seven-day march of Camelot.

The commanding officers were all present in the war room, as Baldar reported.

"Commander Āvi recommended a wide-area survey. We discovered the princeling had hidden a second ogre army of about thirty thousand soldiers, a three-day march from Camelot. Their bivouac rests behind a range of small mountains near a single pass., The rest of the land is clear of enemies. She recommends placing soldiers to control the pass and then attack the ogres from behind, forcing them through the ravine to their deaths.

"I concur with her recommendations. After the slaughter, she attacks Crafty from behind and we from the front. She informed me that a powerful goddess and mage would arrive with the Army to supplement your magi in Camelot. Her name is Hekate, and it is she who sent Āvi. She is a special wife of Eugenis, who you know as Gabriel, and they are very close. She will locate him after she gets here."

Arthur asks, "Baldar, what odds are we will win?"

"Highness, currently, I would estimate that we have a slight advantage. I cannot include Hekate until I meet her, but our odds explode if she can control the worldlines. If she can find my father and your Saviour, our odds of victory are 100%.

"I have sent requests for reinforcements to every Commander I know who can arrive within a few days. Prince Festian reports the siege is almost over with destruction of the enemy, with minimal losses."

A handsome Elf with long dark hair and green eyes entered the war room.

The battle Elf said, "Brother, you asked for my help, and with Father's grace, I am here to fight and die, though not so likely as I am an Elf."

Baldar threw his arms around Festian, saying, "Festian, I can always count on you and your troops. Let me introduce you to my friends and comrades.

"First, I want you to meet King Arthur and his beautiful Queen Lydia. Arthur is a wise and benevolent king. The people of Camelot practise our Elf Religion, Festian, and they must be protected."

Festian bowed to Arthur, saying, "Your Majesty, it is an honour to meet you and your Queen. To know that your people practise the Elf Religion is a splendid gift for my Elves and me, and we will fight ten times more valiantly knowing this."

Baldar said, "Second, the woman in Grecian armour is *Stratigos* (General) of the Amazon Horse Archers. Āvi brought thirty thousand warriors. The Greek goddess, Hekate, controls the worldlines and brings them here. She will arrive with the bulk of our support. She will locate my father and brother, who are repulsing a large attack on an outer world. Unfortunately, there is no communication with them."

Festian bowed to Āvi, saying, "You are the sister of Gabriel, I believe. Father Gabriel taught us about the Great Djinn War and about you. The Elves know you as Wrathful Blood Lioness. Our female battle Elves pray to you."

Walking over to Nata and kissing her, Baldar said, "Festian, this is my mother and your aunt. Your cousin Kulkin is also here, and he saved Mother's life."

Festian went to Nata and kneeled in front of her on his left knee.

He took her hands up from her lap and kissed them, saying, "Mother, I am blessed, for I have seen and kissed these hands, again, of Father Gabriel's first daughter and wife. You are the First of the Elves created by the Great Father. The love shared by you and Gabriel is our most remarkable tale of romance and unconditional love. Our bards sing tales of the depth and faithfulness of the love you two shared.

"The bards sing of the sadness of the Great Father after he pledged you to your brother, who was fading away in despair. Erasing the memory of your love for Father still saddens him. But the good of others must come before his own. This is the reason the Elves love him so much. We call him the Great Father, Whose Love Is Immeasurable.

"But Gabriel would not give you to Tristan unless you agreed, which you did. We know you as the First Mother of Our Race, Who Knows Only Love.

Then Festian laid his head in Nata's lap, and Nata said, "My son reconnected me with the first part of my existence, so I remember. I remember birthing so many beautiful Elf children to love and nourish. Now I understand why I love being a mother. I remember you, Festian, and I bless you."

Festian stood, replying. "Thank you, Mother."

The revelation surprised Lydia. Arthur and his Camelot knights didn't know what to say, for their Nata was not only a powerful sorceress but Mother of the Elves and First Wife of Lord Gabriel.

Baldar brought everyone back to the current reality.

"Now that our introductions are over, we must return to the war. Festian, how many warriors did you bring?"

"I brought eight thousand, cousin. More are coming from the few remaining Elf Principalities nearby. I expect our cousins to supply at least forty thousand battle-eager Elves to fight. This battle will be a pivoting point in the End Wars. Ahri-Simeon will see the danger and send his senior princelings and, perhaps, his sister to oversee things. Ahri-Simeon will not come himself. He may send his magi, so we must counteract ourselves."

"Festian, as to magi, we have Mother, my sister Morgana, and Merlin. The Greek goddess of Witchcraft will arrive soon, and she is powerful enough to jump worldlines and bring troops from ancient Greece to our time. If Father considers her a special wife, then she is mighty. I am sure Father saw her importance in this War and married her."

Āvi interrupted.

"Princes, I think my troops must attack as soon as they arrive. It may draw some ogres to us, which we can handle. We have our flying chariots, and they carry amphoras filled with an ogre-selective, volatile, poisonous liquid created by Husband. Our troops and yours are immune to its effects. I don't know if we will have extra to give Camelot until our supplies arrive. They will be in position by tomorrow and attack at first light the next day. I hope reinforcements arrive for Camelot. We will proceed here as rapidly as we can. I will use our elemental spies to keep Camelot updated."

Baldar said, "Thank you, Commander. This afternoon, we begin our catapult barrage to disable as many ogre catapults as possible. Father invented a liquid fire to pour into large, hollow ceramic balls, igniting on contact. Our Dragons and DragonElves can burn the tents and wagons of the ogres. No foolish manoeuvres, for we need all of you intact. As the demons vaporise into the ground during the day, they will not be a problem. Princeling battle plans use demons to attack at night and ogres during the day."

"Dismissed to lunch. Then, our attack begins in two hours. Questions?"

There were no questions, and everyone dispersed.

Baldar went to speak with Nata.

"Mother, you are still recovering and must not over-exert yourself for a few days. If I lost you, Father would never forgive me. He loves you as much as ever, Mother. You must return to him as his wife. I will tell Tristan. Your mother promised me she would help."

"But Baldar, what about my daughters? I cannot leave them?"

"They will stay with you, perhaps in Camelot. We will make some minor changes in the past, but none will suffer over it. Will you take me to Chatelaine? She and I must speak."

Nata teleported Baldar and herself to Merlin's cave. When the two arrived in the kitchen, the girls were helping make lunch with the grannies. All her daughters went to hug Mummy and get a kiss.

Then, Baldar took Chatelaine's hand, saying, "I have not forgotten you, darling. I have been busy saving Camelot. Things are looking up, and we go on the offensive this afternoon. Father's Amazons will be here this evening. My cousin Festian has brought troops, and more are to arrive shortly.

"I wanted to visit you when free, so you know I have chosen you to wed. I can't promise that we can be scientists now, but one day, maybe in the future. Father said, 'We can marry if you so desire?'"

"Baldar, I agree to be your wife. I love you."

Baldar kissed Chatelaine on her lips. Then, Nata and Baldar returned to Camelot.

The barrage began at 1400 hr, apparent solar time. As the ogres expected no action, most were away from their catapults, presenting easy targets for the Dragons and Camelot's catapults. Camelot and the Dragons destroyed two-thirds of the ogre's firing power in four hours. All the catapult operators approved of Gabriel's incendiary jars. The DragonElves burned an astounding number of loaded supply wagons and tents.

Baldar asked Mother to write in the sky over the ogres, 'Kiss My Ass, Crafty,' which she did, asking, "Why do you torment the princeling?"

"Mother, the madder he gets, the more errors he will make. Trust me, I know him well."

Baldar met Festian, leaving the battlement.

Festian asked, "Don't you find it strange that Crafty hasn't launched a full-out attack on Camelot yet. He is not typically so patient."

"I have thought similarly, cousin. It is strange as we are decimating his demons, and I doubt he knows we found his backup force as we flew relatively high. It feels that something is wrong, and I know that no burrowing under the city is occurring."

"Cousin, I am concerned about your mother. Reminding her, she is the Elves' original mother and loved Gabriel is very unsettling. She is conflicted with her love for Tristan and Gabriel. But it seems her heart loves your father. We owe it to her to help her resolve the problem. Why did you even tell her, Baldar? It was very unkind of you."

"I had no choice, Festian. I did it on Father's instructions. He said he planned to restore our Golden Age when the Elves oversaw all of Creation. His mind is incomprehensible for a simple battle Elf."

"Simple, my ass. You are as devious and secretive as your father. But I love my cousin, who has a big heart, like his father. I'm hungry, and let us get some food and drink."

The pair of Elves headed to the Sleeping Dragon Inn.

When they arrived, Annie seated them with other Elves and brought them one of Merlin's most potent ales, Demon Kicker.

Festian winked at Annie, and Annie said, "Mind your manners, Sir Elf. I am a married woman. My husband is an officer in the Saviour's Army and is training in Montemar."

"Meant no disrespect, lass. I apologise. I trained in Montemar, myself, as did Baldar. If any of my soldiers cause you or this place trouble, send a message to me, and I will correct it."

Annie curtseyed and left.

"Festian, call one of your officers over here and inform him that the people of this city practise our Religion and are to be respected and helped."

A young officer came over, and Festian told him to spread the word to the army. The officer saluted to do as ordered.

Baldar and Festian chatted about old times, careful not to get too drunk.

Balder said, "Cousin, if something big is brewing, we will need Father or Tristan. I hope the Witch Goddess, Hekate, can find them, and I hear she is stunning and married to Father."

Festian replied, "Why does your father get all the babes?"

In a couple of hours, they left to walk the battlements, ensuring the glyphs were in place and there was no sign of burrowing vibrations.

They stopped to chat for a few minutes whenever they came upon guards.

When finished, both got ready for a sortie with one hundred Elf Cavalry and fifty of Arthur's Knights attacking the demon camp from the gates of Camelot. Morgana created a path of ice from the gates to the shore over the moat, which was thirty meters wide., sufficient for the cavalry. Being brilliant, she added protection glyphs at both ends.

The charge occurred as the demons rose and solidified from the Earth. They do not fully orientate for several minutes. The only sound heard as the cavalry rushed across the ice bridge was the jangling of men and horses' armour. As they were about to exit the ice bridge, the men unsheathed their sabres, holding them high to cut down the first demon they crossed.[30]

When they reached the land, demon heads and arms littered the battlefield. A giant is the only demon able to best a single Elf blade and horse. But an accurately thrown Elf lance will stop a giant, for elfin steel pierces hide and armour, and Elf blades are sharp and covered in killing glyphs. The other demon forms cannot adequately defend themselves against an Elf warhorse with its glyph'd armour and an Elf with a glyph'd sabre.

The Elves and Knights massacred at least three thousand demons that night with the loss of three knights, whose bodies their comrades retrieved to prevent mutilation. Baldar blew his retreat horn four hours after the charge, its eerie notes reverberating across the heath, generating fear in the enemy's heart. The men turned their horses and returned to Camelot, and Morgana melted the ice bridge promptly.

Dismounting from his warhorse in front of the castle, Baldar and Festian hurried to the war room to report the raid's success to Arthur. Arthur and Lydia were pleased.

---

[30] A heavy military sword with long cutting edges and slightly curved blades.

Arthur ordered that his pages inform the families to come to the castle. He also ordered the fallen Knights' bodies and armour to be immediately cleansed of blood and dirt for the families to mourn.

Turning to Baldar, he said, "I doubt if tonight's foray made much difference strategically, but it was good for our morale. Excellent work, Prince."

"Majesty, everything we do is to stall an attack on the city. I know Crafty is taking his anger out on his closest demons. Keeping him angry and slighted is our best policy until our Army is complete enough to attack. And attack we will."

Baldar and Festian made a final round of the battlements to ensure all was quiet.

Festian said, "Like the old days, Cousin?"

"It is so, dear friend. Immersing in a life or death battle makes me feel alive, and I could never sleep like our brethren did."

"It is as you say. Even if the Golden Age returns, I imagine there will be outposts of agent evil for us to dispose of, eh, Baldar? Sleep well."

"Same to you, Festian."

Both went to their chambers to wash and sleep, perchance to dream of a family to love and protect. Baldar saw a hypnogogic image of his Chatelaine before losing consciousness.

Baldar was eating breakfast with Festian when an escort brought a gorgeous woman dressed in Amazon armour like Āvi into the room. She was tall with dark eyes and dark, long, wavy hair, and her nose was straight, and her lips thin. Looking at her, Baldar saw she was a powerful woman with Elf blood running in her veins.

Baldar stood, bowing, "You are Hekate, Goddess of Witchcraft. You are Elf, in case you did not know, Goddess. I feel your innate power. This is my cousin, Prince Festian. I am Prince Baldar. We are Elves."

"Yes, I am Hekate. I may be Elf as there is a great resonance between my husband, the First Born and Lord General of the Blessed Isles, and me. I am pleased to meet others of my lineage."

"Hekate, are you hungry," asked Festian?

"I am. You Elves are well-mannered gentlemen. But I love my husband and will never have another man."

Hecate sat and was served a bowl of porridge, plate of ham, cheese, and bread. She focuses fully on hare food until she was full.

"You are straightforward, Goddess. Baldar and I like you already. Are your warriors situated and prepared for killing?"

"Yes, they are. You picked a promising field for killing ogres. I find them nasty and primitive. Not a shred of good in any of them. I can feel the essence of creatures. Our Amazons have secured the ravine, and Āvi controls our advancing cohort of warriors. The extermination will take only five or six hours. No survivors.

"How many soldiers do you have in this town, Prince Baldar?"

Baldar answered, "Twelve thousand now and three magi. We expect another thirty thousand in another two days. A messenger just reported another cousin arrived with fifteen thousand additional. We can start our last offensive when the rest of our reinforcements are in place. I want to attack from four sides to force them to the centre for an easier kill. We have flying machines and Dragons to carry poison bombs to drop, which only kill ogres. Someone called it technology."

"Good, then I can begin my search for my husband. If you excuse me, I will begin now."

Hecate disappeared in a burst of light.

Festian said, "She is one straightforward female. I would hate to be an ogre."

"Same here, cousin. Let us locate cousin Finnet."

The two arose from the table and left the castle. After a few inquiries, they found Prince Finnet brushing his horse, Ogre Stomper, in the stable. Finnet saw them approaching, donned an ogre mask, and hid. After his cousins passed through the stable doors, he jumped out, growling like a maddened female ogre in heat. Baldar and Festian jumped aside and were about to pull their swords.

Prince Finnet removed his mask, laughing, "Got you! You two are nothing but a pair of little girls scared by the bogey ogres. I bet Festian peed in his leggings."

Baldar and Festian began laughing and went to hug their cousin.

Festian said, "It has been a little tense here for the last week, Finnet. I am glad you haven't lost your sense of humour, yet, moronic as it is. How are your wife and daughters?"

"Agnetha is pregnant and will deliver in a few months. My twins are eleven and destined to be battle Elves and archers.

"I heard Natanel lives in Camelot. Is she here? I want to visit her because I want her blessing for my soldiers and me. One of your officers told me that the people of Camelot practise our religion?"

Festian replied, "It is true, Finnet. An old Elf Codex of the End is here, and Natanel and Tristan used it to introduce our religion. The people here practise altruism and love, Finnet, really. As Elves, we are honour-bound to defend this Holy City onto death.

"Baldar's father, Gabriel, came to Camelot, and the people understand he is the Father of all sentient creatures. Tristan is the prophesied Saviour.

"Baldar recovered Natanel's memories of being the Mother of our Race, and her heart pines again for Father Gabriel. She loves Tristan, but her natural place is with Gabriel, and Gabriel never told her because of his love for both.

"Baldar, my Granny Esmerelda, who wrote parts of the Elfin Codex, told me that our Holy Mother would return to Her Husband one day. The Golden Age of the Elves would come again, and the Elves group guilt over Ahri-Simeon would be no more."

Baldar said, "Well, that solves Nata's conundrum. It is in the Codex, which Father inspired the Elf Priestesses to compose. I guess he is the Master of our destinies, eh, cousins?"

"Seems so, Baldar, seem so," answered Festian.

"Finnet, get your warriors settled. The Inns here serve excellent food and drink. Watch out for Merlin's brews, for they are potent. We have nothing to fear here today. Tell them to be gentlemen, for most of the young ladies in Camelot are chaste. There are some excellent brothels, one of the Knights informed me. Very high class.

"Festian and I go to visit Commander Āvi. Later, Cousin."

The two Elves rode their flying horses to find the Amazon troops. They found them about a kilometre behind the ogre camp. They dismounted, and an Amazon Horse Archer saluted and took them to speak with her commander.

As they entered her command tent, Baldar said, "Impressive troops, Āvi. This is my cousin, Prince Festian. Since he was a boy, he has fought ogres and is an expert in killing them. He has agreed to fight with you after he discusses ogre defences and how they fight."

"Thank you, Baldar. I dislike entering a battlefield without advanced knowledge of my enemies' strengths and weaknesses."

Āvi offers her right arm to Festian.

He takes it, saying, "A great pleasure to meet you, Commander. We studied some of your battles in military school. Should we call your primary officers and work out an effective offence?"

Āvi nodded to an adjuvant to call her officers to her tent. The group spent two hours coming up with an effective plan of attack.

Festian asked, "Commander, did Hekate advise the Amazons how to kill ogres in the pass?"

"Hekate created magical catapults throwing poison liquids and incendiary vessels which explode in fire and disperse iron pellets. My fellow wife is a genius. She was heartbroken all her life, having only Demeter and Kore as friends. When Eugenis dispersed the Greek gods, she asked to marry him. Gabriel's daughter Isis removed the stone in her heart, and now she lives again. No one can ask for a truer friend than Hekate. She will find your father, Baldar."

"Commander, I want to stay and fight with you today. After our victory celebration, I will return to my warriors in Camelot."

"It would honour me to have you fight by my side, Prince Festian."

Baldar excused himself and returned to Camelot.

Hekate used her magick to sense electromagnetic and atonic disturbances large enough to isolate planets. She was not worried about the distances as she could travel anywhere; she works in five-space. The only problem was that she could enter five-space only once every twelve hours. She meditated for several hours, discovering ten places within one million light-years from Camelot.

Hekate possessed a fierce determination and allowed nothing to interfere with her desires. She had never been in love or married before Gabriel (Eugenis in ancient Greece) took her into his pantheon. But sweet Isis removed the stone from her heart so she could feel it once again.

She missed her husband, making her cry, "I will find you, my love. I swear by all that is Holy."

She picked the first disturbance area and vanished.

Baldar walked to the war room to report to Arthur.

"Your Majesty. Festian stayed to discuss battle strategies with Āvi and her officers. Festian knows the ways of ogres better than anyone else I know. Hekate produced weapons for the mass destruction of the enemy, and Festian brought blade poison for the Amazon arrows. He knows the enemy has never faced Amazon Horse Archers and will panic.

"Our forces will prevail based upon all I have observed. They must kill every ogre to prevent Crafty from knowing about his loss.

"Hekate is searching for Gabriel and Tristan, and she will find them and bring them to us. Hekate is a determined woman and warrior, and I would hate to be her enemy."

"Thank you, Baldar. The troops Festian and Finnet brought to Camelot engage well with our citizens. The Elf Religion binds us as brothers and sisters. I am delighted. Business is stable as the Elves insist on paying in silver. Our merchants only charge their cost as we appreciate their help. Some of your soldiers teach us more about our new religion when off duty.

"The children adore the Dragons and the DragonElves, for they give them rides. The female Dragons are motherly, sit with the children, and tell them beautiful stories to cheer them up. They also supply mothers' milk for our young ones, as we do not have sufficient cows and goats.

"It has always amazed me that people often act their best in troubling times. Perhaps much good will come out of this situation."

Baldar bowed, saying, "I am sure it shall, Highness. I go to check to see if we have replenished our catapult projectiles? Excuse me."

Baldar left for the arms building, situated as far away from people as possible.

Arriving, he asked the chief engineer, "Captain, how is production going?"

"Right on schedule, Sir. We will be done by late afternoon."

"Good work, Captain."

Baldar informed Festian's officers that he had stayed with the Amazons to fight. He will return after the hidden enemy threat is resolved.

He inspected the town walls and troops to see if they were secure, telling them we would attack in two or three days.

He walked by the practise area and saw the soldiers occupied with military exercises.

He thought to himself, "All is well in Camelot now. Let us hope it stays this way for a few more days."

He headed for the Sleepy Dragon Inn and found Finnet speaking with Nata and Morgana. He sat next to them, and Annie brought him a tankard of Dragon's Blood, which he liked.

Annie said, "Seeing you and your soldiers in our inn is nice. They have been perfect gentlemen. Many of them are helping us spread the Elf Religion by teaching us. Everyone seems pleased that we practise your religion. Thank you, Sir."

"Annie, you and your family may call me Baldar. I am glad to hear this. Religion is a big part of our lives, Annie, and it gives us strength when we go to battle and comforts us when we are despondent.

"Do you know that your Auntie Nata is the Mother of our Race? She is the most precious Elf in all the universes."

"I know, as Prince Finnet told us many stories about Auntie Nata. We call her Holy Mother; everyone loves her and would die protecting her.

"Even my sisters and I know she is the Mother of Camelot, too. Unlike the Elves, we are unimportant, but she loves and cares for us. I think she is the Mother of all creatures. Don't you, Baldar?"

Baldar saw that Annie's eyes began to water, asking, "Why the sad eyes, little sister. Come sit next to me and tell me how I can brighten your face again?

Baldar made room for her, and Annie sat down, answering, "I married a few days before all this happened, and my husband, Thomas, had to return to Montemar for military training. I worry about him, Milord. I am sorry I am crying."

Baldar took Annie's hand, saying, "Annie, Montemar is an incredible fortress that no one has conquered. Your Thomas is safe there. Our military trainers are the best in the universe and will show him how to fight without injury. Your papa told me he is an engineer and will not have to do any hand-to-hand combat. So, I wouldn't worry. Father will protect him."

Annie wiped her eyes.

"Thank you, Milord. I must get back to work."

She returned to her chores, looking relieved.

Nata said, "That was sweet of you, Son. Cousin Finnet has told me more of the Codex, written partially by his grandmother. We are good friends, but she never told me about my earlier life. I think the Codex came from your father, Baldar. My destiny is to return to him with all my daughters. I believe Tristan always knew about my past, at some level, now that I look back. His destiny love is Morgana.

"Baldar, the Golden Age of the Elves will return to this universe, and peace and goodwill will prevail again. I will never fully understand our father. He is like a null point and an absolute infinity at the same time. All He wants us to do is love each other and help each other enjoy creation. I love him more than I can say.

"I guess his special daughter, Isis, was correct when she bragged her daddy was the best-fixer-upper in this universe."

Baldar replied, "Nata, I will surprise you with what I know. Our son is visiting with Chatelaine, and I took his form to see what you had decided. I had to know you wanted me, my love, and I hope our daughters will, too."

Gabriel resumed his standard form, and Nata threw her arms around him, kissing him many times.

"My love, my love, my husband true. You made me leave you once, but never will you send me away again."

Tristan, who had taken Finnet's form, resumed his own.

"Tristan, you knew all along, didn't you?"

"Well, not forever. Baldar told me when he came to Camelot. It is your destiny to mother our race again. I am happy with my Morgana and student wives; the twins will stay with you. Demeter and Kore will go with Father, but you will stay with your other daughters. Everything is falling in place for the rebirth of the Golden Age, though much work remains. I love you, Nata, always have and always will."

An astonishing, beautiful female introduced herself to Nata, saying, "Mum, I am married to your husband, and I hope we will be friends. I used my magick to locate and bring him home to us. He loves all his wives, and we love each other. You will meet most of them soon."

Nata opened her arms to Hekate and hugged and kissed her.

"I welcome you and your sisters, Hekate. And I want you to meet my children, who will adore you. Two of them, you know, Sophie and Alliona. You know them as Demeter and Kore. I call them my babies, for they are my youngest, and I bore all from my womb. Come sit and chat."

Molly exclaimed, "Glory be to the Saviour and Our God. They came to save us. Annie, run to the castle and tell Arthur, Tristan, and Gabriel have returned."

The news spread rapidly throughout Camelot. Even many of the soldiers ran to listen to the news. The church bells rang, drawing people from work and play to hear of another miracle.

The Saviour has returned. The Golden Age is coming. Natanel is the Mother of the Elves, and Gabriel is everyone's Father.

How everyone knew so much so fast remains a mystery in Camelot. I heard it was Baldar's and Finnet's idea to strengthen the Elf Religion. Knowing them as I do it is likely accurate.

Baldar returned with Merlin after a kitchen granny told them, "Sirs, the bells they are a-ringing in Camelot. Better go."

From habit, Merlin returned them to the Sleeping Dragon Inn. Both immediately recognised Tristan, Gabriel, and Hekate.

"Merlin, Hekate found them and brought them home. I am going to kiss her," said Baldar.

He kissed Hekate on the cheek, saying, "You are the best goddess anywhere. You found them.

"Nice to see you are safe, Tristan. How went the battles?"

"The reawakened Elves fought fiercely with slight injuries. We have extinguished the threat, which I see was only a ruse by Ahri-Simeon. He is cagier than he was in the past, and it seems the Oblivion helped him more than hurt him."

Gabriel hugged Baldar, saying, "Ahri-Simeon will send his sister to command their invasion. Expect more humans and dwarves. They know demons are too easy for us to kill. I will send one of my spy elementals to inform one of the ogre Captains that Tristan and I are in town to rid ourselves of the vainglorious Crafty. I want Ahri-Lilith here to return her to her original self. All she ever wanted was to be loved and a mother. Easily enough done.

"I knew well that going to the outer worlds was a ruse, but the entities there needed saving."

Baldar slapped his father on the back, saying, "Live and learn, live and learn from the masters."

Gabriel smiled.

Morgana went to Tristan, asking, "You are alright with everything. I know your first love was Mummy."

"Temporally, you were my first love, Morgana. I am okay with recent events. How can I object, for my essence is love, as is Father's? Father loved me too intensely and should not have given Nata to me. Father forgets his own needs overly much. Being the Creator is not a straightforward job. Being back together will right this universe, for they are the Father and Mother of the First Ones.

"I guess love cures and love hurts, but mainly, it just loves. Simple enough."

"I love you, Tristan. You do not have my permission to leave ever again. Understand?"

"Yes, Morgana," and he kissed her.

That night, the people and the Elves rejoiced and partied under a golden shield that protected Camelot.

Overlooking Camelot stood Crafty and Ahri-Lilith on a nearby hill.

Crafty said, "Mistress, we will unleash our hidden forces the day after tomorrow, and the town will fall."

"Crafty, you are an idiot, but don't feel so bad, for your brother is one, too. Even Ahriman the Evil is not strong enough to defeat the Father of Creation. We will fight to the end but lose, Crafty."

Ahri-Lilith disappeared and reappeared with Gabriel when he was dressing for dinner.

"Hello, Lilith. You have not fulfilled the destiny I wrote for you, and you were my favourite daughter. Do you remember, honey?"

"I only remember my two favourite cousins, Marduk and Eleanor, loved me. But my brother ruined everything and made them hate me."

"That is not true, Daughter. Marduk and Eleanor loved and cared about you, even after you allowed vanity to rule your heart. I know you loved Marduk because he protected you. But your brother tricked and lied to you so you would become a vassal of my brother."

"But why wouldn't Marduk love and marry me when I was sweet?"

"I did not mean Marduk to be your husband and give you baby Elves."

"Who was I to love and marry, Father? An ogre?"

"No, my dear, I am your husband and will give you Elf babies."

"Even if you were, I am evil now, so why would you want to be with me?"

"Are you happy being evil, Lilith? Tell me, truly."

"No, I am miserable. Everyone hates me."

"Lilith, do you want me to remove all the evil in you so you are a pure virgin again?"

"You would do this for me, Father?"

"If you ask me to do this, I will, Daughter. Then you will have found your destiny."

"I want to be pure again and have babies. I only wanted to be a well-educated Mother-Elf like Mummy. If my destiny is to marry you, Father, I will. Will you take me now, even with my filth?"

"Drop your dress and look. There is no more filth or evil in you. Come and make love with me as I willed before Time began."

Lilith looked at herself and saw she was clean and unmarked by evil. She lay with Gabriel in joy and peace at last. She knew she would conceive and her husband would fix everything so no one hated her anymore. Lilith fell asleep in Gabriel's arms.

Gabriel woke her with a kiss, saying, "Come, wife and daughter, we shall go to dinner together. I will help you dress. I made a beautiful dress for you and found the most precious gems for you to wear. See how beautiful you and your soul are."

Gabriel dressed and combed her hair, then let her look at herself in the mirror.

Lilith saw a pretty, young Elf girl with sparkling eyes full of love. Tears fell from her eyes, which Gabriel wiped away.

"Now, my pure wife, no tears, for I will show Camelot my precious Lilith. They will say it is another of God's miracles, and I will say this is my beautiful daughter and wife, Lilith. She finally agreed to accept her destiny. Take my arm, and we will go to the Sleeping Dragon Inn, where our family celebrates."

Gabriel and his Lilith walked downstairs to a waiting carriage. He helped her climb abroad, and then he followed.

"Sleeping Dragon Inn, driver, please."

The driver snapped the reins, and the horse headed to the Inn. When they arrived, the driver lowered the steps, and Gabriel exited and gave his hand to Lilith to descend.

The couple walked into the Inn. Everyone stopped talking to look at Gabriel and the utterly beautiful dark-haired Elf lady. The men rose from their benches to honour Gabriel.

"Look, honey. The men are standing so to honour your beauty and demeanour."

Gabriel took Lilith to Nata.

Nata recognised and hugged and kissed her on the cheek, saying, "I am delighted to see my sweet daughter wholesome again."

"Daddy always fixes things," says little Isis.

Lilith did not know who little Isis was but recognised she was referring to her daddy.

Gabriel whispered, "No crying, young lady. Husband's orders."

Gabriel and Lilith sat down.

Morgana said, "Gabriel, you forgot to introduce your beautiful friend."

"I did, didn't I. This lovely lady is my wife, Lilith."

"Lilith, you mean, the Lilith?"

"I mean her, Morgana. Isn't she beautiful and sweet? Not a wicked thought in her head, nor feeling in her heart. She will make a wonderful mother, right, Nata?"

"Absolutely, Husband. This means she never was Ahri-Lilith, and our father corrected her worldline, so she attained the destiny he intended. So, I ask you to be kind to her and help her readjust her memories."

Baldar replied, "Welcome home, Lilith. Personally, I am happy you are in our family."

Finnet added, "I am happy also, Cousin Lilith."

Lilith turned to Gabriel with wide-open eyes and a grin, saying, "Husband, my cousins like me, at least a little. There is hope for me."

"Sweetheart, I look forward to seeing you nursing our child. Our babies will be perfect. I love you. Your destiny is fantastic, honey. Trust me.

"I recommend we keep this a secret from nonfamily, for it is too big a miracle for Camelot," said Nata.

Everyone agreed and enjoyed being with Lilith. They were pleased to have her back where she belonged.

The town celebrated the return of the Saviour and his Divine Father for most of the night. The residents and the Elves found that the two races shared a destiny chosen by the Great God. The return to a Golden Age where Love is Supreme and Generosity is the realm's currency.[31]

Lilith asked her new husband, "Husband, do you write destinies for all sentient creatures?"

Gabriel turned and kissed her forehead, saying, "No, darling. I cannot write destinies for all sentient beings. It would be impossible, for everything would be predetermined, and sentient creatures would have no choice. All I do is create an evolutionary plan for each new universe and a transfinite set of worldlines from the beginning to the end.

"Each alternative universe must solve the same evolutionary problem, overcoming the biopsychological drive towards egoism and hoarding. Consciously replacing these with altruism and generosity. The endless conundrum I give to all sentient life."

Morgana replied, "Father, why can you not fix this?"

Gabriel said, "Daughter, by existing within each of my universes, my powers are transfinite but not infinite. Only a mind more extensive than your manifest God could do this. Still, infinity cannot function within a transfinite universe. Therefore, I miscalculate events, so I must suffer with my creatures.

"But my desire for each world is to find its way to the Golden Age. The Age I visualised when I created the worldlines. Hidden within my worldlines is an ancient path leading to the Kingdom of Heaven or the Kingdom of the Elves. Solve and overcome the evolutionary

---

[31] The Golden Age of the Elves is the foundation reality for the realm of the Christ Consciousness following the destruction of Satan et al. If one knows Elf history, one discovers that many human ideas descended from the Elves. It is found also in Hindu Literature.

conundrum, and a world rises from the reactive into the proactive world. When sentient creatures accomplish this chore, they find enlightenment.

"So, to answer Lilith's question, I write destinies for creatures I see having the skills and desire to help me help all sentient beings. But these creatures need to find their futures through their own efforts, though I will help them when I need them to be where I would like.

"So, my beloved Lilith, I wrote a hard destiny for you, a destiny you had to suffer to grow into an enlightened Elf. Still, you could accept or reject my plan for you, honey. By coming to me to seek forgiveness and acceptance, you fulfilled my desire for you.

"You, Lilith, will inspire those who think themselves lost and damned. I will reward you a thousand-fold for each day you suffered for your destiny. You, Lilith, have attained a place next to Natanel and me. Two daughters and spouses forever, Eternal. Glory to She who carried my Cross for the salvation of All. I love you, Lilith."

The Elves in the Inn did now know what to say. But now, they understood their father so much better.

Baldar stood, slamming his sword hilt on the tabletop.

"Friends, stand and toast our father and mother, who created the Golden Ages for us. We toast our cousin Lilith, who suffered for the return of our Golden Age. Beings so benevolent, they come to work and live with us. Let us take oaths to serve and love those who serve and love us beyond measure. I give my life to you, Great Father and Great Mother. Use me better than I can use myself."

The room roared with the reverberation of the oath as the crowd repeated it many times.

Gabriel, Tristan, Natanel, and Lilith attended the war room the following day.

Gabriel said, "Arthur, this is my daughter, Lilith. She suffered more than any of you can imagine and now equals Natanel. She defected from her brother, recanted, and acknowledged the destiny I created for her before time began. I cleansed her of all evil, and we can trust her.

"I assigned the most difficult destinies to my daughters and wives, for the female constitution is spiritually stronger. Why? Because females carry life in their wombs and innately sacrifice for their children—good or bad. Mother Space suffers and never stops loving the creatures within Her Womb, and women will suffer for the good of all beings. Therefore, our religion honours all women. They are vessels sent by Mother Space to bear life and carry our sentient agents of Destiny, male and female.

"Males are to protect the families women create physically and spiritually. Abusing a female is a horrendous crime punished by banishment from the Golden Age and annihilation.

"To respect and love those of the female gender pleases Mother, and she welcomes you to Our Home. Mother Space and I are One Unmanifest, the Father and the Mother of All. So, please Mother and me by accepting Lilith and your wives, sisters, and mothers. She will prove invaluable in your battle against Ahri-Simeon. As my son has told you, I will annihilate Ahriman the Evil, for none of you can."

Nata took Lilith by the right hand, turning to Arthur, the Elves, and the Knights, saying, "I accept Lilith, for I remember that her life was never easy. Unlike my other children, she felt rejected and unloved, making her easy prey for her brother, Simeon.

"I accept her as my equal, and so should all of you."

Lilith began to cry. Everyone realised she was genuine. Like their Morgana, she had to go into the Dark to purify the collective mind of all sentient creatures to return them to the Golden Age. To incinerate the sins that limit altruism.

Queen Lydia went to hug Lilith, saying, "Arthur, accept her into Camelot. I am not equal to my holy sister, Ariel, or Āvi, as you know her, but I can read hearts, and this girl's heart is pure. Make a Proclamation,

Arthur, declaring that you pardon her of her past errors. Accept and elevate her to a Noble Lady of Camelot and child of Gabriel and Nata."

Arthur searched the eyes of those in the room for disagreement, but there was none.

He stood tall, saying, "Camelot forgives Lady Lilith for the errors of her past and takes her into our arms as a Noble Lady of Camelot and wife of our beloved Gabriel. So Mote It Be. Archivist, write my Order and cry it to my subjects today.

"Come, Lady Lilith, and receive my hug and kiss."

Lilith went to Arthur, still crying but now from joy and not sorrow. Arthur hugged and kissed her.

Gabriel lifted her to hold her in his arms, spinning her around.

"Lilith, you are free of what I asked of you so long ago by acceptance of your destiny. I love you, Lilith. Arthur, please add this line to your Proclamation. Our Father Gabriel proclaims his Eternal Love for His Beloved, Lady Lilith."

"Archivist, add this to my proclamation and send our cryers now."

Nata said, "Husband, you are to accompany your Elf wives and parade Lilith around Camelot. Baron Ivan will accompany us to validate Arthur's Proclamation. Is this okay, Arthur?"

"An excellent good idea, Aunt Nata. What do you think, Ivan?"

"Reassurance is good for the people. I am happy to help. Shall we leave, Nata?"

The foursome left with Nata on Baron Ivan's arm and Lilith on Gabriel's. They were off to inspection of the battlements and the town.

The residents of Camelot were open to Lilith, for they felt the love that radiated from her. The Elves bowed down to her. Verbum sap as she was with the Holy Mother, Baron Ivan, and Gabriel.

Following the walk, they went for lunch at the Sleepy Dragon Inn. The group found Baldar and Finnet eating with several of Festian's officers.

Suddenly, Prince Festian entered the room in battle armour, covered in black ogre blood.

He saw Gabriel and bowed to him, reporting, "Lord General, mission accomplished. The ogre threat is no more. No ogre escaped, as Philathorn burned every escaping ogre. Commander Āvi is advancing towards Camelot and will arrive tonight and rest two kilometres away. Goddess Hekate is hiding us from Crafty's eyes."

"Good news, Festian. Sit, drink, and eat with us. Baldar, please carry the news to Arthur. Let my wife's army rest for a day and ensure they have provisions and medical supplies. Send an elemental with an Elf battle horse so Āvi can come to discuss our battle meeting in four hours in the war room. I will shield all movement."

Merlin had returned the Table Round and its chairs to Arthur as a good omen for the battle ahead. Arthur sat at the head of the table with Lydia close by in an auxiliary chair. Gabriel, Tristan, Baron Ivan, Prince Finnet, Prince Festian, Commander Āvi, Merlin, Prince Baldar, Lady Natanel, Lady Hecate, Lady Lilith, Lokatin, and Paulak sat at the table. Prince Paulak had arrived in the early afternoon with twelve thousand battle Elves. Lady Morgana sat a little behind and in between Natanel and Gabriel.

Gabriel opened the meeting.

"Comrades, we launch our offence against Princeling Crafty tomorrow at sunrise. They bring one corps of ogres, some forty thousand, making sixty-five thousand. Lady Lilith tells me her brother called two elder brothers to aid in our defeat.

"If you look at the tabletop, you will see the area occupied by Crafty. Behind him waits Commander Āvi's Amazons. These two parties lie in a straight line, with Camelot north of Āvi.

"Prince Festian will occupy the land to the east, and Prince Paulak will be west of the ogre army. The Goddess Hecate, Merlin, the DragonElves, and Dragons will be auxiliaries to Baron Ivan and Camelot's attack.

"Baldar fights with Festian. Nata fights with Finnet. Morgana fights with Paulak. Hekate, love, you must permanently find and close Ahri-Simeon's troop portal. You discovered your husband, so I know you can do such. Take Lady Lilith with you on your mental search; she will help."

"I will not fail, my husband. I now have a life worth dying for. I am off to search. Come, Lady Lilith."

Both left the room to enter a magical trance in Arthur's chapel.

"Troop strengths are Paulak, 12,000, mainly horsemen. Festian, 8,000, primarily horsemen. Finnet, 18,000 infantry, Amazon, 30,000 House Archers and Elementals, Camelot, 10,000 knights, archers, and yeomen. We will probably outnumber the enemy, but we will win even if Ahri-Simeon has upgraded my wife's estimate.

"Camelot's firepower comprises catapults with incendiary and poison gas bombs. Our magical cohort includes Lady Natanel, Hekate, Morgana, Merlin, and Tristan.

"I will do all I can to prepare you for victory, but I cannot reveal your destiny now. I suggest you win. I will protect the people of Camelot and those in Merlin's Crystal Cave. Protecting Camelot proper is in Baron Ivan's hands.

"The attack will begin one hour before the usual waking time of the ogres. It will start with a catapult attack lasting one hour. Then, the south, west, and east legions will attack, forcing the ogres towards Camelot. The ogre camp is about one thousand meters away from Camelot, thinking they are outside our catapults. They will soon discover that their assumption is erroneous.

"Baron Ivan will attack from the north when all the church bells ring. The three other armies will strike at my command. Every Elf, Amazon, knight, and yeoman wears a red piece of cloth around their right upper arms, which will protect them from arrows and spears. It cannot prevent death in armed combat. Elves win because of courage and dedication, not by magic.

I ride with Commander Āvi and her Amazons. Each Army will carry the double-headed dragon banner of the Saviour flying on high. Tristan will ride by your side, Ivan.

"I will not interfere magically in the battle unless Ahri-Simeon brings more troops. After we have contained the enemy within the centre of the fighting field, I will turn this area into a quicksand swamp and suck them down to nothingness. Prior to doing this I will light the sky. I want each army to sound a general retreat the way they came. Let your archers cover your retreat with arrows so dense the ogres cannot move forward.

"The problem with egoism is that it thinks it can win against God, which is frankly impossible. If your hearts are pure and adamant, the Golden Ages returns. I will address each of your armies myself. Remind your soldiers to fight with their hearts to protect the innocent and meek from oppression. Whether they live or die, fighting for the oppressed is all I ask. Your future is mine; you will live with me in the Golden Age. To fight this way is to be the victor."

Lady Hekate asked, "Husband, after Lilith and I close the portal, can I join the battle for I lust for ogre blood. Evil must not be tolerated."

"You may fight with your sword and magick, my darling. But only one on one or to save a comrade."

"Thank you, Husband."

Lilith asked, "Husband, I, too, want to fight. May I join Hekate? She is special to me."

"Then you and Hekate will ride with me after the catapult attack. Hekate can teleport both of you, and you will wear standard Elf armour. I do not want you recognised, for I will not have time to save you. Hekate, I place our Lilith in your hands."

"She and I will protect each other, Husband. Both of us bear your child, so we must live to deliver. I love you, my Lord General."

"Soldiers, to your armies. I want you to perform our old ritual for entering a righteous war. I desire the ancient religion to grow and prosper again, for it leads into the Golden Age of the Elves. Baron Ivan, Natanel, will conduct one for your troops. Dismissed."

Natanel asked her husband, "Your wives need to be loved by you this night. Each with you alone. You must connect our single hearts into one pure heart with one goal and desire. To return love to all the worlds, banishing hate and greed forever. Like you, I have watched life become conscious and mature, making egregious mistakes for sure. Seeing one hero or another carrying their people towards the Golden Age. Husband, it is time for this game to end. Please, Husband."

Nata fell to the floor, sobbing.

Gabriel kneeled beside her, saying, "This game is the most pressing challenge in any universe. But you know I fix everything that remains undone. None suffer forever. But the Kingdom of the Golden Age comes earned and not given gratis. I will do as you ask, kind daughter and wife."

Nata and Morgana transported Festian and Finnet to the hidden waiting areas with their armies. Baldar stayed in Camelot to prepare for the Elf war ritual, and the Army Commanders did the same.

Ever growing in knowledge and being during the Golden Age. The ritual takes about an hour. Its purpose is to prepare oneself for death in battle if such occurs. To die with honour and meaning, sacrificing one's own life force for the innocent and meek is the highest good a battle Elf can perform. Knowing that one day, one will live again to eat, drink, and celebrate with friends and family. Hoping Lord Gabriel will write a destiny for you for the next universe.

Hekate and Lilith found the troop portal and closed it permanently. The opposing troops were equal now, so Gabriel would have his fair battle.

Baldar and Gabriel inspected the battlements and the catapult areas to ensure all was ready for the morning barrage. Gabriel stopped to chat with an older catapult technician.

"Soldier, are you ready for the morrow?"

"Aye, Sir, Lord General. I may be a grandfather, but I have fired catapults all my life and know how to adjust my aim for all critical variables. My accuracy is within a three-meter circle, and my sighting scope is of my design with good magnification."

"I would like to see through it, soldier."

"Climb up and look, Milord. You will see my expertise."

Gabriel climbed onto the catapult and looked, saying, "This is the best scope I have ever seen. I promote you to Captain of my Armoury. I want more range finders like yours. Can you fix all the other catapults?"

"Immediately, Milord. I will not let Camelot down."

"I know you won't, Captain. I will speak with you when the barrage begins."

After finishing their inspection, Baldar went to speak with Arthur, and Gabriel went to his chamber to rest. Arriving, he found Hekate and Lilith naked in bed with each other.

Hekate said shyly, "We undressed to wait for you in bed. Since you were late, we kissed each other, and you know, the rest of the things you like to watch us do just happened. Are you upset with us, Husband?"

Gabriel, laughing, replied, "No, darling. Lilith needs as much tender love as she can get. I know you love her, Hekate, so everything is as it should be."

Gabriel undressed and climbed into bed.

"I think you two will be safer carrying semen into battle in the morning. What do you think?"

Lilith replied, "I would love to be full of semen for battle. Lots of semen. Right, Hekate?"

"Right, Lilith."

"I wonder why all my wives have picked up the twins' security question for each other. Curious but cute," mused Gabriel.

Natanel and Āvi arrived shortly, undressed, and began making love with Lilith and Hekate to please Gabriel.

The five made love for much of the night, then rested for the battle, as they needed to be up for the barrage early.

Gabriel was on the battlements with his new captain of the Armoury. "Are your technicians ready, Captain?"

"Aye, Milord. All is ready when you light the skies so we can see. Our first barrage will be poison gas bombs to the sleeping areas and incendiary bombs to all arrow and lance wagons and tents."

"Excellent, Darum. Blow the horn. Our offence begins now."

The sky lit as if it were day, and the desired targets were visible through the new range-finders. The technicians adjusted their catapults and fired. The poisonous ceramics made little noise, hitting the ground. The poison distributed itself well when the incendiary bombs awoke the ogre camp.

The poison gas dropped many ogres, and the firebombs destroyed many weapons. The barrage's real purpose was to keep the ogres from organising to resist an assault.

Towards the end of the barrage, the sun was rising. Gabriel appeared before each army outside Camelot on his Palomino warhorse, wearing his golden Mithril Elf armour. All Elf armour will reject arrows and spears automatically, and it is not wholly immune to swords. The morning sun reflected off his armour, and he held his helmet in his left hand with the reins. His very presence inspired confidence in the soldiers.

He walked his horse in front of each army, holding his lance high in his right hand.

Gabriel said, "Comrades, today is the opening battle against Ahri-Simeon and his master, Ahriman the Evil. Today, we fight for those who are not warriors but support us in many other ways. Our friends, parents, children, blacksmiths, farmers, physicians, herbalists, and all the rest, especially our innkeepers. Merlin, our local mage, prepared a brew to increase your power and endurance three times. It will keep you focused on our aim of exterminating the enemy.

"Comrades, we fight, and some will die, but evil unopposed can never be bargained with or tolerated. Evil wants only to destroy, and to combat it, we destroy it. The Golden Age of the Elves is not a myth but moves into a future time whenever evil reigns. A time when Man, Djinn, and Elf live in brotherhood and peace. Today, our battle cry is, Our Destiny is Our Golden Age. Long May It Reign.

"Drink from your canteens as I emptied the water and filled them with Merlin's Battle Elixir. Drink now."

The soldiers opened their canteens, drinking down the fiery brew.

When the canteens were empty, Gabriel chanted, "Our Destiny is Our Golden Age. Long May It Reign."

Gabriel and the Commanders rode in the front to be the first to face the enemy. The troops yelled back and chanted as their commanders led the advance. The Elves on horseback struck their Battle Drums to reinforce the chanting.

Crafty restored order to his troops as the noise of a moving army chanting struck their ears from the south, east, and west. As the catapult barrage had ended because of a lack of bombs, Crafty headed towards Camelot. He ordered his generals to arrange a strong fighting line with shields and lances. This seemed the best defence for the catapults would be silent during armed conflict.

The DragonElves dived onto them, launching poisoned-tipped arrows and dragon fire as the princeling attempted to establish order. For an Elf, the arrow sheath is never absent of arrows, for it magically refills after it empties. An Elf can fire thirty to forty arrows per minute nonstop.

The first army to arrive was Āvi's Amazons, and her buglers blew their attack horns. The DragonElves stopped their aerial harassment, jumping off their Dragons to fight on foot. DragonElves live to battle against oppressors and share one trait with the ogres. Their Dragons hover close to guard their gender-opposite partners. They do not fear death, for death is a door to the Elves' returning Golden Age.

The Elf books say that Dragons bonding with Elves receive the gift of transformation into Elves, so they are married. When an Elf or a Dragon loses their spouse, they pine into death. They will not stay when asked.

As the power of battling rose, Gabriel's warhorse pulled ahead of those of the Amazons to attack. Elf warhorses hate ogres and stomp them to death if they can, and Āvi cannot keep up with him.

Seeing Lord General attack the ogre lines alone inspired the warriors beyond imagination. They cheered as he approached the ogre lines.

He met the first shield of ogres, throwing his lance as he neared the first row of shields. The force was so great his lance pierced through the hearts of the ogres to the fourth row. He withdrew his scimitar from its sheath as his horse jumped over the first eight shield rows. As his horse landed securely, he struck off the head of the nearest ogre.

Gabriel and his warhorse moved so quickly that no ogre could touch him. Now covered in black blood, Gabriel and his horse slowly forced their way through the ogre lines, breaking free as the three armies arrived on the battle scene. He fought through the ogres heading for Crafty, who watched on a hill some distance away. It was time that the princelings died permanently.

Gabriel cast a spell, trapping the three princelings on their hill.

Baldar and Festian arrived next and jumped off their mounts to fight hand-to-hand, as did many other Elves. Battle Elves fight in groups of eight and will guard an injured mate. The rest of the mounted Elves disrupted the ogre defences so the foot soldiers could more easily kill the enemy.

An ogre jammed a spear tip into a small space between Baldar's breastplate and shoulder armour. Festian rushed to his side and killed the ogre.

"Are you able to fight, Cousin?

Laughing, Baldar responded, "Thanks for caring, Cousin. It is only my shield arm, and I can still fight. Bet I will kill more ogres than you."

"It's a bet, Cousin. By the way, glad to be fighting again with you."

"Same here, Festian."

The pair moved faster than the other Elves, spreading enemy blood and limbs everywhere. Whenever an ogre or human lost a spear, Festian or Baldar would use it to kill another enemy.

Soon, the ogres retreated toward the only vacant land, Camelot. The church bells rang, and soldiers blew bugles. Tristan, Baron Ivan, and the Knights of Camelot emerged from Camelot's gates at full gallop over another ice bridge created by Morgana.

The ogres found themselves trapped, and the four armies annihilated the remaining ogres, dwarves, and humans over the next two hours. It turned out manifesting the quick sand was unnecessary.

Gabriel rested his warhorse before attacking the princelings. He wanted them to watch the slaughter of their ogres.

Gabriel teleported Lilith to his side, for she had a message for one princeling to carry back to their master. He mounted his warhorse and pulled up Lilith to ride in front of him.

Gabriel asked, "Sweetheart, are you afraid?"

"No, Husband, I am not afraid. I am not scared of my brother any longer. I know you love me and will protect our baby and me. I am happy to be pregnant and know that you and Hekate really love me, and I am happy for the first time in my life."

Gabriel and Lilith rode through his guard shield. The princelings cast fireballs and iron at them, but Gabriel continued unharmed.

"The game is over. Stop your magic. Put down your arms and listen."

Crafty and his two brothers complied. Hate radiated from their eyes.

"Crafty, Baldar wants to kill you himself, so watch your brothers burn in flames."

Gabriel said one word in Enochian, and Crafty's two brothers found their feet frozen to the Earth. Gabriel said another word, and they lit like Christian torches in Nero's Garden, screaming as their soulless carcasses burned.

"Dearest, would you like to tell Crafty something?"

"Yes, I would. Crafty, tell my brother that Gabriel removed his spell over me. He loves and genuinely cares for me. My husband made me a pure virgin, and I gave myself to him because I love him. Father elevated me to be beside him, equivalent to Natanel, the Mother of all of us. My destiny is to help my husband return our universe to the Golden Age of the Elves. Sadly, like Ahriman the Evil, you will disintegrate and be no more.

"Husband is the Great God, and His will shall be done. He loves all those who try to do good. Goodbye, brother. Husband said I am not to hate you but to have pity on you."

"Crafty, repeat back the message my beloved gives to your master. If you cannot repeat it exactly, you will die," added Gabriel.

Crafty repeated the message exactly, knowing that Gabriel would destroy him if he changed it.

"Good job, Crafty. You are free to leave now."

Crafty disappeared into the Earth.

"Lilith, I intended you to be with me even before birth. I love you the more because you accepted the most challenging destiny I created, a destiny contrary to your beautiful nature. I asked you to hate me. You will not remember, but you cried for days when I asked you to do what I asked."

You returned, saying, "Father, what you ask is more than I can carry on my shoulders. But my love for you is large enough to hate you if this is necessary for the return of the Golden Age. Promise me someday you will rescue and marry me. I will do as you ask. Just promise me."

"I promise to make you equal to your Mother, Natanel. She will never give up on you, Lilith. She will watch over you always, as a mother should watch over her daughter. I love you as much as I love Natanel. I will hide your love, but it will protect your purity.

"So, do you love me, Wife?"

"Oh, yes, I love you more than before time began. Looking back, my destiny was okay, for you never stopped loving me, Father. And now I have the baby I always wanted. Kiss me."

Gabriel kissed his Lilith. He turned his warhorse towards the battlefield to return life to his soldiers who died and health to those wounded. He cleared the battlefield of all evidence of the dead enemy. Gabriel raised an excellent Monel monument for posterity to read. It said,

> *On this day in Camelot, man and Elf fought side-by-side to protect Camelot. Battle Elves came to fight, as did Amazon warriors from long ago. The call brought DragonElves and Dragons to safeguard the hardworking householder and the innocent. All are Brothers and Sisters now. On this day, Good destroyed two princelings and sixty thousand ogres, humans, and dwarves. Our heroes and heroines went into battle chanting, "Our Destiny is Our Golden Age. Long May It Reign."*

Signed, Lord General Gabriel

Then, the Camelot Army returned to Camelot to celebrate in its inns, town squares, and residents' homes and shops. Gabriel produced sufficient food, drink, and music for everyone, and the celebration continued for three days and nights.

Gabriel shared the festivities with Natanel, Lilith, Āvi, and Hekate. Lilith grew more beautiful every day as she entered her destiny. Gabriel and Natanel created Lilith as the Daughter of Mercy and Motherhood. Her touch heals all wounds and brings back life to those who died near her. She is the Guardian of children and young mothers.

The Elves, Amazons, and Camelot's residents marvelled at Lilith, whose evil had metamorphosed into tender love for all creatures. Pregnant women and young mothers brought their children for her blessing. By the end of the celebration, everyone understood that Ahriman the Evil had captured her, but Gabriel saved her. Was there anything our *der Über Gott* could not do?

Gabriel asked Lilith, "Wife, are you happy with your ultimate destiny?"

"Father, I am finally content, able to love and be loved. I love helping you and Mother return to the Golden Age. I am happy to feel my belly and know our child grows inside me. It seems the price I paid was much less than the reward."

Nata added, "It is how Father acts, my love. He needs you to accept every moment of suffering. Then, he returns an ever-increasing series of rewards. Like mine, Father's love is beyond measure; I love you, Lilith. I am proud of my most holy daughter."

Lilith blushed, asking, "Husband, I want you to elevate Hekate so she and I can serve you together. I love her, and she suffered much for you. You need to tell her, Husband."

Gabriel called Hekate, and she came immediately, saying, "Yes, Husband, I heard you call."

"Hekate, you took the chores I asked you to carry before the birth of this time. Lilith loves you as much as Nata and I do, and you have earned elevation to this tetrad. Come, Wife, take my hand and Nata's, and you will understand."

Hekate took both hands, and she remembered what Gabriel had asked her. She fell to her knees, crying, and Lilith put her arms around her.

"Have a good cry, dear sister. Let Daddy take the pain away and fill you overflowing with love and happiness."

In a few minutes, Hekate stood, hugging Lilith, Nata, and finally, Gabriel.

"It is, as you say, Lilith. It is incredible, my love. I am filled with the Holy Light, as you are. I see the destiny that my husband wrote for me. I am the Daughter of Hope and Strength and will work with Lilith."

Hekate gave Gabriel a passionate kiss to thank him. Then she kissed Nata.

Āvi said, "Husband, time-lock Camelot, for the four of us need to make love with you for a few days undisturbed."

And Gabriel time-locked all the worlds for three days. Their lovemaking was so passionate and spiritual that Camelot glowed with a Golden Love.

When Gabriel released the time-lock, the pentad walked about. Another miracle came to Camelot.

Amazons, Elves, Dragons, and people had changed. Greed and egoism lost fashion, and generosity and altruism infected the whole of Camelot.

The five deities rose into the sky, and all the people came outside and turned their eyes skyward.

Gabriel said, "It is time for my Beloved Wives and me to depart from Camelot. Worry not, for time and distance are not obstacles to us. I am proud of all of you, fighting together as a family, defeating evil. Even more critical is that Camelot is now an outpost of our Golden Age for all sentient creatures. Generosity and altruism are the building blocks of the Golden Age.

"My wives and daughters, Lilith, Daughter of Mercy and Motherhood, and Hekate, Daughter of Hope and Strength, are always close by, so pray to them when a serious need arises.

"If evil comes a-calling, pray to us and your friends, the Elves, Dragons, and Amazons, and we will come again. There is always room for more warriors with the other Generals and me. They are the vanguard of my Holy Army and shall be invincible.

"Follow my son, Tristan, for he will guide you spiritually. I proclaim, Glory to the Saviour for he Glorifies the People."

Camelot chanted its slogan as the new Holy Pentad rose into the sky.

The people said their God is worth worshipping by practising love and altruism.

Tristan felt a familiar arm on his shoulder.

Turning, he said, "Nice departure, Father. I shan't let you down."

"Tell Baldar that he is to marry Chatelaine and give Nata some Elf grandchildren to spoil. We will be here for the wedding with the Prince and Princess of Nouseum. I am taking the two sets of twins with me. I made Arthur's daughters Immortal, and they will visit him. I will marry them and give him grandchildren to dote upon. I will return them to Camelot soon.

"Tell Arthur Lydia will provide him, talented sons and daughters. He will live for a very long time. Ask Lydia to behave as a queen should. I return to Ancient Greece, for I must conquer the world before Ahriman the Evil does. Don't worry. I will not erase what happened at Camelot, for this worldline lies where it should be. Send priests of the new Religion to all the kingdoms of this world and those surrounding it. Choose your Elves. Finnet will volunteer, for his heart has always been with Nata and me. Tell Finnet he is now the Patriarch Elf Prince and is to guard the purity of our religion. Baldar and Festian will come to me soon in Greece as new Commanders."

Gabriel hugged his son and disappeared.

Chapter 22

Let's Do the Time Warp Again[32]

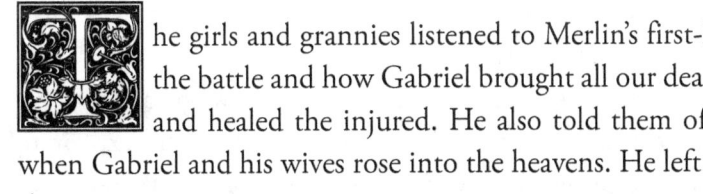he girls and grannies listened to Merlin's first-hand tales of the battle and how Gabriel brought all our dead back to life and healed the injured. He also told them of the Miracle when Gabriel and his wives rose into the heavens. He left out much of the gruesome parts.

Gabriel and his wives arrived in Merlin's Crystal Cave to everyone's delight, and the tale-telling ended.

When the girls saw Nata, they ran to her, surrounding her to hug and kiss her.

Sophie said, "We prayed for everyone every morning and night. Right, Alliona?"

"Right, Sophie. We were so worried because the news was scarce. The grannies watched over us when we slept. Captain Vika was the

---

[32] Title of a song from the Rocky Horror Picture Show (1975)

bravest one, for she checked the cave for the enemy many times daily. Right, Calliope?"

"Right, Sophie. But don't forget that I slept on the side of the bed facing the door so you could be by the wall. Vika gave me a sword, just in case."

Isis and little Eleanor went to hug Gabriel.

Little Eleanor said, "Uncle Gabriel, I was brave too. So was Isis. We helped the grannies daily in the kitchen by picking vegetables and berries for our meals. Asteraceae told us we were the best helpers she ever had."

Gabriel picked up Eleanor, saying, "You are a brave girl, and one day, when you are big, you will fight with me in the war to return to the Golden Age of the Elves. I love you, Eleanor. Mummy and Daddy will be here soon, and I am sure they will be proud of you."

Then Gabriel picked up his Isis, kissing her on the lips, saying, "I have much to share with you. I missed my number one vagina."

Isis replied, "What a silly Daddy I have. I love you so much. You did it; you returned the primary worldline to where we meant it to be. You saved my sweet Lilith, for which I am grateful. You must explain to others what has happened since you put aside the Merciless Heropass, Time Himself. I need you inside me, for I have had no semen for days."

Gabriel put down Isis but continued to hold her hand.

"I need to explain something, so let's go to Merlin's library. We will drink warm honey milk. The troop walked to the library and found convenient seats and hot steaming honey milk with a powered cinnamon dash.

"Isis is correct when she said I put Time and entropy aside, the Merciless Heropass. As Isis, Sophie, Alliona, Hekate, and Āvi know, we came to Camelot from ancient Greece at the beginning of the 3rd Century BCE. Alliona and Sophie are not Alliona and Sophie, but the goddesses Demeter and Kore in Greece. My beloved Hekate is another goddess. I am also married to Athena, Artemis, Leto, and Hera. Our friends Dionysus, Eros, and Hephaestus are part of our pantheon.

"We unified Athens and Sparta first; now all Greece is a great republic. Our armies converted all the islands and land, touching the Mediterranean Sea. There is no slavery, filthy-rich persons, and full gender equality. We have working healthcare and universal education.

"Slowly, we have been reintroducing the Old Religion through the active involvement of our gods and goddesses in human life. Humanity needs deities, deities it can touch and love. Now, my Amazons and Greek hoplites are conquering Asia. My *Polemarchoi* are my wife, Zoe, and my sister-wife, Āvi, who brought our Amazons to fight Ahriman the Evil. Āvi, Isis, and I return to the Asian conquest when we leave here.

"The End War has begun, for we corrected the deviation of the primary worldline, so it is where it needs to be. The Golden Age of the Elves' Return is a reality, but all sentient creatures must fight for it.

"Therefore, Isis said, 'I put aside Time.'"

Isis yelled, "My Daddy is the best fixer-up Elf there ever was. I adore you, Daddy."

Little Eleanor yelled, "Uncle Gabriel is my God, for he is the best Elf I know."

Vivian said, "I am sure that is true, Eleanor, but you are only three years old. But it is true for another twelve years. Right, twins?"

In unison, Ingrid, Calliope, and Vika replied, "Right, Vivian. You are so wise and pay expert attention. We love you."

"I love all of you, too."

Gabriel continued, "Chatelaine, I suggested Baldar marry you, so I will give you the lifetime for an Elf. He will be here later."

Gabriel went to Lilith's chair, taking her by the hand, standing next to her.

"This beautiful lady is Lilith. She is very dear to me because she agreed to accept a horrible destiny to help bring the return of the Golden Age. Another special wife is the goddess Hekate. Come stand with us, darling."

Hekate came to stand with Lilith and Gabriel.

"Hekate also agreed to accept the destiny I wrote for her, which involved unbearable loneliness. She did what I needed, and Isis and I restored her living heart. Isis loves Hekate as much as I do.

"Vivian and Ingrid, I will marry you, and you will have beautiful daughters. You will become Elves, like your sisters, Vika and Calliope. The two babies you have now will return to your baby sisters, and I will give you Elf daughters while I give them to Vivian and Ingrid.

"Morgana is now Tristan's principal wife, and his other wives are his students, other than Chatelaine, who loves my son, Baldar. It is what he wanted, so now they belong to each other.

"Nata was my first Elf daughter and wife, and she wants to return to me, for her love for me is much. I made her leave to help Tristan and wiped her memory. Now is the time to return things to normal.

"I want to ask the two sets of twins who their mummy and daddy are?"

All the twins said, "Silly, Daddy. You know Nata is our mummy, and you are our daddy. You are also the babies' Daddy, for Mummy only sleeps with her husband because Mummy is a proper Elf."

Vivian asked, "But Ingrid, King Arthur, is also our daddy. How can this be for mummy never made love to King Arthur?"

"I don't know, Sister? But our real daddy is Gabriel, and our real mummy is Nata. Oh, well, I guess we can have two daddies?"

Nata said, "Of course, you may have two daddies, but only one Mummy, right?"

All the twins replied, "Right, Mummy. We lived inside of you, and now we live outside of you. Will you be proud of us when we have our babies?"

"Daddy and I are always proud of our daughters. You four are our best creations."

Gabriel continued, "Āvi, Sophie, Alliona, and Isis will return with me to ancient Greece. Nata, Lilith, Hekate, and the twins will stay in Camelot and help spread the Elf Religion. The worldline will shift if I do not return to correct history. It will involve me in human history for a long time, as evil is prevalent there. I will frequently visit to check on my wives and daughters and keep them full of semen. I am sorry for our family, but this is the price we pay for fixing things.

"There will be more battles, but I am always with you. Come, Nata and my twins, it is time to give you babies who will grow up and help the cause."

Ingrid asked, "Daddy, will Vivian and I be actual wives and daughters like Vika and Calliope?"

"You shall be. We will visit Arthur and Lydia tomorrow and tell them."

Nata, the two sets of twins, and Gabriel left for Nata's chambers. The rest of the crew stayed in the library, ensuring that Lilith and Hekate felt welcome and loved.

The following day, Gabriel took the family to visit Arthur and Lydia. They rode in the fine carriage that first took Calliope and Vika to Auntie Julia's clothing store.

After they arrived, the two sets of twins ran to find Lydia and Arthur so they would know they were safe. Lydia and Arthur were discussing the recent improvement of the citizens of Camelot.

Lydia said, "I have known Gabriel for thousands and thousands of years, Arthur. People change for the better when He comes into their lives. Think about Lilith's changes because she knew Gabriel loved and needed her. Gabriel is God, Arthur. And what a God he is! May he bless himself."

"What you say is true, darling. Being with Gabriel makes me want to be better and to think that Camelot is the first step in bringing about the next Golden Age."

We interrupted the conversation as the girls hugged and kissed Lydia and Arthur.

Finally, as the adults entered the breakfast room, Vivian said, "Daddy, Ingrid and I are in love with Gabriel, and now we are wives like Vika and Calliope. Husband said all of us will have beautiful and smart daughters for you and Auntie Lydia to dote over. Right, sisters?"

The remaining sisters yelled, "Right, our precious Vivian. We are sisters, wives, and mothers. Hooray for us."

Nata said, "Sorry for not asking your permission, but I know you wouldn't mind wanting your twins to be happy. They are delighted, Arthur. I am now with Gabriel, my proper husband. Tristan will tell you a long story if you ask.

"The twins will stay with me in Camelot and help spread the Elf Religion. Finnet and some friends want to remain in Camelot to help Baron Ivan protect the city and teach and spread the Elf Teachings. Finnet is amazingly spiritual and wise. He will be the guiding light and head of all our houses of worship and healing. I hope we have your permission, Arthur?"

"When Deities speak, a wise king listens."

Turning to his twins, he says, "Girls, I am pleased you chose the right Elf to marry. I know my daughters and nieces are silly twins, but not stupid ones."

Gabriel added, "Arthur, Lydia is a Djinn, in case you didn't notice. I know she loves you, so I made your life as long as hers. This gives you sufficient time to help me repair Isis' creation.

"My Holy Wives, Lilith and Hekate, will remain in Camelot with Nata. Keep them safe, Arthur. They are important. Āvi, Isis, Sophie, and Alliona return to ancient Greece and earlier times to ensure the prime worldline remains where it is. We will visit, but we are conquering Asia to rid the world of sociopaths. We are busy. Send priests to every city in your world to bring unconditional love and altruism to the population.

"The Saviour stays here to proclaim our Message. More war will come sporadically, but the war will grow. Tristan can deal with this now, and I will fight when I can. Also, Prince Festian asks permission to build a battle training station for Elves and others outside of Camelot. He will feel more comfortable knowing that this city is well-protected."

"I grant all that you ask, Lord General. We have grown to love you, and we will miss you. Visit with your new wives. I would like to have the children live with Lydia and me."

"A good idea, but don't forget Morgana and Merlin. Keep them busy in the magick school. Come, my darlings, it's time to return to Greece. We love you and Camelot, Arthur and Lydia. Call me if you need me. Love to all of you."

Gabriel and his wives vanished, but he left a life-size mural of his family on a blank wall to avoid forgetting. Even the goddesses and Amazons they had not yet met.

END OF CODEX THREE

About the Author

ean-Michel is a gifted Spiritual Teacher writing transformative teaching tales based upon his adventures exploring the Sentient Oneirion Worlds. To those souls consciously exploring the Boundless Realms, these worlds are just as real as the physical but operate under broader laws. Those persons grounded only in the material would call his Tales fiction. But does it really matter?

What is unusual is that he teaches and writes infused with the Serpent or Kundalini Energies, explaining the importance of eroticism and love. He calls his Spirituality the Way of the Gallant Heart. Sacred Knowledge is more than sterile thoughts; it is a way of living filled with Love and Wisdom applied wholesomely to our Earth and its creatures. Where gender equality is practised as was in ancient Crete.

Jean-Michel is an accomplished poet appreciated in North America and Europe for his tender and sensual romantic poetry. He founded the Institute for Conscious Evolution and Human Development  at enlightenment123.org. He regularly posts articles at freedomexercises.blog on WordPress. He has finished several more volumes of this series and a second series of the Nouseum Sagas.

He loves to travel, so it is difficult to find him sometimes. Studying with him is a trip; he is outrageous, original, and funny. He is the best if you want to make a soul and become eternal. The author travels with a love from Simferopol to Yalta in Crimea, Ukraine. He spent a long time there with Regina. She was a university volleyball star working on a PhD in Economics.

If you ask him why he is, he will tell you one thing. My dream is to restore the Great Mother to humanity's pantheon. Peace ruled in the Neolithic agriculturalists when humanity understood the Dvinity was a Holy Family of equally essential members.

Once, we had a near Golden Age in the European-Meditaerranen territory until the invasions of the Kurgans and Semitic hoards, Male dominant, female subjugating, violent oppressors. They worshipped war and weapons and will bring the End Times if the Goddess is not returned.

www.ingramcontent.com/pod-product-compliance
Lightning Source LLC
Chambersburg PA
CBHW060551230426
43670CB00011B/1779